Prai
INSERT GIGGLE GIGGLE

"I know firsthand that Kay lives the wisdom, success, and love that she shares. She demonstrates great leadership-wisdom through her results . . . Her humorous stories and keen insights in this book—so clear, practical, kind, and down-to-earth—I got to see in application, and what she shares in this book works! It works as a guide to a truly meaningful life, to a successful and humane business, and, most importantly to me, as a rich guide to bringing out the best in children and parents."

—Bob Lancer
Coach, Trainer, Speaker,
Author of *Parenting With Love: Without Anger or Stress*

"I laughed. I cried. I remembered. I learned. This book is so practical and full of common sense, it's almost ridiculous. I sincerely hope that young parents will read it and have an awakening of good ol' common sense in their life and parenting. And the rest of us can glean some truth nuggets as well.

"I love the 'asides.' These are funny, powerful, illustrative, and sometimes all at once! Love the way they are woven into a story and then bounce back to the subject of the chapter.

"Everyone. Read. This. Book."

—Felicia
a minor character in **INSERT GIGGLE GIGGLE**

INSERT
GIGGLE GIGGLE

INSERT GIGGLE GIGGLE

Laughing Your Way through Raising Kids and Running a Business

Kay Paschal

BOOKLOGIX®
Alpharetta, GA

The author has tried to recreate events, locations, and conversations from her memories of them. In some instances, in order to maintain their anonymity, the author has changed the names of individuals and places. She may also have changed some identifying characteristics and details such as physical attributes, occupations, and places of residence. Although the author and publisher have made every effort to ensure that the information in this book was correct at the time of first publication, the author and publisher do not assume and hereby disclaim any liability to any party for any loss, damage, or disruption caused by errors or omissions, whether such errors or omissions result from negligence, accident, or any other cause.

ISBN: 978-1-6653-0293-7 - Paperback
eISBN: 978-1-6653-0294-4 - eBook

Library of Congress Control Number: 2022920643

Printed in the United States of America 110222

♾ This paper meets the requirements of ANSI/NISO Z39.48-1992 (Permanence of Paper)

Author photo by KO Photography, LLC

To my husband, Steve.
That's why I hitched my wagon to your star.

To my boys, Hayden and William.
Gnm and LTD.

CONTENTS

Chapter 1: Why Did I Write This Book
and Why Are You Reading It? 1
Chapter 2: Opening a Preschool
—Where Did *That* Come From? 7
Chapter 3: What Do I Do *Now*? 15
Chapter 4: Why Do We Have Kids—*Who Does That?* 23
Chapter 5: The Power of the Brain! 35
Chapter 6: What Kind of Mother *Are* You? 41
Chapter 7: Being a Father, Being a Man, Being a *Dad* 49
Chapter 8: What Kind of Parent Are You?
Do You Treat Your Children the Same? 55
Chapter 9: Making School Choices—No Size Fits All! 69
Chapter 10: "Redshirting" and Role Models 81
Chapter 11: How Did It Get So Late So Soon? 89
Chapter 12: You Can't Make This Up! 103
Chapter 13: Our Millennials and
Millennials in the Workplace 113
Chapter 14: You Have to Pick Your Battles 131
Chapter 15: Our Techno-Savvy Kids!
Not Just for Geeks Anymore! 143
Chapter 16: Are Our Kids Safe in Our Schools? 155

Chapter 17: Social Media in Today's Workplace 163

Chapter 18: Are *You* a Victim?
What Are *You* Entitled To? 173

Chapter 19: You Can Lead a Horse to Water . . . 185

Chapter 20: How Does Customer
Entitlement Drive Customer Service? 197

Chapter 21: Hot Fun in the Summertime! 209

Chapter 22: It's Our Tradition 221

Chapter 23: Thankful Is as Thankful Does 233

Chapter 24: Might as Well Face It . . . 243

Chapter 25: Always Remember to
Insert a Giggle Giggle 251

Acknowledgments *257*

CHAPTER 1
WHY DID I WRITE THIS BOOK AND WHY ARE YOU READING IT?

Those are two great questions! I'm no celebrity—you've never heard of me; why would anyone be interested in what I, just a random woman and a mom, have to say?

Well . . . the answer to the first question is that boredom had set in after about the first three months of retirement. Boredom is not really the best word—I guess I will use "purpose" as a better word as well as a better way to look at how I was trying to figure out how to fulfill myself as well as *fill my day* (insert giggle giggle). Maybe some of you are wondering that same thing about yourself now that you might not be working outside the home any longer and/or your children are no longer at home . . .

The answer to the second question (besides I can't imagine why . . . insert giggle giggle!) is that hopefully you will find something of use or value in not only the business component of the book, but also in the parent–child interactions, *or* maybe just an acknowledgment that we all have the same issues as everyone else in running a business or being an employee, and more importantly, being a parent in the process. No one seems to be immune to the problems and joys of either. I bet so many of you, as you read this book, will see yourself in some of the same situations as me or think of your own situations where you were pursuing, just like me, to "have it all."

As I was coming to grips with my retirement at the age of sixty after working since I was eighteen, I wanted to find a way to memorialize what my husband, Steve, and I had created—really, out of nothing—just an idea and a leap of faith—the preschool. This period of time does not count as a "job." When you own your own business—not only own it, but built it from scratch—concept, building, and everything else—it's a part of your life, of your soul. It's hard to walk away from, but walk away I did, as so many of you may have done with your business or will have to do at some point in the future. One of the most important things about knowing when to sell your business, or leave any other type of situation behind—indeed, a relationship of any type—is to read and acknowledge the signs, sort of the "know when to hold 'em and know when to fold 'em" advice. I hope some of the stories about starting and owning a business, service to customers, and integrity in your business dealings hit home and shed light, whether you are an owner, a boss, or an employee.

You will also find a lot of personal stories, noted as asides. You may wonder why these stories are in these chapters and sometimes why these asides seem to stray so very far away from the original intent of the chapter. Just hang with them a little—I try to find a way by the end of the aside to weave it back into the chapter's meaning . . . hopefully (insert giggle giggle). In the early writing of the book, I sort of thought the only people that would ever read it would be my family and others close to me, so these stories would not be so boring to them. I hope they aren't too boring to you (insert giggle giggle).

You will also see the "giggle giggle" inserted a lot throughout the book. You may wonder why. The reason is because I find a lot of humor, or maybe my parental naivete, in some of the stories I tell or some of the opinions I assert. Stay tuned or flip to the chapter on social media about why my "giggle" is expressed this way! If you ask anyone that knows me, I laugh at myself a lot. I believe it's best to not take yourself so seriously while owning a business, especially one such as mine that was as delightful as taking care of children *and as stressful* as taking care of children (and parents), as well as dealing with the rest of the aspects of your life. Sometimes, the *giggle giggle* (in the book and in my life) might mean I was nervous about what I was doing or saying.

As I reminisce about all the business decisions and parent and child interactions throughout twenty-five years of PPP (the acronym of my business's name), you will see a lot of reference to the "early years" and the "later years." I became very close to so many people. I learned a lot about people and a lot about myself. I learned about jobs I didn't know even existed—so many times I would say to a parent, "There's a job for that?"

I was surrounded by the most interesting people through twenty-five years of working closely with parents and with my Fabulous Faculty (this phrase would become how I referred to my teachers). We are all so different, yet so similar. I had one mom tell Steve one day that she loved that her children attended PPP, but just as important, PPP had become a safe haven for her to voice her concerns as a mom and also hear about our (not just mine, but those of my administrative staff as well) experiences raising our children while being businesswomen and wives. We had this sort of relationship with a lot of moms.

In the "later years" of PPP, we also had these kinds of relationships with dads. You will see in one of the chapters how the dads' roles noticeably changed through the years, as we had dads enjoy their morning coffee standing around in our lobby discussing all sorts of "dad/kid" things as well as enjoying the typical sports talk. We had one dad, who was working on his PhD, tell me afterward that he wrote a business thesis that included components of what he perceived as the "PPP business model." This was an exciting revelation for me. He told me he could not imagine all that went into the daily, monthly, and long-range planning of PPP and the responsibility we had. All the "normal" things of running *any* business are immense, but roll into that educational decisions, implementations for young children that were so successful, all the faculty issues, and the customer service considerations, as well as meshing together all the different parenting styles, and it must be exhausting and countless. However, he said that we always "seemed" laid-back and always made the parents (the customers) feel that we had all the time in the world for them. Funny enough, there were parents we really got close to, and sometimes we would have to say to them, "You have to go! I've got to get to work!" (insert giggle giggle).

As the title of the book states, the chapters run the gamut from owning a business and supervising people to business integrity in all aspects of difficult situations, as well as being an employee . . . and, oh yeah, being a parent in the process (insert giggle giggle). None of us are alone in the situations and craziness of either being "the one in charge" *or* of being an employee working for someone who, day by day, is just trying to figure it all out.

I think if you are a business owner or one who supervises others, you may see yourself in some of the business-related examples and dilemmas presented in this book, *and* if you are an employee, you may be able to get a glimpse that, most often, it's not as glamorous as one may think, to be "the one in charge." Of course, there are many rewards for running your own business or being a highly compensated employee "in charge," but sometimes this comes at a high personal cost and times when "the one in charge" would love not to be.

I was an employee myself for the first eighteen years or so of my working life before I started my own business, and I have a better appreciation of "seeing both sides" now that I have been on both sides. I hope this vantage point served me well in dealing with my employees.

A majority of this book centers around parenting tips and topics that I wrote about and were published monthly in magazines and newspapers throughout Atlanta during the years of owning PPP, featured as "Kids & Kay." I tackled situational ups and downs based on my own experiences raising my two boys, Hayden and William; observations of friends with their children; and advising parents in my preschool on questions and situations they had about raising *their* children. I'm not sure which was the hardest (insert giggle giggle).

I want to very clearly state that the examples I put forth of parents dealing with their children at PPP, of myself, or of friends of mine are in no way a remark on good or bad parenting. Parenting, for all of us, is a crap shoot, and we are all just doing the best we can. Sometimes we get it right and sometimes we get it wrong. Sometimes what someone sees us doing in isolation is not representative of the type of parent we really are. If you are like me, you may look askance at something you see a parent doing that you "would never do" but then do something yourself just as "questionable" in other situations. Just like the examples of parenting I give in others, I give so many more about myself, so I hope as well that I am not judged unfairly in some of the examples I give of myself. So let's all just giggle at ourselves a little and move on to the next issue . . . maybe a little wiser . . . ? (Insert giggle giggle!)

One of the hardest things to do, and it may seem weird, was putting the chapters in order—they were written in no particular order and I skipped from one to the other a lot! I know in my own reading, when I purchase a book such as this, I tend to just skip around—unlike a fictional book that must be read from cover to cover. Sometimes one chapter seems a lot more interesting to me than others. If you do this with this book, you will note a lot of references to "other" chapters, which was one reason why it was so hard to ultimately put the book in chapter order. My apologies for any dissatisfaction this causes in your "hop-around" reading.

During the writing of this book, no one read a word of it. The only people that even knew I was writing a book were my husband, Steve, my sons, Hayden and William, and my best friend, Felicia. I was so insecure about putting down my thoughts that I knew if anyone said one negative word, the writing would stop. Once I felt "done," I felt I could take on all the criticisms during the immense editing process, because I would at least have the thoughts down, and if it was a big, fat flop, at least my family could read it, tell me I did well, and throw it in a drawer. Even this, I felt, would be a successful endeavor, and reassure me that all the time spent on writing this book had served a purpose. To think of it being published and read by others was just too much to think about or hope for. During this process, I also created a website, which sat unlaunched for over a year. It's also now open for view, titled the same as this book—InsertGiggleGiggle.com with lots of fun content.

I call some people by name in the book, and it's possible that some unnamed examples of things I mention may be recognized by others or by the person/people themselves. All of these examples were either given in admiration of or illustration of the point being made in the chapter. These stories, as well as my own, are vital to the understanding of what I am trying to accomplish in this book. While I could have chosen other examples, these came fresh to mind. I note some research through the years I did on various topics in my published articles as well as in the book. I have not cited any . . . most of the things I note as researched you can easily search on the internet on your own. Believe me, there's nothing "rocket science" about my opinions and stances on anything I write about—book or blog.

So relax, get a cup of coffee or a glass of wine, get in your comfy pants, hop around the chapters, read what you like, don't read the rest . . . but don't miss the part about loving your kids.

CHAPTER 2
OPENING A PRESCHOOL —WHERE DID *THAT* COME FROM?

You cannot imagine, through twenty-five years, how often I was asked that question. To be one, if not the only, preschool in the community that was completely privately owned and directed, was a fascination to a lot of families when they were touring the school. So here's the short version . . .

Steve and I had never lived anywhere but Atlanta, Georgia, our entire lives, but, in 1990, found ourselves living in Houston, Texas, due to Steve accepting a transfer there from the international bank he was working for. I found a great job in Texas that I loved and we were excited about building our life in Houston. However, when the decision was made, in early 1993, to close the Houston, as well as the Atlanta, offices of the bank, Steve was given that responsibility, and after closing the Houston branch, we were transferred back "home" to Atlanta so he could complete that task. Hayden was three years old and I was in my final trimester of pregnancy with William. During this period, it was discussed that Steve may have the opportunity to join the company's "expat" program, which would involve our family moving to Singapore. We gave it some thought and decided the time was not right for us with two very young children to move that far away from home. So, when the closing of the Atlanta office was completed, both Steve and I would be jobless.

Oh my! We were not jobless people! By choice, we had waited

through ten years of marriage to start our family due to both of us being very career-minded individuals and enjoying the benefits of very lucrative careers. We were anxiously trying to envision what our next steps were going to be. *Ah-ha!* What about a day-care center? Where did *that* come from?

So here we were, a toddler and a new baby, neither one of us with a job, and a business plan to be formulated and seen through, no matter the cost. Of course, neither of us knew anything about owning a business, much less running a day-care center. Steve, however, with his MBA in finance from Georgia Tech and his incredible business-honed sense and experience, turned out to be a genius at business-plan models and implementation. He made indescribable and somewhat unbelievable things happen during the two years it took to get the school opened, but open we did in August 1995, with six students, which *included* Hayden and William.

As for me, all I really brought to the table were my people skills and a shared "drive-to-succeed" attitude for our young family. Boy, I had a lot to do! For those two years prior to the opening of PPP, I immersed myself in early-childhood education books, conferences, and curriculum, as well as the rules and regulations of the Department of Human Resources (DHR) and the criteria set forth for developmentally appropriate practices by the National Association of the Education of Young Children (NAEYC).

Then there was the development of our marketing plan, parent procedures, and the strategy of how we were going to market our very upscale day-care center to parents in the affluent area of North Fulton County, which Steve had chosen for our location. This was perhaps the most genius move on his part, to recognize the growth potential of this untapped area where our preschool was being built in the middle of (what looked like) a wheat field. I was a nervous wreck! Where were our student enrollees going to come from? Just who were these people who were going to trust an untested preschool opened by two people with no day-care experience in a community that had few neighborhoods and few businesses?

But explode this community did, and quickly (as Steve had expected), and a mere two years after opening our first location, we were excitedly looking for our second location, which ended up being barely five miles from our first preschool. In January 1998, the North School of PPP was opened, and PPP was off and running to become among the recognized leaders in academic excellence by several measures, as well as be branded as providing elite customer service, coupled with a longevity of teachers unparalleled in the day-care industry statewide, if not nationwide as well. It was a foundational component of PPP to have a fabulous faculty, which was appreciated and lauded by the families and students of PPP over the next twenty-three years, that brought joy and fulfillment to us all. PPP was in a class by itself, and nothing was left to chance in maintaining the high standards for the faculty, students, and families of PPP.

On a personal front, our two boys, Hayden and William, were growing up and becoming very active in school, with friends and extracurricular activities. For the first seven or so years, Steve and I worked together each day at PPP while the boys were at school. Steve, upstairs, doing all sorts of financial planning and the "numbers" type stuff, and me running the day-to-day, downstairs. Steve also handled all the handy "honey-do" projects during the weekends. However, it eventually evolved into Steve being on site less and less as the boys needed him more and more, and we were able to hire people to do some of the tasks he had been doing for "free." Hayden started Irish dancing at the age of eight, which would last until his college years, and William started his love of baseball that took him through a college scholarship and into professional umpiring as an adult.

> An aside: William's hobby and love of baseball is easy to understand, but Hayden—Irish dancing, you may ask? Well, let me explain it this way: The other day, I was bingeing on *Law & Order SVU* and there was a scene where Olivia and her young son, Noah, were

> walking down the street. She had to stop and take a phone call, so Noah had the opportunity to just look around, and he saw, through a full glass window, a group of teenagers dancing. It looked like Irish dancing, or maybe some sort of tap/modern dance. When Olivia got off the phone, Noah pointed to the window and told Olivia that he wanted to do that . . . not baseball. She thought he liked baseball, but he really didn't. At the end of the episode, it showed Noah going into the dance class, all smiles, as well as Olivia, knowing her son had found a hobby that he truly would enjoy.
>
> Okay—that is totally Hayden's story! Tried baseball, didn't like it. Tried piano lessons (next to the dance studio), didn't like it either. But one day when we were leaving piano lessons, he saw the dancers, and a love was born that would take us all over the world and, ultimately for Hayden, to compete in the World Irish Dance Championships in Ireland and Scotland. Someone must have written to *SVU* and told them Hayden's story and they found a way to incorporate it into an interesting storyline. Just saying . . . (Insert giggle giggle!)

Back to PPP. Running two very successful preschools (we never referred to ourselves as day care) was such a joy. In the early years of PPP, I was a mother of two young children, the same as the moms who were enrolling in the preschool. We were experiencing the same joys and challenges as mothers, and our children were friends. I even loaned some of my maternity clothes to another mom (customer) at PPP. There was such a feeling of friendliness in those early years, this didn't seem to be an odd thing to do at all; in the later years of PPP, this would have seemed very odd for a variety of reasons.

Years happily passed, and before we knew it, PPP was

celebrating the 20th Anniversary of serving families in North Fulton and the surrounding counties. It started slowly but built into a year or so of what we referred to as "mystical connections" to PPP families of the past twenty years. Families we had not seen or heard from since their children graduated from PPP starting calling and stopping by to offer their congratulations as well as their appreciation of what PPP had meant to their child and, indeed, to their family.

All of a sudden, so many of us were just randomly running into students out in the community. Why now, we asked ourselves. We received photos from high school and college graduates from all over the country, from the most prestigious colleges in the country, and a lot of these photos included "Preppies" (what we called our preschool students) who were still friends with each other now as young adults. We heard stories of family connections that had started at PPP and had lasted throughout these twenty years, which was something that was always among my proudest achievements of the business—family and children friendships that had withstood the test of time.

Over the years, we had numerous teachers who had kept in touch with a lot of PPP families—had been invited to their homes for celebrations, to graduations, and even weddings of these past PPP students. This had always been a heartwarming "aside" of the business of PPP, the feeling of family that was always a big part of anyone who was a part of PPP.

We had T-shirts made up to honor PPP's 20th Anniversary and the Preppies of PPP, which said, "I WAS A PREPPIE." We gave out hundreds of these shirts, and photos poured in of these young people from middle school, high school, college, and beyond, wearing their anniversary T-shirt. We were thrilled! I felt compelled, as more and more "mystical connections" happened and emails, phone calls, and visits continued to stream in, to write a letter to my Fabulous Faculty. In a nutshell, it plainly said that each of us, myself included, came to "work" each day to do a "job." How could any of us have known that this "job" would translate into the incredible and sustaining influence that we all made in the lives of so many people, including our own? It was palpable to anyone who went to or worked at PPP . . . an extraordinary "ah-ha" moment.

All this to say that if you are looking for a preschool for your child, whether due to being a working parent or using preschool as a social and educational tool, make sure to find one that has a teacher connection, a student connection, a family connection, and a community connection. If you are successful at this, you will have found not only a treasure for your child when their young brains are establishing patterns they will continue to search of positive experiences for the rest of their lives, but also a treasure for your family. Take this very first foundational step for your child—indeed, for your family—very seriously.

Moving along, just like the opening of PPP twenty-five years previously seemed to come out of nowhere, now so did the thought of selling PPP. I can't really recall how the conversation and the seemingly quick eventuality of selling PPP started; however, it was now full steam ahead, and once again it was Steve who was in the driver's seat, after years of not really being that involved in the day-to-day running of PPP. I was continuing to go to work each day, continuing to develop new programs, marketing strategies, and coming up with the next thing to separate PPP from any other preschool, just business as usual for me. If I am being honest, I didn't really know if I thought it was time to sell PPP. What would happen to my daily routine, what would we do, and how could I give up all those leg hugs from those precious children?

The reputation of PPP had grown to such a heightened level that we were constantly asked by parents to open more schools. Certainly no one thought there was a possibility that PPP might cease to exist! Any time we had a young couple tell us they were moving away from the ability to bring their child to PPP, another community, or maybe another state, the thing they seemed most concerned about was how they were going to find a preschool to replace PPP. While this stroked our ego, it was sad to see the angst in these parents. We heard constantly, "You could make a fortune," trying to entice more and more PPP locations, if we would build a PPP in "name-a-place-anywhere-parents-were-moving." As enticing as "a fortune" sounded to us, we sincerely thought continuing to expand past our two existing schools, much less franchising into different states, would spread me too thin and we would lose that owner-concept feeling that made PPP, PPP. It just didn't fit our business model. But selling PPP? Heresy! And what about the subterfuge during the selling process? Deceiving my staff, my faculty, my parents! I couldn't imagine what was about to happen—to all of us.

But Steve had, again, the unbelievable foresight and wisdom to seek out a company whose business model was the acquisition of existing preschools and maintaining the unique brand that had made these preschools successful and sought out in their respective communities. Very little would change for the faculty and families of PPP. Months of negotiation and meetings went by, until Steve and I were satisfied that we were placing our beloved PPP in the best of hands and that we could start our retirement years with the peace of mind that PPP would live on and thrive. Now, almost three years since the sale, there are still so many teachers and administrative staff making sure that PPP is still PPP. I will never be able to express how much this means to Steve and me. As I always said, it is a Fabulous Faculty.

From the summer of 2018, when the thought of selling PPP was floated, until the somewhat unbelievable closing of the deal in late November, things were moving quickly while seemingly in slow motion for me. The faculty were told, amid protests as well as congratulations. The families were told, with the same mixture of feelings. Funny enough, our months-ago-planned holiday party was scheduled for November 29 at a local restaurant, and the acquisition team was still in town—a wonderful group of ladies, whom I invited to our faculty celebration. It seemed like a wonderful way to merge the old with the new, and everyone had a delightful time getting to know one another.

The next day, Friday, November 30, 2018, the sale of PPP was finalized. A twenty-five-year labor of love had come full circle—our two boys playing in the dirt mound as the first PPP building went up, both of their very first jobs (Hayden's as a summer camp counselor and William's as a summer baseball coach to our Preppies) happened at PPP, and then there was the privilege of participating in thousands of families' lives who placed their children and their trust in Steve and I, and in PPP.

During these twenty-five years, I became a board member and committee chair for the Georgia Child Care Association, a designee on the Legislative Advisory Committee at Bright from the Start, and a published writer in several community and Atlanta-at-large magazines on parenting tips and educational articles, most of which this book is based on, while, most importantly, being a wife and a mom.

Steve and I celebrated our success that evening at our neighborhood Chick-fil-A.

CHAPTER 3
WHAT DO I DO *NOW?*

PPP has been sold. You would think that my daily planner (a traditional journal I have kept for over twenty-five years) should and would memorialize all sorts of things, meetings, thoughts, etc., about what was going on during this time, but no, almost nothing! Was this just my busy inattention to this matter, or a subliminal disregard that it was really happening? I knew a letter was sent to the parents, which again solicited all sorts of reactions similar to the faculty's, ranging from *Congratulations* to *Please, not now, wait until* my *child graduates PPP.*

> A funny aside: A much-loved parent came into my office and said, in his somewhat broken English, "Why you retire? You not old!" Isn't that the best! And *precisely* the point of retiring *now,* so that Steve and I could easily enjoy our retirement years before we are either physically challenged to do so or maybe start having a passel of grandkids and don't want to travel . . . (Insert giggle giggle!)

I have been a working person since my graduation from high school. What was I going to do *now*? I started talking to my "non-working" and retired friends about what occupied their day if you didn't have a job outside the home (and didn't have children at home to raise). Without exception the answer was, "Whatever I want to do" or "You will wonder how you ever worked!" No, I wanted to know *exactly,* "What do *you* do?" Give me a snapshot of your daily/weekly activities. No one really could. It seemed, to me, an elusive ideal, but one that everyone seemed to really enjoy. I wasn't so sure.

The First Stage of Retirement (for me): Joyful! The first thing I enjoyed was that I didn't have a specific time I "had to be up" in the morning. A couple from the neighborhood where we lived during the PPP years always made a point of telling me how they used to see me leaving each day before six in the morning to go to PPP as they were just getting up. Of course, I hadn't done that shift for many years, but I can still recall those early years of twelve-hour days, leaving home in the dark and coming home in the dark.

Another joy was the particular time of the year I retired. It was December, and I had a new house to decorate and presents to buy and finally all the time I wanted to shop! I was in bliss! Hayden would be coming home from New York City for the holidays and spending almost two weeks with us. Steve had arranged for William and Crash (our Lab mix rescue granddog) to bunk in with us from his apartment in Atlanta during this time too. So, a full house. I was just . . . joyful!

Steve surprised me mid-December and swept me off to order a 2019 Mercedes GWagon to replace the GWagon that I had driven for over ten years. Also, Steve and I were looking forward to an early-January, five-day cruise with eight couples we had been friends with since before the boys were born, and we were looking forward to reconnecting with them. Steve insisted, as our first retirement trip, that we book the royal suite, and I cannot tell you what an incredible experience and what a nice trip this was. For Christmas I gave Steve tickets to *Les Misérables* at the Fox Theatre and two nights at a bed and breakfast in downtown Atlanta—on a Tuesday and Wednesday no less! It's just one endless weekend when you are retired (insert excited giggle giggle)!

We were totally enjoying this whole new world open to us. No timelines, no issues to worry about, just enjoying life, lunches with old friends, doing things around the house, going to the gym daily, cooking at home (after not doing this for many, many years), and enjoying spending the day with Steve all made retirement look very easy.

Little did I know the second stage was coming . . .

The Second Stage of Retirement (for me): What is my purpose? I have no purpose. For the past forty years of marriage, I had a purpose. Steve was finishing up his senior year at Georgia Tech during our first year of marriage and we decided for him to get his MBA during years two and three of our marriage. My purpose was to support us and support him during the rigors at GT. The ten years between that and the start of our family was to continue working, Steve and I bought our first house, and we were doing all the things young, upwardly mobile ("yuppies") couples do. And then from the age of thirty to fifty-nine, my purpose was to help raise our two boys and run our family business. *Now what . . .?*

How much shopping can you do? Boy, I had given that a good run for the past two to three months! How many friends can you lunch with? I was getting dressed some days to do nothing more than go to the grocery store, post office, bank, and dry cleaners. That was my busy *planned* day. These things used to be a mere by-product of my work day—just a lunchtime, hurry-up errand. Now, I was making a *plan* to do these things to actually take up a day! Oh no . . . were couple's trips to the doctor far behind?

Everyone told me just to take my time. Something would spark my interest to get involved in. But what? I was almost leery of coming up with an interest—what if that took hold and I didn't have my free time? It was a conflicting position to be in, to get involved in something *or* continue a life of doing anything I wanted to at any time. The trouble was, I was running out of the "doing anything I wanted to do" mindset.

Was I becoming depressed? I didn't think so . . . I mean, I was still enjoying being retired and not having the responsibility of dealing with issues of owning and running a business. And of course, Steve and I were really enjoying ourselves, too, as noted in my first stage of retirement, but was this going to be enough for the next, hopefully many, years to come? Some days I was beginning to wonder if it was a mistake for me not to be a working person . . .

The Third Stage of Retirement (for me): How did I *ever* work? It finally came! It took about nine months, but boy, are my days full, and in a good way. To address how I used to spend my retirement days illustrated in the Second Stage of Retirement, I have a bunch of clothes at the dry cleaners that have been ready for two weeks! I just haven't found the time to go pick them up—isn't that wonderful? I have an app on my phone for banking. I have found a drop box for mail at the nearby CVS, and thankfully Steve and I are very healthy, so no couple's doctor appointments!

So let's see, the million-dollar question: what do I do? Just like the friends I had badgered before about "What exactly do you do," it's hard to capture on paper really. For one, I've started this book. It may never go anywhere except on my computer, but I am having such a good time with it.

Each morning I got up an hour or so before Steve and enjoyed coffee and reading. Then I sat at the kitchen island and would work on this book on days I was able to do that. I would get so wrapped up that some days it was lunchtime before I realized it and I pretty much made myself stop. One of my Fabulous Faculty gave me, as a retirement gift, a book to put down all my thoughts. It has a red "heart tree" on it, very representative of PPP. I filled it up with snippets of ideas for this book. Sometimes as I wrote one chapter, a totally unrelated thought popped into my head and I had to jot it down for another chapter. I am very grateful to this person for this journal and for thinking my thoughts were worthy and might be interesting to anyone other than myself.

To find a day convenient for both myself and my other "non-working" friends to meet for lunch is getting hard. Steve and I have renovated and furnished two condos we own in Atlanta for corporate rentals, and we purchased a condo in Florida for our pleasure as well as rental.

Steve is also heavily involved, and to a small degree me as well, in the negotiations and the opening of my brother's hardware business. It's very possible I will work there two to three days a week in the beginning just to help him out. *How will I work this in?* I still enjoy going to the gym every day. And even though in my Second Stage of Retirement I made fun of making a whole day of going to the grocery store, it has now become a *luxury* to spend the time going to Publix, Kroger, and Fresh Market for certain things that Steve and I like specifically at each of those stores and enjoying having the time to do so! My refrigerator is a work of art after being empty pretty much since William left for college eight years ago!

I have a separate notebook I keep all sorts of "running my life and home" reminders, and it's always full of things to do that sometimes take me weeks to accomplish and mark off. I also have more time to visit my mom and help handle her affairs and take care of her. As I am writing this chapter, it's Labor Day 2019, and Steve and I only managed to go to our club pool once the whole summer! During the past couple of years of my work life, we looked forward each weekend to relax with "Sea Breeze Saturday or Sunday"—and sometimes both! But between the sixteen-day European cruise we took in July for my sixtieth birthday and our fortieth wedding anniversary and four trips from April to September to Florida, we just never had the weekend spare time to sit at the pool. How great is that!

The point being, I think retirement (at least for me) will probably rotate through the above three stages again and again. I think I will once again be *Joyful* when we have completed this period of frenzy in getting these three condos finished, and hopefully successfully rented, right about the time that the holiday season hits and we can sit back and enjoy the family and the beautiful house Steve created for us. I think I will enter into the *What Do I Do Now?* stage when we finish these projects, and I wonder what's going to occupy my time and mind. And finally I will get back to *How Did I Ever Work?* when I once again find something different to occupy myself in a meaningful way.

I can't ignore that I have days where I wish I were still working. I miss the old routine of getting dressed in the morning and walking out to where Steve would be watching morning news. He would admire what I was wearing and would tell me how beautiful he thinks I am. That was a great way to start my work day. I sometimes look at all my clothes and wonder what I'm going to do with most of them in my current retired phase! Is it bad to be in your pj's by 6:30 p.m.? I used to think so, but now I'm totally okay with it!

I get nostalgic when hearing about things going on at PPP, and indeed in the preschool education world, and I wish I were still a part of this rewarding field. I continue to get invited to stop by and visit PPP or to attend a fun event happening there, which I really appreciate. However, it's with a mix of making sure I'm not interfering in any way with the somewhat new acquisition period, as well as just a sadness to be around what's no longer mine, that I don't do that. I don't receive many calls or texts from the teachers or others on the administrative team, and as surprising as it is to me, it's really as it should be. The loyalty of the staff has, rightly so, passed. The twenty-plus-year friendship I share with two of my directors goes beyond the job and I will be eternally grateful for that.

Last week, while in Florida, I got a call from an associate at GCCA asking if I would consider being a part of a panel of owners at the Fall GCCA Conference to discuss topics and field questions from everything to hiring, training, rules/regulations, marketing, etc. from other owners/directors attending. Boy would I! I was also asked if I would like to be considered for a position, sponsored through my prior association with GCCA, on a potential committee being discussed with the governor of Georgia on child-care advocacy, which will meet four times a year. I do hope this committee is formed and that I am confirmed for this position. These two things would connect my professional self to the world and help establish a connection for what has been my life's work for the past twenty-five years.

Maybe I *have* hit my stride as a newly retired person. I think so. I am open to all sorts of possibilities for my future, and I feel confident that the best can still be "yet to come."

UPDATE

I have entered into—what may be long or short term—the hardware business with my brother. I am helping him with staff scheduling to maximize his workforce to complement his sales, inventory, profitability, and customer service as well as shaping up the store in organization, and finally to help with staff policy and procedures implementation that he needed to get in place. And once again, it was Steve who had this idea for me and for the business—can't say it enough, he's a genius!

The store is one hour from my home; I work five to six days a week, eight hours each day, and I am loving it . . . for now. Felicia asked me the other day (when I "took off work" to have lunch with her and attend to some other neglected errands) why I was working so much. Well, I don't know any other way to work! One hundred percent is the only way I know to be. So again, for now I am enjoying helping him out, which in turn is giving me a purpose, which I have always needed. I appreciate his needing me and I am enjoying learning something new about myself in this new position at a hardware business. And, *of course,* gabbing with all the parents—oops!—customers. Go figure (insert giggle giggle)!

CHAPTER 4
WHY DO WE HAVE KIDS —*WHO DOES THAT?*

Because we want them? Because we planned for them? Because it was an accident? To save a marriage? To satisfy social expectations? How about "bonus babies"?

There are a lot of reasons a couple or a person has a baby. I mention several times in this book that Steve and I were married ten years before we had a baby, and we have been a couple since I was twelve years old and he was thirteen. We were together all through high school, the college years, and every year since. Everyone thought we would get married as soon as I got out of school, but we waited three more years before we married. Of course, a baby couldn't be far away. My goodness, we had been together already for many years by the time we married. But no, we waited *ten* years before having a child, by choice—*who does that?!*

My mother held off for about five years into our marriage before she started asking, "When are you going to have a baby?" For the next five years, she told me (and she tried to do so jokingly) that Steve and I were the most selfish people she knew. I told her many times that I did not want to have a child because Steve and I were enjoying each other and our life too much (that's why she kept saying we were selfish). I told her I didn't want to "have to" say no to Steve if he called me in the afternoon and said, "Hey, come downtown and let's have cocktails and dinner," or "Let's go somewhere this weekend," which happened quite often. I told her

I would resent a baby tying me (us) down. She told me that would not be the case, that I wouldn't feel this way toward my child. And you know what, she was totally right! Maybe we didn't feel that way because we *did* have those ten years of an unfettered lifestyle, or maybe because we were thirty and thirty-one and were ready to settle down. Or maybe it's just because it's a fact that when you have *your* baby, those feelings that made you question whether you wanted one reversed. For whatever the reason, Steve and I couldn't imagine ourselves without our baby.

> A funny aside (I was going to say "personal" aside, but most of the asides *are* personal (insert giggle giggle)): So, Steve and I decided we were going to start thinking about having a baby. After many years of being on birth control, the school of thought at that time (1980s) was that it may take many months, if not years, to get your body back on track and successfully get pregnant. The *first month* I went off the pill, I got pregnant. We were not ready! What? After ten years we weren't ready? No.
>
> I found out on Easter Sunday morning, and all the cute plans I had formulated in my mind about how I would tell Steve I was pregnant went out the window. He walked downstairs, and I blurted out, menacingly, even accusingly, "I'm pregnant." He couldn't believe it either.
>
> It was our year to go with his mom and grandparents to their church for Easter Sunday service, and I told him I was not going. He could go and just make some excuse for me; I didn't want to see anyone just yet. I was in shock. We both had several days of silence—I guess each of us was trying to come to grips with this unexpected news. One night I was walking our dog, Catfish, and Steve was working late. In the dark, Catfish and I were heading home, and here came

> Steve's BMW down the street. He stopped, got out of the car, grabbed me, and said, "We are going to have a baby." And that was it—we were in bliss!

So, maybe we were selfish. The above story really makes it seem so. So many people can't have children and yearn for them that it seems that any of us who can have children should be incredibly happy to do so. Life continues to be a funny thing.

Our nephew had his first child a couple of years ago in his forties. His younger sister, our niece, had two children, ages eighteen and sixteen by this time. To be fair, she looks more like her children's older sister than their mom, but she and her husband just knew when they married that they wanted children and didn't waste any time. They are fabulous parents, raising two very accomplished children, our great-niece and nephew. Just imagine how young they are going to be (presumably) when they get to enjoy grandchildren. Steve's dad enjoyed grandchildren and great-grandchildren for many years before his recent passing. Steve and I are wondering *if/when* we are going to be grandparents now that we are in our sixties. I guess payback's a b*tch (insert giggle giggle)! It was so sweet when I talked with our nephew after the birth of his first son and he was so joyful. I said to him, "Just like Steve and I, you just didn't know." I'm not saying that either of us are regretful of our life *before* children, just an observation of the *after*.

> A funny aside: One day, several years ago, William called me on a Saturday morning as Steve and I were getting dressed to go about our day. He asked if I could meet him for lunch. I said, "Just me, or me and Dad?" He said, "Just you for now."
>
> Oh no. What was the problem that I might need to know first to soften the blow? Of course I met him (with instructions from Steve to please let him know as soon as I could what was wrong). I speculated to Steve, "Someone's pregnant." Steve said, "Well, what

> are you going to do or say?" I said, "You mean after I yell 'YES'?" (Insert giggle giggle!)
>
> Of course, part of me was just kidding, but part of me wasn't. Well, it wasn't that (or believe me, you would have already heard about my grandchild in this chapter, or in this book somewhere). It was just an issue he needed advice on before he may get Steve involved. So off I sneaked to the bathroom and told Steve it wasn't very serious, just William feeling me out on how to proceed with something, so all's well.

But how does society push the concept of having children or not? A very popular political figure is asking young people these days to really consider if it's wise to bring a child into the world under the current global situation that she sees as being a mess. Not because of this politician, certainly, but young people *are* seemingly giving the children thing a very hard and cynical look (as discussed briefly in the Parents and Millennials chapter). There is already a decline in new population, and several years ago China lifted its only-one-child law to allow couples to have more children due to a decline in their new population. *Do we see the possibility of a* Handmaid's Tale *child-bearing regulation nightmare in its early phase?*

In my parents' day, if you didn't have a child after a couple of years of marriage, something was wrong, *with something*. I have joked many times with my mom that only my older brother was "planned." I say this because he was barely two when I was born, which meant she got pregnant with me when he was not even a year and a half—*who does that?* (Insert giggle giggle!) Then he and I were seven and five when our younger brother was born—*who does that?* (Insert giggle giggle!) She tells me her plan was to have two children, wait a few years, and then have two more—two pairs of children. That fourth one, the other half of the pair for my younger brother, unfortunately did not happen.

> A funny aside: Just last night I was reading a fashion magazine, and the feature was on Kylie Jenner. She was talking about how close she is to all her siblings and that her mom, the consummate "momager," decided to have three sets of children so that everyone would have a partner growing up. This plan worked out for her. So the ultimate fashionable Kardashian mom channeled my "unfashionable" mom's pairs-of-children philosophy before anyone ever heard of a Kardashian! I guess my mom is the real influencer (insert giggle giggle).

I have a good friend who has what's called Irish twins. A funny story she tells is that one Father's Day, her husband was not a father, but before the *next* Father's Day, he was a father of *two*! Both of their children have June birthdays, and there's a couple of weeks in June when they are the same age, so I will leave it up to you to figure out the math on that one! Again, I ask, *who does that?!*

So, why do we have kids? There obviously is not one model. It's all over the place. It was always so funny when a family left PPP after so many years and sometimes I couldn't resist saying, "Well, you never know, we may see you again." Of course, they would all—and I mean *all*—say a resolute "NO WAY!" And what happened in so many instances? We would see them back with either a new husband/wife, thus a new baby, or the same spouse with a bonus baby! I joked with one family that had two girls go through our school (I mean, they were at PPP for ten or more years with their daughters), and when I said that goodbye-haha-phrase to her, she said, "No way. We are putting our monthly PPP money into a lakehouse!" A few years later when she brought her third baby girl to PPP, we laughed! What lakehouse? She said a lakehouse was nothing compared to this bonus baby girl. We agreed with her.

Another wonderful story: We had a fabulous family bring their beautiful baby to us in the Infant Suite. She grew through our program and graduated at six years of age from the PPP kindergarten class. This is an *extremely accomplished family*—mom, dad, *and* daughter. They were a perfect set, seemingly missing nothing in their family's makeup. This family lived in my community, but I never ran into them in any way for the next eight or so years, like so many other families after seeing them every day for years at PPP. When we had the 20th "mystical connections" Anniversary, here came the dad and the now *teen* daughter walking up to the party. I was overjoyed seeing them and this beautiful young lady who used to be a PREPPIE. So I said, "Wow, I haven't seen you guys in forever!" And the dad said, "Well, you are going to be seeing a lot more of us soon. We are having a baby in January!" Same family unit, new baby. When they brought their baby boy to us, I told him, "You just didn't realize you weren't through." They could not have been happier to have this child.

Again, *who does that?* But, I think I've shown we *all* "do that," there is no *one* way, and it all works!

It was always funny for me to talk to parents, specifically moms, about how we decided to start, and continue, our families. There's not a single one of us who doesn't enjoy sharing our pregnancy stories and birth stories; we practically talk over each other. Moms, you know what I'm talking about! I could make the rest of this chapter about my pregnancy adventures (insert giggle giggle). Hayden and William were both premature, so I had a *lot* of ups and downs: months of bedrest, hospitalizations, both were C-section births—William was a placental abruption emergency birth, which could have been fatal to either or both of us—and on and on. When William was three, we had our own bonus baby pregnancy, or accident (I really can't honestly say which), that ended in a twenty-two-week miscarriage. Several other moms at PPP were pregnant at this time, so you can imagine how difficult this was for me, and for them, as these particular children grew through PPP. But, like millions of women who have had miscarriages, you go on, especially if you are blessed with other children.

It's also very interesting how a couple becomes experts on handling a child the minute you have one of your own (insert giggle

giggle). One day you have absolutely no idea what to do, the next day, voilà, it's your child and no one knows how to hold it, bathe it, feed it, and love it better than you.

My mom came over to our house after Hayden was born to help out. What she really was, was a cleaner and a cook. I handled Hayden, except when I needed rest, and then she took over. In fact, in my experience with myself and my friends, the grandmothers were a little afraid (not really afraid, but maybe nervous is a better word) of handling or telling their child how to care for their own baby. What if that was wrong now from when they had their own baby? I think God gives us a certain window of instant knowledge and security on how to care for *our* baby. I don't think it's necessarily a natural instinct until you have your own, but from what I know, it's instantaneous when you get home with your baby. When I had William, my mom again came to help, taking care of Hayden. I took care of my baby, William.

So many young, first-time moms would come with their baby to PPP and have all sorts of instructions on exactly how our caregivers should care for their baby, sometimes pages of instructions they expected the teachers to read (insert giggle giggle). These ladies had taken care of thousands of babies. They were experts. Obviously these moms and dads trusted these ladies, or else they couldn't have walked out, leaving their baby with us—what an unnatural thing to do!

I often said to parents, as a way to validate their feelings of trusting us with their baby, that their baby was in the best of hands and not to worry, it was okay for them to do this. I did it myself when Hayden was born, as do millions of parents every day, and I thought the babies at PPP had the best care in the world, other than with the parent, of course.

And isn't it a funny observation when you see how much equipment is needed for a baby's care these days? I thought it was a lot when I had my babies, and that's not even a scratch as to what parents have these days! But to see moms in a store with a HUGE stuffed diaper bag in their cart, almost no place to put their groceries or other items, it makes me giggle. What in the world do they think they need that bag for? Can't they run out to the car if some situation arises that they need *multiple* diaper changes and *multiple* changes of clothes? Is their child playing with the assortment of toys that are housed in that bag? Are they eating all the snacks crammed into the bag? It's a, what, thirty-minute grocery or Target run . . . what does the baby really *need* during that time? I mean, grab a diaper and wipes and stuff it in your purse—take a chance, live on the wild side (insert *huge* giggle giggle)! Just a funny observation.

> An aside: I told you about the conflicting emotional way Steve and I handled finding out I was pregnant with Hayden. When I got pregnant with William, it was an exciting, uplifting announcement! We now knew what was unknown when I found out I was pregnant with Hayden—we love kids! In fact, we wanted several!
>
> Here's what happened. We were living in Texas and Hayden was three. Steve was on a business trip. I purposely waited until the middle of the day, when I knew Steve would not be in his hotel room, before I made a call to him. There were no cell phones at that time, and when you called a hotel, you left a message with an actual person at the hotel to pass along (I know, it seems like cavemen days compared to now). So after the operator rang his room several times, she came on the line and said he wasn't there and asked if I wanted to leave a message. The message she took down said, "We can't wait for you to get home, Daddy. Love Hayden and Natalie." For some reason, Steve thought it was up to him to name our children (insert giggle giggle). Way before we had Hayden, he came home one day from work and said, "If we ever have a boy, we are going to name him Hayden." He

also said he wanted his daughter, if he ever had one, to be named Natalie (he thought the actress Natalie Wood was a beautiful woman), so that's how I broke the news to him. I knew he would get the meaning. When he got this message, about midnight that night when he returned to his room, he called me and was over the moon!

Of course, Natalie turned out to be William, which was just perfect. William was named after Steve's uncle Bill, who played football in the 1940s for the New York Giants and was one of my and Steve's favorite family members. What a character Uncle Bill was! William has lived up to his name in many ways!

As you can see, in whatever way we have our children, it's the perfect way. I used to not be able to imagine not having a daughter. Someone I could dress up, show how to apply makeup and do her hair, shop with, have girl days with, gossip with. But I had two boys. Everyone who knows me knows that I am *thrilled* to be the only girl in my little family—go figure! All three of my boys (insert giggle giggle!) spoil me. I am deferred to in every way! I *cannot* imagine sharing this spoiling and attention with a daughter (insert a HUGE giggle giggle!). See, my mom is right again about my being selfish.

Hayden satisfies the shopping and gossiping part, and William satisfies the love of sports in me. Perfect! But, of course, anyone that has one of each, or a mix of boys and girls, feels they are the luckiest of all. See? Steve and I think we "did right" by enjoying our younger years and then settling down with children. Other friends of ours who had children young now enjoy being "still young" and enjoying grandchildren . . . I'm sure none of us in our situations feels we didn't do the *right* thing. And it was right, for each of us in our situations at that time. I know I wouldn't have done anything differently.

> A funny aside: I mention Crash, our granddog, in other chapters. He belongs to William, and it's a funny story how Crash became a part of our family. William was eighteen and just finishing his freshman year of college. For some reason, he got in his head that he wanted a dog.
>
> So one Saturday, he went to a nearby animal shelter and he found ten-week-old Crash (who was named Chuckie Finster at the time). What was he thinking?! I told him when the time was right, whenever that may be, he would find another dog he liked just as well. But no, *this* was the dog he wanted.
>
> So William "thought" that the dog he had picked out and wanted so badly would be a dog that would like to hunt with him, a big dog that would be a protector, a real testosterone companion. Hahahaha! What he ended up with was Crash the scaredy-cat. He runs when the vacuum is turned on, he doesn't like the sound of flipping out a trash-can liner, and when it thunders, it's the saddest thing to see that big dog shake in fright. And forget about going hunting where a loud gun is fired!
>
> But you know what? William wouldn't have him any other way. Crash is now almost ten years old, and a better granddog we couldn't have asked for. William gets mad at Steve and I when they visit because we do everything that William has taught Crash is wrong, mostly as it pertains to begging for food (insert giggle giggle). We've told William, "If you think this is bad, just wait and see what we do to your kids!" (insert giggle giggle).

So, what do our children think of our choice of when we had them? I don't believe our children can imagine having parents who are in any way different from the parents they have, *or* having a different sibling situation. Sibling relationships have always been interesting to me. Boy, that could be a book in itself, so complicated a dynamic sibling relationships are.

> An aside: Like so many families that don't live in the same community, or even the same state, Steve and his sister did not have the traditional relationship of seeing each other regularly or celebrating holidays together with their families and things like that as they got older. Really for no reason other than living out of state, having different life experiences, and just busy times (and as I'm typing this, I also realize I did not have the traditional relationship with my older brother, since he lived out of state his entire adult life until recently and came home pretty much *only* for holidays).
>
> Steve and his sister would have spurts of not seeing each other for a bit and then reconnecting. They would have periods of being closer, but busy lives would happen and time would go by. His sister was the mother of the niece and nephew I mentioned in the beginning of this chapter. Steve and I love them very much, but due to the fact that they lived out of state, and just busy lives on both ends as well, we missed out on being very much involved with them growing up, which lasted into their young adult years. Of course, we visited and kept in touch on some level with them through the years, but not as closely as we would have wanted or thought when they were children.
>
> Steve's sister, their mother, passed away two years ago. For some reason her death brought Steve and I very close to our niece and nephew and their families. Maybe it was the realization in all of us that any type of a reconnecting through her could now never be, so that brought out the strong desire for all of us to

> become a closer family unit. Who knows. But her death was not without meaning. We now call and text and visit with them and enjoy a loving relationship with our great-nieces and nephews.
>
> So, for all the ups and downs of the years before, and how sad it is that Steve's sister passed away so young and unexpectedly, she ended up giving her remaining family a great gift. Her passing brought us all together in such a way that I can't imagine ever being without them in our life. I love and thank her for that.

So, why do we have children? I know for me (even though I waited ten years into our marriage), not having a child was never an option. I knew I would be a mother. But what if I—*we*—couldn't? I was involved with many parents at PPP who had fertility issues. Some of these couples went to great lengths and expense to become parents. Some of these parents adopted children. We had a wonderful story of a couple who had one child, struggled to have another, decided to adopt, and once that was a certainty, she got pregnant! You hear that sort of thing happening a lot. We had one couple who barely got one child out of our Infant Suite before the next one had to start, and really, we could have kept the older one in the Infant Suite a month or two longer than we did. The different ways we decide to have kids, or maybe don't decide, are too numerous to write about.

I always told parents that whatever their path to children was, whatever gender they did or didn't have, or how many children they ended up having, or when, was perfect. I never had anyone disagree.

Who Does That? was *never* a question.

CHAPTER 5
THE POWER OF THE BRAIN!

Sometime during the first ten years of my "baby-free by choice" marriage, I attended a baby shower with a friend of mine for a friend of hers that I didn't know. Sounds odd, but during those halcyon days in the '80s, friends just did that sort of thing and it didn't seem socially awkward. Anyway, the shower occurred *after* the baby was born due to some pregnancy complications prior to the birth (which later happened to me with my first baby shower as well—so once again, odd).

During the small talk at this shower, the proud mom, holding her six-week-old baby boy, declared, "Well, I can tell you, he's all boy!" and I wondered, *What in the world could this tiny, seemingly non-genderish human being possibly be doing to qualify as being "all boy" instead of "all baby"?* I mean, do baby boys eat differently or poop differently than baby girls? Was he already throwing a mean curve ball or zooming his tiny baby racecar around the floor? What was this proud mama trying to sell us on her baby boy?

Well . . . fast-forward to when my first child was born. There was no type of proud moment, glib comment, or well-worn cliché that went unspoken about Hayden. He was, no doubt and without bias, the smartest baby that had ever been born (insert giggle giggle). *Now* I totally understood how the above-mentioned mom could recognize in her six-week-old baby boy the characteristics that made him do things that were, so proudly, "all boy"—I mean, I could tell how smart and special my five-week-old premature baby boy was too—and not just me, the whole family could—and if we all could see it, it must be true (insert giggle giggle).

But seriously, babies are a wonder. Just look at what they accomplish *in a year*. They go from living *inside of* and *off of* another human being to living on their own outside of that human being (if this wasn't just accepted as the way we reproduce, it would be the stuff of a truly sci-fi movie). And if *that* incredible achievement is not enough, they also learn to eat, walk, communicate, and yes, eventually they learn to manipulate grown, educated, and life-worn people all around them, and not just their parents or family members. Just let this sink in a minute. *Babies achieve all this in just twelve short months!*

Babies can, with a smile, a whimper, or a full-fledged screech, control not only their parents and family members, but waitresses, caregivers, flight attendants, shop clerks, you name it. Have you ever witnessed a parent in a restaurant giving a child anything they want just to keep them quiet? I once observed a young couple reduced to asking for a bowl of maraschino cherries because their child stood up in a chair and they were only able to coax him back down by giving him the cherry from their drink. Of course, they were proud of themselves for this quick and smart thinking of *controlling* their child, but not so fast—*never underestimate a child.* The child stood up again (of course to get the same result) and these, now *outsmarted,* parents had to keep feeding him the cherries in order to get him to sit down and keep the restaurant-peace, just to stand back up and so on.

Smart kid or a brat? Oh no—that's a motivated child learning life cues on how to control a situation and get a desired result, a wonderful life skill to have. However, this is an early learned skill, *taught by well-meaning adults,* that can have adverse outcomes when used by an immature child of any age.

I wrote an article entitled "The POWER of the Brain!" If you have had the opportunity to read anything about brain research in babies and young children, ages zero to five, that information will amaze you. Again, the achievements of an infant, toddler, and preschooler in the first five years of their life is really an incalculable miracle. We look at infants and toddlers as eating/sleeping/pooping machines, but what their bodies and brains are going through and what they are capable of learning is mind-blowing. We cannot wrap our adult brains around what's actually going on inside the brain of a baby—again, just sit still and *think about that for a moment.*

As an adult, look back on, let's say, the past five years of your life. What have you learned, achieved, or accomplished? And I don't mean building on achievements or skills you already had. I mean totally and completely a brand-new skill, and I'm just asking you to come up with one—in five years, not twelve months! Infants are doing so much at once—again, it's mind-blowing! Adults cannot—repeat, *cannot*—compete with the brain power of an infant. It's just *not possible.* Again, let that sink in for a minute.

In the article I wrote on this subject, I mention two movies, *Baby Geniuses* and *Lucy*. Both movies, one a comedy and one a thriller, respectively, deal with the power of the brain. Specifically, *Baby Geniuses* highlights the complete and total knowledge that babies are born with and eventually lose as they get older due to us, as the weaker and dumber adults, teaching them what we know, which *ensures* they become just mediocre and "normal" human beings. A vile scientific corporation understands this "baby genius" and tries to harness this power for disreputable reasons before it slips away from these infants/toddlers. But of course that doesn't work. We smart adults get to them, with the best intentions of course, too quick.

In *Lucy*, the main character knows how to use the 90 percent of her brain that her fellow human beings don't know how to access or use, and you get the picture, she's just too cool for school, as they say, and all sorts of havoc ensues. While being Hollywood flicks, these two examples are correct in theory.

Specifically in the case of a baby's brain, the unused or unnourished as well as the overabundance of brain cells that infants are born with just die off. That's a fact, and these brains cells are lost at an alarming rate. Brain research can show us the density of a child's brain at different ages and how this concept works. I state in my published article that it is up to us, in the meager ways we can, to nurture and provide the educational, emotional, and social stimuli and skills necessary to help ward off as much cell loss as we can. This brain-density model is a documented and sad fact, as seen in children anywhere from orphanages to poverty-stricken countries and communities that show the brain is significantly less dense and more underdeveloped than those of children who have been exposed to more educational and social stimuli.

In the state of Georgia, where I live, there is free, state-funded pre-K, which is the educational experience for four-year-olds prior to the start of a child's kindergarten year. This concept and program was originally designed to reach at-risk children (possibly in the inner-city areas or rural areas around the state) who might not have the same opportunity for educational exposure as children from a typical suburb or around the larger cities.

As of this writing in 2019, this program is more than twenty years old in the state of Georgia and over the years has now expanded to include *all* four-year-olds, no matter the income level or availability therein of preschool. This program has done wonders for young children across the state to expose them to at least some level of educational stimuli, and the beauty of it is that it is funded by the state-run lottery-gaming proceeds, not tax dollars—genius!

Of course, this program, as wonderful as it sounds, has the unintended (or maybe intended) governmental consequences and political game-playing and problems of a government-run program (sort of like dangling free college for all or forgiving all current student college loans) to garner political votes and clout.

In the current political climate, and with a 2020 election looming, certain candidates for president of the United States are advocating *free* childcare, not just in the year leading up to kindergarten, but for all ages zero to five. This could be viewed as only trying to garner votes (I mean, if you have ever had to pay for childcare, who wouldn't want it to be free?), but one has to hope they are advocating this in an altruistic way to help capture the importance of the zero-to-five learning years.

Of course, the desire of some parents to educate their child outside of a government-run system will always exist, no matter the cost associated. It's interesting to note that Georgia pre-K classes in many areas of the state (typically middle class and above) are not filled to capacity as one might think they would be. As the owner for twenty-five years of a private preschool that did not subscribe to the free Georgia pre-K program, I could justify the significant differences and advantages of my private-based program, unencumbered by any government regulations.

At many of the GCCA board meetings, I listened to most of the members discuss the problems and inadequacies of the Georgia pre-K program. Most of these preschools had no choice but to participate in this free, government-sponsored program due to either the community's demographics, the interest of the parents in their area, or because of the needed financial resources pumped into their center by the government with these state funds. But of course, nothing is ever "free," and "free" money (to anyone for any reason) always comes at a high price. And, of course, you have the other side of the coin that discourages group-style learning and the possible emotional detachment of infants and young children of not being kept at home with mom/dad/family member . . . so maybe the government should just stay out of the whole thing—but that's a whole different chapter (insert giggle giggle).

Research also confirms that this sloughing off of a portion of a young child's brain cells will occur no matter what type of educational and emotional stimuli a baby is exposed to, because there are just too many cells to keep.

But, in the sci-fi future, who knows? Will adults be able to find a way to harness the power and abilities of a baby's brain to last into adulthood? Will all the problems of the world be solved? Will diplomatic world peace be simple to achieve? Will everyone know how to communicate in any language? Will there come a time that we no longer need mere computers, calculators, and other "intelligence gathering" or artificial intelligence devices? With as fast as technology is improving, you would never think that we could possibly exist without these advances. But don't be so sure . . .

Because, of course, we have the most advanced device in the world, one that can never *be matched or artificially improved on—our* brain*!*

CHAPTER 6
WHAT KIND OF MOTHER *ARE* YOU?

As moms, we ask ourselves that question a lot. Are we ever happy with our answer? The article I wrote as a Mother's Day tribute reflects on women, as mothers *or* as children, and poses questions on each. I know after this article was published I received both reactions from the PPP moms—being mothers themselves as well as being children, and reflecting on their own relationships with their mothers.

Just last night, I was on the phone with my soon-to-be thirty-year-old son Hayden. We were talking about things I used to cook when the boys were young. He laughingly said he couldn't remember me cooking very much. How this conversation started, funny enough, was he asked what we were having for dinner (which is a *very* typical thing for him to ask being away from the South up in New York—insert giggle giggle!) and I told him we were having Chick-fil-A. So I asked him if he remembered when I used to make homemade chicken filet sandwiches.

That's when he said he didn't remember me cooking very much. About an hour later he called me back after his six-mile run through Central Park, where he reminisced to himself about all the things I used to cook, and he wanted to call me back and set the record straight. He *did* remember a lot of things I used to cook (or maybe it would be more appropriate to say "served for dinner"), and he *did* remember the homemade chicken sandwiches!

A funny aside: One day at William's baseball game,

> when he was probably around twelve years old, a very dear friend told me a funny story in a way that only she could do with her incredible sense of humor. This was a fabulous mom, always laughing and a friend to everyone. She had cooked a fabulous meal for her family of fried chicken, corn on the cob, fried okra, cornbread—all fresh and delicious. Her son, who was a friend of William's, looked at this incredible home-cooked meal and said, "Mom, why can't you ever make Hamburger Helper like Mrs. Paschal?" (Insert huge giggle giggle!)

As I wrote in the chapter about the beginning of PPP, Hayden was five and William two when we opened the school, and I (and Steve) was drowning in that process. Working ten to twelve hours a day for the first several years, cooking was just not high on the priority list. But I don't remember being upset about it or thinking my boys were missing out on anything or were being scarred. Going into the years ahead, when Hayden and William were both so involved in extracurricular activities, which mostly happened at dinnertime (baseball practice and games and Irish dancing practices), cooking dinner and eating traditionally around a dinner table was not even possible, even if I did cook a meal (insert giggle giggle).

Watching the moms in the preschool in those early years when I was also a young mom, I saw mostly professional moms working long hours and struggling to get to the school, in a lot of cases, by our closing time of 7:00 p.m. This broke my heart for them.

In those early years, moms were usually the primary drop-off and pickup person. At that time in the early 1990s, most dads were the "real" breadwinners of the family and were usually the ones who either had to stay at work later, travel, or be out entertaining clients. I know it wasn't only my boys who might have gotten short-changed in the "mom cooking dinner" scenario or eating around the dinner table as a family.

As I write in the Parents and Millennial chapter, this was not the way I, Steve, or most any other baby boomers were raised. Have any studies been done on *why* we raised our children so differently and why we seemed to be okay with that? I'm going to research that and get back to you maybe in another chapter, or maybe another book.

My mom and Steve's mom cooked dinner *every night*. Fresh meats, fresh vegetables, always a bread (even if it was a saucer of stacked sliced white bread—we called the slice "loaf-a-bread"), a dessert was always available, too, and of course, homemade sweet tea. If Publix didn't make sweet tea in gallon containers, my boys wouldn't have grown up on sweet tea since I made it so seldom.

I remember my mom cooking, of course, but I don't really remember having fond memories of bonding around the table discussing family matters or anything like that. I think we were usually in a hurry or wrapped up in our own things to really be interested in drawing out each other's feelings like it seems families do on TV.

I think we get a bad rap these days about not having dinner together as a family and how that has adversely affected this generation. I'm not totally sure that the "dinner table illusion" is true for either the benefit *on* my generation or the detriment *to* the current generation. Maybe it's a subliminal thing about the lost art of family dinners and what that loss demonstrates about the family unit in general these days. Or maybe what it's really about is the feelings of a family—the connections of a family that might not have anything to do with a sit-down family dinner (as nice as it is now to have my boys sit down to a meal with Steve and I, whether at home or at a restaurant). It is more about the importance and power of food, as I have written about in the "You Can Lead a Horse to Water" chapter.

Anyway, as I wrote in the Mother's Day article as a tribute to my mom, it doesn't seem that her influence on me had anything to do with the person I became as far as my aspirations and the way I lead my adult life. She was and is very unaffected by fashion, makeup, and those types of things. I just took her last week for her very first pedicure and she's eighty-five years old! I am very fashion-conscious and spend a lot of time and effort (and money) on clothes and makeup.

My mom never worked outside the home—never. I couldn't wait to leave school at eighteen and get a job, and I worked consistently until my recent retirement nine months ago at the age of fifty-nine—and loved every minute of it.

She wasn't really interested in a social life. Steve and I waited through ten years of marriage to have a child because we were so socially engaged. She doesn't enjoy reading at all and I, sometimes, read a book a week. My mom was great at math. Me? Not so much. My mom is not at all politically engaged and I am a political junkie, the same about sports. But she could sketch on the back of a bank deposit slip how a piece of clothing or home decoration was made and go home and make it. I take my clothes to a dry cleaner if something merely needs a button sewn on, or I give it to Steve to do (insert giggle giggle). She made all my Barbie doll clothes, a lot of my clothes as well, and my cheerleading outfits. She could quilt beautifully.

And listen to this: I found Hayden's baby crib linens at Saks Fifth Avenue, very expensive, but my mother found the exact same fabric and *made* everything and surprised me! It was beautiful and saved me hundreds of dollars. I used the bumper pads, ruffle set, pillows, and comforter for both Hayden and William, so beautifully made by my mom. I have it wrapped up still, thirty years later, just in case one of my grandbabies might need it—either at my house or theirs.

This year for Christmas, my aunt gave me kitchen tea towels that my mom had embroidered for each day of the week, each with a saying and a picture of what that day was meant for—cooking, cleaning, shopping, etc. These towels had been lovingly put away for more than twenty years when my mom was able to see and enjoyed spoiling her family with loving gifts such as these.

> A funny aside: During the first two years of our marriage, Steve was finishing up his graduate degree at Georgia Tech and, of course, had a crazy schedule. I worked an eight-to-five job. One Christmas during this time, I macraméd purses and other items as gifts for the women in my family (my mom had talked me into attending a macramé workshop with her). Steve was at home one day, before afternoon classes, fusing the bottoms of the purses for me, doing some laundry, and, of course, studying. Who pops in, unannounced, but my grandmother and two of my great-aunts. This became a funny family story, still told to this day—Kay is at work and Steve is home macraméing purses (insert giggle giggle).

My grandmother was a woman ahead of her time. She worked at the town's cotton mill her whole adult life. When she wasn't working, she was dressed to the nines at all times—matching necklaces and ear bobs, brooches, shoes, and purses. When she retired, she kept her *valise* packed and ready in the trunk of her car. She told me once that you never know when an opportunity may come up, you always have to be ready! How right she was, and this woman never missed an opportunity that came up for her or that she created.

I think my dad told me recently that she had traveled to every state—mostly on church-sponsored bus tours—*wow!* I once got a letter from her when we lived in Texas (she in Georgia) saying she was coming for a visit. Not a phone call, but a letter detailing her *already-made* flight plans. Well, come on then!

On the other hand, my maternal grandmother, Mama, never worked a day in her life outside the home and never learned to drive. I don't believe she ever went five miles or so from where she was born, except when we would bring her and my granddaddy up to Atlanta for the holidays in their later years. She had the sweetest heart of *anyone I have ever known*.

I was surrounded my whole life by wonderful Southern women—my aunts and great-aunts could be a book of their own. They were loud and proud—strong women, all of them. They were soft and loving. They were fabulous cooks and loving wives and mothers. I hope I have some of all of them in me.

My mom was a part of everything my brothers and I were involved in. One year she was the carnival chairman at our elementary school. Back then, those types of school events were *huge* community extravaganzas, and it took a special kind of volunteer to be in charge and successfully organize. She was PTA chairman (I guess it's correct these days to say "chairwoman" or "chairperson," but back then it was still seen as honorable to be called "chairman"). I never really did the hands-on work of volunteerism with Hayden and William. I bankrolled these types of things at school events or their hobby interests and told the boys that all moms had their place of importance—some had the time and talent to help organize and create things, some moms helped to pay for the things that went into making the events possible, but both are equally as important (insert giggle giggle). I always loved when William was in the class with a set of twins in our community because I knew their mom was an excellent, stay-at-home-mom organizer and that William's class events would be well taken care of!

My mom is an old-fashioned Southern lady. She took us to church, she cooked, she cleaned, and she made sure we were always where we were supposed to be. She made every birthday and holiday special, until just recently, which is a source of real sadness and despair for her. She never shirked her duties as a daughter to her parents, and she was someone my two brothers and I knew we could always count on to do anything necessary for our health, safety, comfort, and happiness.

For all the things I didn't get from my mom, what my mother *did* instill in me is how to love my boys and how to be there for them. Funny, though, I don't remember her really ever *telling me* while I was growing up that she loved me. My boys have been told that an infinite number of times in their lives. In talking with

Felicia, my very best friend in the world, she says the same thing about her mother, *and as I am typing this,* a very strange thing just hit me this very second! Felicia's mom was one of a very few moms I knew who worked (and she had a very good job), but Felicia chose the stay-at-home-mom route for herself. What the heck? A mother's influence? What impact does it *really* have on the way we are as adults? Just take these two examples of myself and Felicia and our moms, and both of us turned out pretty much the opposite of the role our mothers had in the household.

When I was a young mother and a lot of women were joining the workforce (baby boomer women hit their work stride during this time), we were inundated with the "quality vs. quantity" theorem. My reflection on this was that it was meant to be a societal justification for *not* spending time with your child. As long as you had quality in the time that you *did* spend with your child, you were good.

Not so fast. My mother really didn't have *quality* in the time she spent with me. What I remember is that I could *always* count on her *being there* for me. When I got home from school, when I had friends over, when a mom was needed to volunteer for *anything,* she was always there; I could always count on her without even asking her—it was a given. My hand could be raised, and yes, my mom can do that. I think a certain segment of children of my boys' generation maybe didn't feel they could count on their mothers always being there—and I mean that from both a working and non-working mother standpoint. The term "latch-key kid" was phrased during this era. Carpooling began in this era. I'm not being derisive of either of these practices, just stating that my generation of moms started these practices that largely didn't exist between a mother and child before. Maybe one needs to wonder why?

What kind of mother are you? I don't think you really know until your children are grown and you can have funny stories and shared memories with them. It is really telling on how they view you as a mom, I think. When Hayden was telling me he didn't remember me cooking (before he called me back and said he did), he said what he *did* remember was me waking him up every single morning and fixing his lunch in the kitchen as he ate breakfast before school. He went on and said he remembered telling me one time that some of the other kids only had snacks for their lunch and that he wanted that, too, and then a couple days after that he opened his lunch and I had packed only snacks! I didn't remember that at all, but he went on to say, "That's because you were the best mommy," and I replied, "I think that sounds like a terrible mommy!" And we laughed.

It's when William told me a couple of years after that terrible college baseball loss that I write about in another chapter, that he *knew* I would still be there waiting to console him or just be there for him even though it took him over an hour to come out of the locker room. It's about me getting a bouquet of flowers on Hayden's birthday *from Hayden* thanking me for being his mom. It's about William putting something touching on his social media page about me (or about Steve and I) that he *knows* we will never see, but someone else sends it to me. (And now that I wrote this, he'll know that I know!) It's about when William calls me to go out for lunch because he needs his mom for advice, or just to listen, about a personal issue or decision. It's about Hayden calling multiple times during the day just to check in and chat. It's about William telling his girlfriend I wouldn't miss his very first umpiring job.

This is when you know, that for all your mistakes, for *all* the things you could have done better, you were "the best mommy" in the eyes of your child.

And to end this chapter on mothers, since the time I had my own children thirty years ago, I bet there hasn't been a phone conversation or a visit with my mom that hasn't ended in her saying to me, "I love you."

CHAPTER 7
BEING A FATHER, BEING A MAN, BEING A *DAD*

If we moms thought it was tough being a mom and what impact our choices have on our children, no doubt dads have had the harsh glare of the spotlight on them in the last few years. As women, our choices on how to be a woman *and* a mother have been elevated and celebrated by society. No matter which way we have chosen, there seems to be a respected place for all of us. For men, not so much. Absentee dads, male toxicity, the "wussification" of the man—how does a man know how to *be* in the eyes of society or, sometimes, in his own home?

In my article on how moms have changed from the time of my mom to now, this is even truer for men. At least when I was a child, there were a few moms who worked and had fewer traditional traits than most other moms; but for men, fathers—they were all pretty much the same. There were *no* stay-at-home dads. There were no dads who worked from home. Everyone's dad left in the morning for work in a suit or their work clothes and didn't come home until dinnertime. I don't remember anyone's dad ever volunteering for anything at school. Dads coached (the boys) in sports and dads were the disciplinarian at home. Who of my age doesn't remember their stay-at-home mom saying, "Just wait until your father gets home"? Poor dads. They had no idea they were going to have to come home and be expected to get all geared up and mad for something they had no part in just so they could be the one to discipline their child—to be THE FATHER. Oh well.

Fast-forward to today. As I chronicle in a Father's Day article I wrote, over the twenty-five years we owned PPP, the roles of dads changed so much. The role of Steve in our household changed so much. After being the "real" breadwinner of the family and the strategic and driving force of opening PPP, Steve stepped into the stay-at-home-dad role after the first five or so years of working seven days a week for our family business and was excellent at it.

Hayden has a vague memory of going to his dad's big corporate office. William has no recollection of Steve "working" in the traditional way. William, however, has a great recollection of him and Steve driving to school, singing tunes from Fleetwood Mac or Lynyrd Skynyrd, and throwing the baseball to each other a million times, and Hayden counts on Steve for professional "work advice" as he climbs the professional ladder. Both boys know without a doubt that Steve is the better cook of the two of us. That trait is also true of my younger brother, David, who, like Steve, is an awesome dad. Both he and Steve can concoct the best things in the kitchen for the family, among their many other talents as men and dads.

Growing up, my dad went to work every day. He was a sales representative for a huge trucking company and he entertained a lot. He had a company car. He always had a lot of money in his pocket. He coached my brother and Steve's baseball team for years. As I am writing this in November 2019, he's turning eighty-five tomorrow and he doesn't look a day over seventy-five—really! He can retell those long-ago baseball games from start to finish—who was on base, who got a hit and to where, how Steve pitched against what team, and how my brother did at every bat. He's as passionate about it now as he was then as the coach. When we were growing up, he could play basketball with my brother's friends like he was one of them, he played a mean infield with our church softball team, and he let us have the rare cocktail at home a little bit before we turned eighteen (the drinking age then). As he is turning eighty-five, we continue to wonder when he will ever *begin* the aging process!

> A funny drinking aside: His trucking company was based or had routes (I can't remember which) out west. Whenever the trucks would come from Colorado, they would (I guess) sneak Coors Beer in the trailer. Sometimes my dad would bring some home. We were the *only* people in our social circle who had access to Coors Beer at that time (I'm talking about the early '70s). We thought—and our friends did too—my dad was the coolest!

My dad rarely, if ever, laid an aggressive hand on me or my brothers. Our rules as teenagers were more lenient than most due to his fun-loving and trusting nature, but when he *did* issue a rule—an instruction, if you will—that we knew he was serious about, he expected it to have the weight and respect of being our father and for it to be followed. We knew when not to tempt his temper.

One night I was having one of my seasonal coughing fits and my mom concocted the dreaded whiskey, lemon juice, and honey home remedy prescribed by my pediatrician. Like any medicine, it tasted awful and I would not open my mouth for it. It was the middle of the night and I had kept the whole house up with my coughing. Through my coughing, I kept saying I would stop so that I wouldn't have to take that spoonful of medicine (insert giggle giggle). After a long period of cajoling and trying to get me to take the teaspoon of medicine, my dad told me, "I'm counting to three, and if you don't take this, I'm throwing it against the wall. One, two, three . . ."

I didn't open my mouth—splattered against the wall it went! I couldn't get my mouth open fast enough then and the medicine did the trick. This was how a dad acted back then—with force and enforcement when needed.

I don't think something like this would be looked on very well these days. For some reason, lessons learned "the hard way" as a child don't fly nowadays so much. Don't they say that these types of lessons will last a lifetime? Of course, I'm not talking about any form of child abuse being condoned in my youth's time. But getting a spanking or getting a "swat on the fanny" was something accepted—and expected as a form of discipline—in most all households, as well as in schools, back in the day.

Recently, one of my high school cheerleader friends recalled a memory of an issue that we experienced as senior cheerleaders: a conflict with our teacher cheer sponsor. The problem had gone on all year and our parents were fed up with it. My dad was the spokesmen for the group of parents, and in the *second meeting of the day* about this issue with the school principal, my dad said, "I have three children, one older than Kay and one younger, and this is the second time I have *ever* had to come to a school because of an issue with any one of them. The first time was this morning." She said she never forgot how impactful he was at that meeting.

My father, Steve's father, and every other father I knew of in my youth was the head of the household. I am not embarrassed to say that Steve is the head of our household; in fact, I depend on it. I also know he would contradict that. Steve and I truly are partners, we make decisions together and always have. I have a strong personality, and I am a tough businesswoman and a fierce protector of my family. (William has called me Leigh Anne Tuohy from *The Blind Side* . . . insert giggle giggle!) But, when push comes to shove, we *all* look to him for answers, for guidance, for the solution to any of our specific problems. He has never failed us.

Steve is tough as nails *and* has the biggest heart of anyone I have ever known—and that's not just my biased opinion, you can ask anyone that truly knows him. I have joked with many, "You just think *I'm* the nice one!" (Insert giggle giggle!) Steve roars like a lion and hugs like a teddy bear. He has been the benefactor (most times, anonymously) to so many people and counts among his closest friends people that others may least expect or maybe would never even acknowledge themselves. His generosity to his family and to people known and unknown to him is limitless—sometimes to his detriment, I tell him. (Insert giggle giggle!) He's, at times, an enigma, but *never* when it comes to his love and loyalty to those he loves. On that subject, he's crystal clear.

So, what does it mean to be a man these days? I do think being a dad today is akin to walking a daily tightrope in the eyes of society. Are you involved enough? Are you involved too much? Are you too "wussie"? Are you too chauvinistic? Are you too manly? Exactly what defines a man and a father these days? Is there any one answer?

When Hayden, and then William, turned twenty-one, I asked my brothers, their great-uncle, both their grandfathers, and, of course, Steve to write them a letter giving them advice on what it means to be a man. Hayden and William even wrote each other a letter to be included when each turned twenty-one. These letters were compiled and put into a book for them as a birthday gift. The letters were accompanied by photos of the boys with each of these wonderful men in their lives during special times. I wish I could share with you in part or in whole these letters.

The advice, the creativity, and the love in all these letters were more than I could have expected or imagined when I asked them to write them, and to do it twice. For the letters and advice to be so different for each boy but just as loving and creative, again, was amazing. No one would be in doubt, after reading any of these letters, about *exactly* what it means to be a man.

Steve's letter to each of his boys, of course, was completely different. Each letter was specific to their personalities, addressing challenges he saw as their father that might be problems they would face and advice on if or when these issues arose, how each of them may choose to attack this challenge. He was as much at ease talking about being tough as he was talking about how to be vulnerable. How to be savvy and smart as well as humble. Most of all he talked about being open to love and how all the joys that giving yourself fully to that one special person can make your life worthwhile. In fact, that nothing else is really as worthwhile.

They are now thirty-two and twenty-eight and when I reread his letters to them, written years ago, it's uncanny, but not surprising, how correctly Steve foresaw each of the boys' strengths and possible challenges as they reached manhood and the accurate advice and love he showed to both. *That* is what it means to be a dad.

Also not surprising is when William was asked, "Who is your role model?" for publishing on the back of his college baseball card, and when he could have chosen any one of the hundreds of athletes or coaches he admired, he said, "My dad, Steve Paschal." Or that Hayden, after admiring Steve's Rolex watch his entire life, counts his own as his prized possession, given to him by his dad upon graduating from Georgia Tech, *their* alma mater. As men, they both seek his advice and help in solving problems or in looking at all sides of an issue they are involved in. Again, he never fails them or steers them wrong. Like me, they depend on it.

Does a man need to give up his status as protector of the family, head of the household, strong and loving to his wife and children in order to fit today's view of what it means, or should mean, to be a man? Does it mean that someone else needs to be "less than" in the relationship in order for a man to actually *be* the man of the house? Not to anyone I know and respect, and certainly that's not the case in our family.

I noted in my Father's Day article how I've watched the role of men change throughout my twenty-five years at PPP. I watched it happen in my own family, and *never* did it mean that just because our roles may have reversed for a portion of our married life, that what it meant to be a man ever changed between me and my husband.

I expect that the roles of Steve and I will go through many changes in our upcoming years. But I also expect him, and depend on him, to always remain the *man* of the house, the head of our household, and the loving, admired, and respected dad to our boys.

CHAPTER 8
WHAT KIND OF PARENT ARE YOU? DO YOU TREAT YOUR CHILDREN THE SAME?

This chapter will merge two separate articles I wrote, which appeared in separate months' publications but are vastly interwoven themes. You will also see glimpses of these two themes in several other chapters in this book. I think the reason for this is that there is just so much to say about being a parent, and so many different paths parenting can take. An article, or in this case a chapter in a book, is not enough to actually examine and discuss fully.

For instance, as I am sitting here writing this chapter, my thirty-year-old son is here from New York for his birthday weekend as well as a business function to start the week. Keep in mind, he's a very successful businessman, a global account executive for a huge company and he travels all over the world—just so the stage is set. He and I have been discussing what may be a recurring medical issue he may need to resume a regimen of medication for. It's a very minor issue, but one that I think, if left unchecked, could *possibly* result in a small medical issue. He's gone off for his business function of the day and I have decided, on my own, that I am going to call our family doctor and see about getting his prescription (of many years ago) refilled or find out if he needs to come in for a blood test, etc.

I'm smiling at myself because, why am *I* doing this? Am I such a helicopter parent that I must do this for him? Am I too controlling? Am I just trying to be helpful? If *he* doesn't think it necessary, why do I? *If* I go through with calling the doctor—for my thirty-year-old!—will he be glad that I've taken care of this for him or will he say, "Mom, why did you do that? I don't need that medicine!" Who knows . . .

> *I'm back to writing after several days of not writing and I'm rereading this chapter. I ended up not calling the doctor, and my son and I have never even talked about this again, which should indicate to all (me specifically) that it was really more of a me/mom concern and not one that really needed* any *attention. I am somewhat proud of myself for holding back*—this time *(insert giggle giggle)!*

A funny aside: You know how I wrote in the Mother's Day chapter that I am really nothing like my mom? Okay, here it is . . . the confession—or really maybe this is just the way *all* mothers act (insert giggle giggle). A couple of years ago, I was getting my hair done, and my salon is somewhat near my mom and my aunt's house. Since they live about forty-five minutes from me, I always tried to pair my every-three-week hair appointment with a visit to my mom's.

On this particular time, I told my mom I would stop by Chick-fil-A and bring lunch for us as well as my aunt and uncle—okay, great! What ensued was several separate phone calls within my hair appointment period from my mom either telling me that none of them needed a drink (that's too much trouble to transport), then that no one really needed french fries (they could just eat chips from home), and then two more calls discussing which Chick-fil-A I should go to, either the one a little out of the way that might be quicker, or the one near the mall, on the way, but might be too much traffic!

> Finally I told my mom if she called me one more time about this simple Chick-fil-A lunch, not only was there going to be no lunch, but I was just going to go home and not even visit! I hung up my phone, looked at my hairdresser, and told her, "Oh my God, I think I do the same thing to my boys."
>
> You see, I recognized in myself things I do with my sons that are an annoyance for me with my own mother. Did she not think that I, a fifty-ish woman at the time, who started and ran two businesses, could not navigate the complexities of this simple lunch? *So what* if I got everyone a drink and fries or went to the Chick-fil-A that might take five extra minutes! But she was only trying to be helpful. She was only trying to make things easier for me. *And that, my friends, is what gets us moms (parents) in so much trouble.*

I'm struggling with where to go from here because I have so many examples and so much content to share for each one of these categories of parenting styles, that my mind is just spinning. How can I keep this chapter focused without boring you with a lot of personal examples? So, bear with me . . .

Let's start with my article "Treating Your Children the Same." I'm sure that you are like me (if you have more than one child): you think your children are completely different in their personalities, likes, and dislikes, as well as how they interact within the family and with society. I don't think in all my years as a mom, as well as owning the preschools, that I ever heard a parent say that they had two children who were the same.

What makes children different when they were raised the same way? You hear parents say that too. In Fredrik Backman's book *Anxious People*, he states, "It's impossible to know if children end up completely different despite the fact that they grew up together or precisely because of that." Interesting, huh? But *do* we treat them the same, raise them the same? *Should* we treat them the same? I propose in my article that we actually *don't* parent our children the same and that we really *shouldn't* treat them the same. Of course, there are traditional values we try to instill in each of our children, such as acceptable and unacceptable behaviors and what is right and wrong. But beyond that, *no,* we don't treat them the same or raise them the same. Be honest with yourself, parents . . .

Birth order plays a huge part in the raising of our children and how they psychologically "accept" our parenting. For instance, take the firstborn. I venture to say that birth order experts, as well as ordinary parents, acknowledge that the firstborn has the most complicated "acceptance" of the way they are raised. As parents, we put so much pressure on the firstborn, or in the case of the only child. We have so many happy expectations for them to excel and they are the recipients of *all* our attention, and (again, be honest, parents) we expect them to give us a huge chunk of their time and attention, as children and then as adults (when they really don't have the time for us). No other child in the family will feel this much pressure *or* have this much attention.

> A funny aside: When Hayden went off to college, I looked at William and said, with a Grinch-like grin, "Well, now you have our FULL attention!" This was *not* a welcome comment or position to be in for William (insert giggle giggle).

How many of us can see ourselves in some form of "first-child favoritism"? So many times at PPP, we saw the first-time parent bring their child to school and be so involved. They didn't miss a party or a presentation, their child's show-and-tell item was academically thought-provoking, and some even called each day for an update on how their child's day was going, and on and on.

Then came the second child. Usually the first child was now in "real school" and there might be a conflict of events involving both children. Of course, *now* the little preschool event was not as important as the *real* school event of the "firstborn." I mean, a mere three- or four-year-old really wouldn't know the difference if a parent was or wasn't at a presentation, or if their show-and-tell item was something found in the car as they were arriving at the preschool, or maybe they even came and got the child before the fall festival or holiday party started because the older child had a soccer game at the same time.

What?! These are things they would have died over if their first child had missed out on or been slighted in any way. And of course, never mind if there was a third or fourth child. Now, I'm not saying that any of us are inattentive parents. In fact, to the contrary. All of us parents can attest to variations of this same "first-child favoritism" theme, the books and books of organized photos of that first child, maybe? And really, the argument can be fully made that maybe the second and subsequent children are more well-adjusted because of this, our more relaxed parenting style.

I joked many times, as we witnessed the first child crawl all over the younger sibling at pickup, almost lying on top of this infant sibling, that none of us as first-time parents would have allowed this type of intrusion on our first child. I mean, just the germs alone, much less the possible physical distress the infant may feel while a four-year-old crawled on them! Heresy! But what do we see instead? We see a baby gripping onto their older sibling, smiling and loving this interaction and intrusion. What we see is a happy, and possibly a more carefree, child's psychological brain pattern beginning. Which one of these children in our family will ultimately be more well-adjusted or happier? That's really not the question here. I submit that children grow up and take on the personalities they are meant to have, sometimes despite our parenting intentions. Nevertheless, it's an interesting observation and question.

> A funny aside: When Hayden was born, we were married ten years before his arrival. So you can just imagine the attention he got! I made his baby food, nothing ever touched his lips that wasn't sterilized, and this was just one of the vast number of germs, injuries, and

> other things I protected him from. He, of course, was potty-trained well before he was three and could recite books by memory around that same time too.
>
> When William was born and Hayden was almost four, we were busy with a four-year-old as well as knee deep in opening our preschool. Parenting William as a baby was easy and stress-free. He napped in the car as we were scurrying around. He always had a bottle or juice cup within his reach on the side of his car seat. He moved around a playground, climbing around on his own. He was a free bird and loved it!
>
> At his third birthday party held at the preschool, his two teachers came up to me and said, "Ms. Kay, when you bring William to school on Monday, bring him in underwear instead of a diaper and leave his pacifier and blanket (a cloth diaper) at home." I jokingly said, "You know you are talking to your boss, right?" and they replied, "No, we are talking to William's *mom*." So, I told William that night what was going to happen to him the next day, and he calmly said, "Okay."
>
> He was ready to grow to the next stage, but I didn't want to lose my baby! For all William's future independence, he gravitated to me and wanted to be with me so much more than Hayden had as a baby, and I loved it. I always called him my "cling sheet."

The above example spills into their early growing-up years and into adulthood. Hayden looks at things a hundred ways before making a decision. He's cautious, motivated, and spot-on about everything he does. William lives life on the fly! Almost everyone who knows William wants to live like that: carefree and secure that all will turn out fine. And you know, life generally works out very well for William as well, it's just not as obvious about his strategic planning.

As parents, what if we could mold together some of the traits of one with the traits of the other? Is this the case of how the third child works out? I don't know since I only have the two, but that would be "the perfect child to be" (insert giggle giggle).

> Another funny aside: When we moved Hayden from his first middle school to a private middle school after only four months into the school year, it was right before the sixth-grade class of the new school would be taking a three-day trip to Jekyll Island, Georgia. These children had either gone to elementary school at this same school together or, at the very least, had known each other for the first four months of the school year. Hayden was coming in as the new kid, and, of course, in protection mode as always, I was nervous for him to be accepted and happy.
>
> So, on the morning of dropping him off to go on this trip, I advised, "Hayden, if the boys you are rooming with want to have a little fun after 'lights out,' don't be such a goody-two-shoes and not participate or lecture them. I mean, don't do anything destructive or dangerous, but if they want to go knock on someone's door to 'scare' them, or go up and down in the elevator for a joyride, go along." This was uncharted territory for Hayden for me to encourage him to act this way.
>
> On the way home, I fell apart laughing at myself. When I got home, I told Steve what I had done and I said, "If that was William, I would be saying, 'You better *not* leave that room if you are told not to and don't do *anything* you are told not to do!" Why the difference? Well, because I knew Hayden would be very cautious to step "out of the box" in any way, but William would be the one to cut himself out of the box! That's just the way they roll. How perfect for one to be just a tad more like the other.

Is it the best way to always take the "approved" or right way, *or* to live life on the edge? Another crazy element in their different personalities is that Hayden's talkative and confident nature often finds himself comfortably the center of attention, which has served him well in his personal as well as professional life. He's fun to be around and always has a spot-on point of view. William, for all the carefree and grab-life-by-the-horns gusto, is more quiet, laid-back, and contemplative in social situations. But when he talks, we listen. He seems to have it all quietly figured out and when he shares his opinions, they are thoughtful and researched. Again, it would be so nice for each of them to exhibit a little bit of the other. Do you see this in your children as well?

In the article, I share that sometimes the different way Steve and I parented the boys caused angst within and frustration between the boys, and still does. We expected more from Hayden academically than we did William. We monitored William's social activities more than we did Hayden. Hayden would say, "Why do I have to study more than William?" And William would say, "Why can Hayden stay out but you want me home?" Well, because they were different and we had different fears and anxieties for each; we thought this was the best way we knew to parent them.

As they got older, into their teenage years, and I was faced with this frustration from either of them, I would say, sarcastically, "Because I love him more." Obviously they were old enough to know this was not true and they would just roll their eyes at me, but this ridiculous, off-handed, sarcastic comment would stop the asking and just let them know I wasn't going to justify myself to either of them. We thought whatever we were letting one do that the other couldn't do, or what we were expecting from one but not the other, was what was necessary for each of their needs or personalities. Was this right? Like I've said in several other chapters (because it pertains to almost everything you do in parenting), you never know if a decision you make at the time is right or not, in most cases not until many years later, but at the time you do the best you can.

> An aside: Several years ago, Steve and I were at a party with a bunch of our friends. A group of us were standing around talking about our *adult* children (insert giggle giggle).
>
> One of my friends was talking about her daughter just graduating from college, getting a job in Atlanta, and how proud they were of her. I started talking about William (they were the same age, right out of college) and she and I said that maybe we should get them together. You know how moms talk.
>
> The conversation progressed, and for some reason I said William had a couple of tattoos you couldn't see. My friend (who is just a hoot, very blunt but in a good way) said something to the effect that she felt successful as a mother because none of her three adult children had ever gotten a tattoo. Another friend, who has no children and was probably very bored listening to this conversation of the two of us blathering on about ours (and she has a hysterically sarcastic personality), turned to me and said, "Well, Kay, I guess you are just a f***ing failure as a mother."
>
> The whole group just collapsed! I couldn't wait to tell my boys this funny story. They have had a good time with me the last few years repeating (lovingly and laughingly) that I am a f***ing failure as a mother at various times when things happen (insert giggle giggle).

But, back to the chapter. After the article "How Do You Treat Your Children?" appeared, I had several of my preschool parents come up to me, and one was in tears, who said, "You know, I finally can see why my parents treated us differently now. As an adult, I still harbored resentment for how they let my little sister get away with so much, but now I understand." One PPP parent even told me they called their mom and had a real talk about some of these issues and admitted to their parent that they didn't recognize in themselves how they are doing the same thing with their own children, but now they see that, and more importantly, they see *why*. It was times like this when I realized that sharing myself with the PPP parents, for all the good and bad, was a good thing.

It was a funny thing to see how my role with the parents changed over the years. From the opening of PPP, as I described, I was the same age as my parent customers and we had children the same age. I didn't have the range of knowledge I had in the later years of PPP. I had not made the mistakes or formulated a parenting style. I was "in the game" just like my customers were, just trying to keep it real and doing the best I could. In the later years, most of the PPP *parents* could have been *my children*. So, it was interesting to see how the dynamics of my relationships with the parents took more a turn from friend and contemporary to mentor and advisor, and even trusted confidante.

Switching to the article "What Kind of Parent Are You?" I think the "typical" parent in current times (2021) sees themselves in variations of the helicopter/hummingbird parent. We enjoy inserting ourselves in every (or most) aspects of our children's (at any age) life decisions or activities. Hovering over our child or swooping in to rescue our child is seen as a normal (even expected) function of parenting these days. I go into more detail and examples of these two types of parenting styles in the "Parents and Millennials" chapter to try and sort out the culture of millennials and parents' role in it. But what about the children of the Free-Range Parent?

This style of parenting touches on a parent leaving, for the most part, decisions and choices, developmentally appropriate, up to the child. These parents feel that by simply raising their child with norms of society's acceptable behaviors, their child will make appropriate decisions for themselves, which will either be for their betterment or not, and that they will have to live with those decisions or fix them themselves. These parents feel that this will make their children more responsible adults, more secure adults, than a child who must seek their parents' advice on every, or most, decisions.

So, here we are. That sounds to me, as I am writing this, that this type of parent has a stronger position of positive parenting than the "hovering" or "swooping in" parent. The Free-Range Parent does not feel the need to fix everything for their child or to always make sure their child is received in the best light by everyone. However, I recall a case several years ago that involved a dad (I think) allowing his children to walk together unaccompanied by an adult to their neighborhood's playground. Some segment of society did not think this appropriate and maybe even dangerous to the children. In fact, I think he might have been arrested or investigated by the authorities. In any event, this private family situation was brought to the public's attention.

> A funny aside: When a friend and I took our three-year-olds to a community park (her first child, my second child), we had very different experiences. My expectation of the outing was for she and I to enjoy each other's company on a beautiful day as our boys played together. However, she was completely absorbed in making sure her son played safely.
>
> She said to me at one point, as William was climbing up the stairs of a slide, "Aren't you afraid he's going to fall?" I was not afraid of this. William had navigated many playground structures, sometimes taking a small fall (as we all did as children ourselves), but most times was successful and carefree in this physical endeavor.
>
> Of course, just like her with *my* first child, when Hayden played on the playground as a three-year-old, I was right there with my hands below him *in case he fell*! Do you see William's first taste of the athlete he was to become? As the question I asked before, was his success in athletics due to Steve and I being more carefree with him when it came to *allowing* him to be more physically unrestrained than we allowed

> Hayden? Or is that just who William was destined to become? Who knows.
>
> The old "nature versus nurture" question that remains a complicated issue about various ways a child "turns out" may come into play here. As in most things in parent decision-making, what success results from our parenting is really more about the child than about us.

Should parents be questioned on how they raise their children? Was this just a busybody sticking their nose into something that was none of their business when they reported this walking-to-the-playground incident to the authorities? Will these two children, whom the *parent* thought were equipped to walk to the neighboring playground without supervision, be more secure as adults to travel alone? Will they be able to make decisions on what is safe to do or not safe to do more than helicopter-parented children who may not have a point of reference because they never had to make a decision on their own or were never left to experience a defeat or problem-solve on their own because of their parents' interference? *Whew!*

How are we to expect our children to make consequential decisions, much less handle disappointments, if we never, or rarely, let them experience any of this? The image of the bubble-wrapped child I talk about in the article becomes vividly clear, and what's so interesting is that, as parents, none of us want our children to be like this illustration, yet we can't help ourselves from acting in this manner to prevent any and everything bad from happening to our child.

Parent after parent, and I'm talking about the new millennial generation of parents, talks about the good old days of more unstructured play and of the childhood ways of the past lost, but even as they mourn this and wish it were the way it used to be, and shake their heads at this hovering style of parenting, they (we) continue to parent children in this manner: hovering over and supervising everything they do. Parents, we are a funny breed.

A funny aside: At PPP, we hosted two teachers each year to attend the annual NAEYC conference all over the United States. The year that Hayden turned twelve, the conference was held in Chicago. The conference is always in November, which is Hayden's birthday month, and he wanted to go with me.

Of course, it would not be fun for him to attend the eight-hour seminar courses, so why did he want to go? What would he do all day? Well, he could get up and order room service and watch movies, he could go to the hotel pool, or he could walk around Chicago's Magnificent Mile. So that's what he did.

I instructed him to either hang around the hotel or walk up and down that *one* street, the Magnificent Mile, and be back at the hotel no later than five p.m. when we would be returning. I did not have any doubt that he would do exactly this and could be trusted to behave and be cautious and careful. Some of the teachers and my friends thought he was way too young to be left alone in a strange city, but I knew he would be fine. I used to say that I could have left Hayden on a street corner when he was little and tell him to find something to do and he would be fine and right back there when I was ready to pick him up!

Boy, I didn't realize back then that I was being a Free-Range Parent, and I bet that busybody discussed earlier would definitely have alerted the authorities on me about this Chicago trip (insert giggle giggle)! Hayden has traveled all over the world, even before he got the position he currently has as a global account executive, and is afraid of nothing—not even scary movies (insert giggle giggle).

Now the latest phrase parents are plagued with: the Lawnmower Parent. This is the parent that far surpasses the helicopter/hummingbird parent. This parent will literally mow down anyone or any obstacle in the way of their child's desires, achievement, or positive perception by society. Further, they will mow the road in a straight and comfortable lane so that their child's path is smooth, free, and clear of any and all obstacles.

To close, I mentioned birth order being significant to the identity a child takes on, as a child and as an adult, and how we parent them. Again, I would venture to say that most children of the current era are parented from a version of the helicopter/hummingbird parent—note the rap millennials have of being so dependent on their parents.

I also proposed that we overparent our first child more than the other children in our family. So it would then logically follow, from what I've outlined, that the first child would be the *least* confident in themselves or decisions than their siblings. But it's very much a universal thought that the first child is more self-motivated and self-reliant, even to the point of helping "parent" the younger siblings, and is the most grounded of the siblings. So what gives? The proposals and examples given don't bear out this logical outcome or the reality of what child is what in most families. Just look at the examples I gave of Hayden and William and the pendulum swing between which one seems the most well-adjusted and confident in various situations.

Can it be, as I also proposed, that no matter how we parent our children, or what influence we have, or *think* we have over our children, *they will become who they were meant to be?*

CHAPTER 9
MAKING SCHOOL CHOICES —NO SIZE FITS ALL!

As you will see throughout this book, so many of the articles I wrote throughout the years pull not only from my experiences of owning two preschools, and the thousands of children who went through their early educational years with us, but also from my own two boys.

We did not have the decision dilemma for our two boys for their day-care/preschool years—we owned the joint! So, the school-choice dilemma for our oldest, Hayden, didn't start until middle school. He was not, however, a preschool product of PPP. We started formulating PPP when he was three years old and I was pregnant with William, and we opened roughly two years later, on the *very day* Hayden started kindergarten and William was two, which was in August 1995.

Hayden's preschool years progressed through a mix of being with my mom, with a nanny, totally at home with me, and then one year of pre-K three days a week, nine to noon, and that was it. When Hayden started kindergarten, he was barely writing his name and had no reading skills. He had to play catch-up (or was right in line with a lot of other "stay-at-home mom" kids) and, being innately a very smart boy and with an incredible kindergarten teacher, he rose to the challenge and had a successful elementary school experience.

When he went into the neighborhood middle school, highly

motivated and equipped with an eager and engaged learning attitude, he had a significant challenge due to the lack of an educationally rich environment for him, mostly due to a lot of student discipline problems and bullying issues at this middle school. He stayed there four months, and at Christmas break we chose to enroll him in a private school for the rest of his middle school years. This was the right choice and an incredible experience for him which placed him well above expectations when going back into the neighborhood public high school.

When it was time for college applications, Hayden was all over it. He was an International Baccalaureate *Diploma* student, which was recognized and rewarded by the best colleges in the country with an additional 0.5 percentage point added to the final grade-point average. He applied all over the country, was accepted to more than a few, and finally decided on Georgia Tech, his dad's alma mater. We were thrilled not only because we are *huge* GT fans, of course, but also because Georgia Tech is one of the best colleges in the country with worldwide recognition *and* right down the road from home, and lastly, being an in-state choice, he was eligible for the state-funded HOPE scholarship program, which pays for some of the college tuition for students maintaining a 3.0 semester average (part of the same Georgia lottery funds that pays for pre-K discussed in the "Power of the Brain" chapter). Golden!

As for William, he was a PPP preschool product from the age of two. He stayed at PPP for private kindergarten, entering with writing *and* reading skills, and stayed on at PPP for first grade to capitalize on the advanced educational experience he received in PPP kindergarten (more on the kindergarten choice issues in the chapter on "Redshirting"). Starting in second grade with these advanced skills at the same elementary school Hayden attended, William's love of sports of any sort—but especially baseball—and his social spirit and athletic swagger put him in another category for his school career experience and ultimately his college choice.

He sailed happily through elementary school, middle school,

and high school on a lot of charm and athletic skill (and all the special considerations that athletes seem to garner), doing what needed to be done to get Bs, Cs, and Ds. He entered his college selection period based not on applying to schools—filling out long admissions forms, getting teacher recommendations, taking the SAT and ACT over and over for a few extra points, and writing essays like Hayden had to do—but instead, attending summer college baseball showcases, playing in summer college-prep scouting leagues, and looking at scholarship considerations from schools that might like him to join their baseball team—his dream. I mean, he was to some degree *asked* to consider a school instead of asking a school to consider him.

William accepted a full scholarship to play baseball at a very small private college where the tuition exceeded forty thousand dollars a year! This small college, however, did not suit William for several reasons, and his college path, still following baseball, led him to accept another baseball scholarship to an NAIA school where the baseball team won multiple national championships and the opportunity to play in the NAIA College Baseball World Series. William received baseball awards and achievement accolades all along the way. Again, golden!

> A funny aside: Hayden, by this time an honor roll student at Georgia Tech, couldn't believe William didn't need to do even the minimum of filling out an admission questionnaire! William was just waiting to see what college wanted him and what they were willing to offer him! Hayden, like so many non-athletic students and their families, wondered, *How is this fair?*
>
> Obviously this has been an ongoing question for many years, and the answer typically, and rightfully, given is that a school's athletic programs benefit *all* students of a college or university, due to the dollars these programs bring in, which is then disbursed, to some degree, throughout the entire college. As I am

> writing this chapter, the NCAA is trying to decide on their position in response to California leading the way in making the announcement that athletes playing in California schools will be paid for the marketing of anything that contains their personal name.
>
> When William received his scholarship, we tried to instill in him that he was getting "paid" already by being given a free education for playing baseball and this was now his *job* to do well on the field as well as in the classroom. This seemed to resonate with him on the baseball field but not always in the classroom, like so many college athletes. Again, the inattention to academics by a lot of athletes and the idea that athletes may not have to adhere to the same academic standards from high school through college, as non-athletes must, seems unfair to so many non-athletes, and you can't blame them. Academic rigor and stress in college is no joke; *however*, couple that with everyday practice, games, travel during the academic week and weekend, and other required athletic events, and it's easier to at least understand a reason for athletes to have a little leniency.

Speaking from my mom perspective of a child who was academically driven and a child who was athletically driven, I sometimes wondered how either one of them kept up with everything that was required and expected of them. I was equally concerned as a mom to know that Hayden was up all hours of the night/morning in the architectural studio, as well as having to keep up with all his other classes, and a member of the GT crew team, as I was with knowing William was trying to complete assignments in the dark of a tour bus after a game, or out of town in a hotel meeting room taking final exams during National Championship tournaments. I could easily see both sides of the college vs. college sports argument.

Which brings to mind another funny aside: When Hayden was in eighth grade and William in fifth grade, Hayden and I pulled into the cul-de-sac of our home and saw William standing at the top of the driveway. So excited and waiting for me—this was William's innocent charm at its best! He had his report card clutched in hand, which showed he got a C in math.

William and Steve had worked very hard to bring up his math grade during the last few weeks of the semester and we were all sweating it, so we were ecstatic with his *achievement* (insert giggle giggle). I got out of the car and as William and I grasped hands and *literally danced in the street*, Hayden looked on incredulously!

Hayden said, "I can't believe y'all are so excited that he got a C!"

William stuck his head in the car and snarked to Hayden, "Well, I started with an F and brought it up to a C!"

Hayden snarked back, "*No*, you started with an A and took it to the F!"

This was repeated for William in tenth grade when, once again struggling in a math class, he and Steve worked together again and William made the *highest* grade in the class on the final! Again, it was repeated in college when William was in danger of falling below baseball eligibility, and when this was brought to his attention, he made the academic dean's list that semester!

Steve and I didn't know whether to be proud of him for this achievement *or* mad at him! See, it was always in him; he just loved sports more than what he saw as the importance of school at that time.

Funny enough, I heard this same story repeated so many times from other parents with children in elite sports. Just recently at our country club, I overheard a mom lamenting to another mom in the ladies locker room that her scholarship-bound tennis son was being courted by various schools but they were concerned about his ability to "get in" and "stay in," which she said had been an academic struggle with him from an early age. I silently chuckled to myself, knowing her challenge of college sports vs. "college" was just beginning.

But back to making the right school choice for your child. The choices seem to be limitless and wide-ranging. At PPP, we decided to adopt an advanced academic environment while realizing that, like almost anything else, including education, you can find an expert to back just about any theory.

Instead of a play-based or Montessori preschool curriculum, we chose to follow the school of thought that, presented in the right way, a child is capable of learning almost anything you put to them, developmentally appropriate, for the age. We very carefully designed an age-and-stage-milestone developmental checklist. This checklist was updated throughout the years because the students were innately getting smarter and smarter! The teachers were trained to utilize the parameters outlined for their specific age group in designing the daily lesson plan, which they posted in the classroom, and we sent via email to the parent.

The parents who chose PPP felt the same about the quality of the academic environment. They were continuously amazed at what their child was learning and the fun they were having in the process. We called this "Loving to Learn," and it was the founding philosophy of our teaching methods.

One of the best, most heartfelt, and in fact most gut-wrenching sentiments ever expressed to me in the twenty-five years of owning PPP was from a dad who came up to me at his daughter's preschool graduation ceremony, almost in tears, and told me that when he thought of the time and money wasted at another preschool before they found PPP, it made him sick to his stomach, and I could tell he *literally* meant that.

One of the many parent testimonials we had started out by saying, "You don't know how good it is until you leave"—a very heartfelt and right-on sentiment. As I told my teachers in a memo during our 20th Anniversary, we all—parents and teachers alike—took for granted daily that PPP was the *best place* to have your child educated and watch them make lifelong friends and forge positive foundations. We just never thought about it as being not "normal" and we always wondered, "Why isn't every place like PPP?"

One of the PPP parents expressed online that "if parents only knew all the great stuff going on at PPP, you couldn't build a place big enough for all the children that would be enrolled there." We had parents fill out an information sheet when they came in for their initial tour. One of the lines on this form addressed the question of how they had heard about PPP. A parent once wrote, "Because you are the best." Humbling. Even though it looks like I'm grandstanding, I never got tired of bragging about PPP.

Everything wasn't always roses, though. As a board member of GCCA, I went up against the government agency that licenses all child learning centers, Bright from the Start (BFTS), several times when they first implemented *requirements* of teacher credentials in order to keep your day-care license to operate. I thought this was absurd and I'll detail why.

By the time of this edict by BFTS, PPP had been in business well over ten years and I had teachers who were lead teachers going into their seventh, eighth, tenth year of teaching at PPP, and they were *fabulous*! If you have ever had a child of yours at a preschool and have experienced a fabulous teacher, you know what I'm talking about. Some people are *born* to be an infant caregiver, a toddler teacher, or a preschool teacher, with or without a college degree.

During the years of PPP, I hired many teachers with a college degree, some actually in early childhood education, that when put in a toddler classroom they had absolutely *no idea* how to handle a productive day for these young students. They idolized, and more importantly learned from, the lead teacher they were working under who, maybe, only had a high school education.

No one knew more about taking care of an infant, loving them, and stimulating their development than the ladies in charge of the PPP Infant Suite. I even had one parent tell me, after having two children with one of these wonderful teachers, that she wanted to have another baby just to be able to have this fabulous teacher take care of it! I had one parent tell me, when we moved one of these teachers for a short time into the Toddler I classroom, that she was putting off having her next baby *until* we placed this teacher back into the Infant Suite! Neither of these wonderful ladies had a college education; in fact, English was not even their first language. However, the state of Georgia wanted to force both of these ladies (as well as others at PPP) to either move to a lesser job within PPP, go back to school for their degree, or take a 120-hour course (CDA, Child Development Associate) in order to keep the job they had had for ten years or more and were fabulous at! Ridiculous.

Both of them could *teach* an infant caregiver course, as could any of the other PPP teachers who faced going through the same time-consuming (and unnecessary) process—and expense. After this pushback, BFTS modified their policy to accept lead teachers as "uncredentialed" (such a misleading designation) if they had worked continuously in a child learning center for seven years and had kept all their required annual professional development training up to date.

I proudly sent in this exception documentation for several of my Fabulous Faculty, at both my school locations, without hesitation. My parents agreed with me 100 percent about the credentials of my Fabulous Faculty. Degrees or not, these ladies had the experience to provide the ultimate in care *and* education for these young children, and it showed in the achievements of these children and the happiness they showed each day of coming to school and being with these wonderful teachers.

During this same time period, other new regulations were deemed necessary to govern who could direct a day-care center/ preschool. Since neither myself or my director had a degree in early childhood education, we were no longer qualified to direct PPP. PPP had proven academic results, through ITBS testing and Scholastic Testing Service, of having more high-achieving students when compared to most other students tested throughout the United States. PPP had the reputation of having the longest tenure of faculty in the state. It seemed we both knew how to run a preschool from the educational standpoint as well as the business standpoint, right? But we had to spend the time to attend a gratuitous forty-hour director training course in order to continue to lead the path of education and the business of PPP—like these forty hours would "magically" make us *more* qualified after running a successful preschool in all regards for over ten years! Again, ridiculous.

But you see, how could anyone stand up and push back on an initiative that requires anyone teaching to have a degree to do so? Seems logical, doesn't it? I think I've shown that, at least at the toddler and preschool level, this is not always the case. You just "looked bad" if you said so, like you were trying to dumb down the preschool teaching process or not be an advocate for better standards. Day-care teachers or preschool teachers should be able to teach based on their merit to do so. Bad or uninspired teachers, at any education level, should not be allowed to teach no matter what degree they have or don't have.

My next position about educating young children I felt was as justified as the previous argument. Steve and I bought a piece of property, put all our financial resources into this endeavor, secured a bank loan, decided on our mission statement, marketed what we were about, and hoped that parents bought into our philosophy and enrolled their children. If they didn't, we were up sh*t creek, so to say. What business was it *now* for the government to tell us how to run our business? We didn't take a penny from them to build our business or to run our business—not a cent!

Of course, I understand licensure and oversight by the government in a host of certain types of businesses—day care being one of those as it pertains to safety regulations. I also understand that any business that takes federal or state funding must play by the rules in order to get those funds. I was fine with BFTS coming in and looking around to make sure the children were safe and their environment, from a safety perspective, was appropriate. But dictating to me the résumé of the people I chose to hire, the learning materials I put in the classroom, what needed to be included in the lesson plan (these things were proposed), was *none* of their business.

I further argued that if I built a business on my own and marketed it to a community of parents that their child would be singing songs, coloring pictures, and read to—and that's *it*—all under the guidance of grandmotherly-type caregivers with no college degrees—my, oh my (insert sarcastic giggle giggle!)—and I was successful in selling that concept to parents, that's *my* business, not the government's to tell me I couldn't do that. Some parents may want *just that* type of environment for their young child! Do I hear an *Amen*?

Of course, I was not successful in this argument, as logical as it is. I just had to be happy that I was perhaps instrumental in the seven-year uncredentialed teacher exception. Right before we sold PPP, there came another announcement that every licensed day-care center must be Quality Rated (another government program with *additional* layers of regulations) in the next couple of years. Up to this point, maybe due to private owners like myself, especially with my voice backed by GCCA, if you did not take government funding, you were not required to be Quality Rated through BFTS and the state of Georgia, but of course, I (and others) discussed with the GCCA board that this was a false sense of security and would not be long-lasting. This QR requirement would be coming for all, and we were right.

I always made the point to PPP parents that I could be totally *unlicensed* through the state of Georgia and it would make *no* difference in the quality of care, level of education, or any service offered at PPP. I was able to justify this same type of argument when a prospective parent would ask me if we were accredited by NAEYC (National Association for the Education of Young Children). I would let them know that PPP standards, in all regards, either met or exceeded NAEYC guidelines and were certainly way beyond state standards. I would let them know that each year, two teachers and one administrator attended the four-day NAEYC conference wherever it was held in the United States, and we pulled relevant information from this conference to enhance our curriculum. However, being accredited through NAEYC came with the obligation to teach the way *they* deemed effective, and I was not willing to, in a lot of circumstances, lower proven PPP educational standards and success just to be in compliance on their form. I was not willing to take them on as my educational as well as business partner. As a private business, the only people I wanted to assess the effectiveness of PPP were the teachers and the parents. This made so much sense to the parents.

PPP standards were so far above the state requirements that there was really no reason for the twice-per-year quality visits from BFTS. Our reports, open to the public, were stellar—keeping in mind that when this type of licensing visit did occur, especially in the earlier years, an infraction or citation was almost *required* to be on your report, and still it was hard to find one at PPP. During the Quality Rated discussions, and my pushback on that, it came to my attention that day-care centers would pool financial resources together, equip their classrooms to fit state regulations for Quality Rated status, and then after the QR evaluation visit was conducted, these centers would box these resources up to send to a sister center for *their* upcoming Quality Rated visit. Exactly how was this program actually benefitting the children on a daily basis?

Form over substance is so prevalent in so many government-supervised programs, and the day-care industry is not exempt from that. But ways around these regulations, some consultants not being as diligent in visits as other consultants, or an array of other subjective arguments made the reasonableness and fairness of assessing these numerous government regulations far-flung. As said in *Jurassic Park*: "Life finds a way."

All this to make an important point about looking at your choice of schools and assessing what's best for your child. Not every school or every type of specialized-school environment is for every child. There is no one size fits all. Ask for answers to some of the specific issues brought up in this chapter instead of accepting the status quo or some "perceived" qualification. When I was growing up, every child in my neighborhood went to the same schools, elementary through high school. Now, as in my own family, lots of families have their children at different schools for a variety of reasons. As parents we can only do the best we can, and, again, as I have told countless parents, "You never know whether your choices were right until years later," which in many cases is too late to fix, if it turned out to be the wrong choice. As parents, this is just a fact for so many of the decisions we make for our children, not just school choice.

What didn't work for one of my boys may have worked for the other. Hayden had a focus on academic achievement. William's path was to focus on the hard work necessary to be an elite athlete. Both of these inherent traits made each of them *happy* and *successful* throughout their school years, and ultimately, these two very different traits and paths paid for each of their college educations. What more as a parent can you ask for?

So, look at your children as individuals. What do you push for one but not the other? What do you foster and celebrate in each, as individuals, to advance their skills and interests to the fullest possible achievement? Sometimes no matter what you do—praise or punish—you can't make a square peg fit into a round hole, and that's okay. Don't be pressured by outside forces when it comes to *your* child. Do you know how many people wondered why Hayden wasn't in community sports and how many people advised that we take sports away from William if he didn't concentrate more on school? To us as their parents, both of these ideas and advice for our sons were just crazy.

Listen to yourself, celebrate what your individual child's strengths are, and make those choices and decisions based on that, not what other people may deem acceptable. Who knows, your child's choices and strengths may just pay for their college tuition *and* make them happy!

CHAPTER 10
"REDSHIRTING" AND ROLE MODELS

> **Redshirting:** the act of postponing entrance in the regulated time frame in sports or academics, with the desired result being that of more developed skills and maturity in a variety of spectrums.

I am a *huge* sports fan! Some nights it's just me sitting up by myself watching a baseball or football game, either college or professional. Hayden—who doesn't know a quarter from an inning (insert giggle giggle!)—will laugh at me when I tell him I can't talk to him on the phone because I'm watching some game on TV. When I tell him what teams I am watching, he will comment, "We didn't go to that school, Mom! Why do you care about that game?" William, who is a sports fanatic, has called me or texted me many times about a play that just happened in a college or professional game because he feels pretty confident I am watching it.

So it's safe to say I know all about the pros and cons of redshirting in sports. But why is redshirting now a term used in education? As I have done throughout this book, just like I did during my twenty-five years at PPP, I used my own experiences to advise or assist other parents. In this case I have both Hayden and William as models of how redshirting might work. Hayden has a November birthday and William has a June birthday. The cutoff in the state of Georgia to enter kindergarten is five years old by September 1. Hayden just missed that cutoff, so he entered kindergarten turning six years old shortly after the school year began.

William, on the other hand, just made the cutoff, so he entered kindergarten barely at the age of five when many of his classmates started turning six just one month into the school year—almost a full year older than him.

It's easy to see which of my boys was at an advantage starting his school career, and there are studies after studies validating the advantage of being more mature starting school, especially for boys. In the last few years before the sale of PPP, discussions regarding moving the cutoff age for entering kindergarten to be five by August 1 instead of September 1 began circulating throughout the state, with a lot of opposing views and opinions on how to implement. Since the school year typically begins in Georgia the first week of August, by keeping the cutoff as September 1, there are many children entering kindergarten at the age of four, turning five with August birthdays.

This has become an educational issue in Georgia. I can't say for sure presently, but for many years most of the private schools in Atlanta had an unofficial cutoff of April 1 instead of September 1 for entering kindergarteners. With so many applicants desiring entrance into private schools, it only made sense to test and accept the oldest, most mature applicants.

Funny enough, parents at PPP who had a child with a September, October, or even November birthday would get so distressed that their child just missed the September cutoff. They saw this as a *disadvantage* for their child to have to wait a whole year in pre-K instead of being in kindergarten merely because of a month or so. These parents would beg me to put their child in pre-K a year early so they would have the chance of going into kindergarten a year early. In contrast, some of the parents whose children—again, mostly *boys*—had late spring/early summer birthdays would be distressed with wrestling with their *option* of letting their child go into kindergarten, just barely making the cutoff, or holding them back (redshirting) a year.

You always want the situation you don't have, right?

As I've said in numerous chapters about numerous topics, as

parents we never know if a decision we make is right or wrong until sometimes years later; and if wrong, it's too late to fix. Well, I would say these words of wisdom to parents in these situations, probably exacerbating their dilemma. However, I would also tell them I never knew a parent who held their child back to be unhappy with their decision, *but* I knew of many parents who didn't and wished they had when those middle school and high school years hit—Steve and I included for William.

Sometimes, the discussion with parents would lead to how other states in the country have a cutoff date of December 31 for entering kindergarten. The argument from the "past-September cutoff" parents would then be that if they lived in almost any other state in the United States, they would not have this dilemma—their child would be in kindergarten, which is a legitimate argument. As transient as families are these days, the argument would then be if that particular family moved, their child would be behind other same-age children in that state. Further complicating the issue, when children go off to colleges all over the United States, they will be entering with students from all sorts of different ages and stages because of when they entered kindergarten way back when. It's really hard to make a concrete argument one way or the other for parents seeking advice. Why don't all states have the same age standards for entering kindergarten?

> A funny aside: As I have written in this book, William is my athlete. From a very early age it was obvious that he had advanced athletic skills as well as the motivation and determination to do well in sports. He took advantage of every avenue available to him to be the best athlete he could be. We did not hold him back from entering kindergarten at the *young* age of five. That really wasn't done so much at the time when William was a preschooler. "Holding back," at that time, alluded to a "developmental delay" of some sort, and was not viewed as giving your child an advantage

> as it's seen now, and even though we were owners of a preschool and maybe should have known better than most parents the advantage of being among the oldest in the class, we didn't. When the high school years came and William was a tenth grader playing as a starter on the varsity baseball team, we even said how great it would be if he was in the ninth grade as a varsity starter!
>
> So, as funny as that seems that you would redshirt a child for an athletic advantage instead of an educational advantage, we knew some parents who did just that. Again, there's nothing wrong with having an advantage due to your athletic skill, just like having an advantage in your academic skills, to pave your way into college.

And to put the "college thing" into a better perspective, Hayden *entered* college two months before turning nineteen (with his November birthday). William *finished* his freshman year of college one month away from turning nineteen (with his June birthday)! Which one do you think had the edge or advantage on academic maturity?

Continuing the insight into the redshirting of boys primarily, whether your son is an extrovert and sees himself hindered in the social scene by being viewed (by girls—giggle giggle) as so much younger than other boys in the class *or* if your son is shy and introverted, this lack of maturity may be even more of a social burden to him, as in possibly being picked on by the "older" boys in the class. In either case, this can cause brain-pattern social problems for developing young men.

As I have told many parents of four-year-old boys whom I have counseled during the PPP years, you are *not* making a decision for your four-year-old, you are making a decision *now* for your twelve-year-old (and beyond) son. It's not a stretch to say the decision you are making now can shape the type of man your son grows up to be. There are many men who will either blame or credit their social experiences in middle and high school with their successes or failures in college and beyond.

A few years ago, there was an article I read in either the *Atlanta Journal*, or possibly a community newspaper, about the disparity and unfair advantage children of higher-income families have over lower-income families on being able to defer entering kindergarten at the age of five. This important decision and outcome for children is seen to be unfairly partial because the children of higher-income parents can afford one more year of paying for a preschool environment, while children who come from lower-income families have no option other than going into free public kindergarten at the age of four or an early five-year-old child. And this doesn't even begin to discuss the advantages of children whose parents have the financial ability to choose a private school education for their child.

I outlined in another chapter that the free pre-K available in the state of Georgia is offered *only* to four-year-olds and cannot be used twice. So, if the desire or need arises to hold your child back a year for any number of reasons *during* their pre-K year, this option cannot come into play *unless* you enroll your child into a private preschool environment for the second go-around, which may not be a financial option. In order to take advantage of this free, government-sponsored preschool year, you must follow *all* state educational guidelines, leaving the choices limited for lower-income families.

Education has always been fodder for political discussions, and a large issue facing today's politicians is "school choice," charter schools, and, in essence, giving the money appropriated for a child's education directly into the hands of the parents to then choose where their child attends school. The "money follows the child" concept. A very interesting concept, and one that has fierce opinions on both sides and from teachers' unions.

For late spring/early summer birthday boys, redshirting seems to be an important decision to be looked at closely. What could be the downside of providing an extra year of growth and development—academic, athletic, as well as social? For parents of girls, who are deemed to be "more mature" as preschoolers—as they are deemed to be more mature throughout school—I hear mostly that the reason for possibly holding them back (when there doesn't really seem to be a good reason academically or athletically to do so) is so they don't go away to college at the young age of eighteen—that's usually the dad talking (insert giggle giggle)!

We were proud to have students placed in all of the most prestigious private schools in Atlanta, either redshirted students or not. I was approached by many of the private schools in Atlanta for a tour of our school due to their recognizing a large portion of their highest-academic-achieving students came from PPP, and they were curious as to our teaching methods that showed such success for our young students. Parents could rely on the reputation of PPP, as well as unbiased test assessments, to add to their child's admission portfolio to private schools or to advocate for accelerated placement in public school. I heard from my director recently that a PPP student we had from eight weeks old through pre-K was offered a first-grade placement as a kindergarten-aged student. Her mom called to say how grateful she was for PPP for her daughter. We had hundreds of these types of calls of appreciation throughout the years. It never got old.

Of all the programs we had in place and of all the attention we gave to ensure our academic standards never faltered, a huge part of the academic success of PPP students, at all levels, was directly related to the Fabulous Faculty of PPP. Enough cannot be said of the dedication over the years of these wonderful teachers, role models all, to the "Loving to Learn" philosophy of PPP. The longevity of the PPP faculty that we enjoyed, and the students benefitted from, was and is unheard of in the industry, when compared to other day-care centers/preschools, statewide as well as nationwide. This was something that was not left to chance, something that we invested time and treasure to ensure, and it paid off in ways that cannot be measured.

The love of learning that these teachers spread to their students was recognized by parents over the years, and PPP was rewarded by these students' academic accolades from colleges all over the country. From academics, community service, sports, media, and celebrity, PPP students run the full spectrum of excellence. For any small part we played in cementing in these young children a love of learning, a desire to excel in many facets of achievements, and for so many of them to return to PPP's 20th Anniversary celebration to give their personal thanks to PPP and their teachers, I say thank you to these incredible children (now adults) and to the Fabulous Faculty of PPP. One of many of these thank-yous was from a once-four-year-old Preppie to one of our fabulous teachers—yes, still teaching at PPP—telling her she has remained a favorite of his. Enclosed was his graduation photo from Harvard.

> An interesting observation about how positive role models in young people's lives affect them as adults: Recently, when William was at his umpiring training camp, there was a rocket launch from Cape Canaveral. He was able to see this from his beach balcony, and he took a video of the launch and sent it to Steve and me. It was fuzzy but still awe-inspiring. William felt very privileged to have this opportunity and experience, and Steve told him that when he was a young boy himself, he and his dad drove down to Florida to see a rocket launch and he had never forgotten the experience.
>
> I told William it was very sad to me, after thinking about this enormous achievement in space exploration, that most people could not tell you the names of the astronauts and scientists involved. But, just the night before, Ricky Gervais had hosted the Golden Globes, and almost everyone could tell you anything you wanted to know about the pampered celebrities that he (rightly) ridiculed about their own elitism. And funny enough, there was a commercial on TV at

> this time about how wonderful it would be if we celebrated the accomplishments of scientists instead of celebrities of the day. It was an eye-opening realization—and a sad one. I was so very proud of the role models the students of PPP had so early in their academic life, and it was always such a joy to hear this expressed by the parents of PPP as well.

At PPP, whether it was redshirted students or students who stayed on the prescribed enrollment path, we celebrate and honor them all. As we jokingly said to each other numerous times during the 20th Anniversary mystical connections we experienced with reconnecting with the students from the past twenty years and hearing about all their successes, accomplishments, relationships, and achievements, "There's not a loser in the bunch!"

We were and are proud of *all* the PPP PREPPIES, and it was a joy and a privilege to play a part in the lives of these young children.

CHAPTER 11
HOW DID IT GET SO LATE SO SOON?

Graduation. What a great time for everyone! But as great as it is, graduation time can also be full of stress, racked with emotions, and incredibly scary. How can one event run such a gamut of opposing feelings?

One of the meanings of "graduate" means to change gradually. But that doesn't happen, does it? You are propelled into the ceremony of graduation and all the attendant events and feelings it entails, and sometimes you, and your child, are not ready, even as it approaches with lightning speed. It's sort of like when we aren't ready for Christmas, shopping and wrapping until the very last minute. It's not like we don't know it's coming; it comes once every year on the same day! Yet it seems we are never ready. That's the same with graduations. It seems that time has gotten away from us and we are left wondering how it got here so soon. Where *did* the time go?

How did it get so late so soon?
It's night before it's afternoon.
December is here before it's June.
My goodness how the time has flewn!
How did it get so late so soon?

This is a Dr. Seuss quote that was read at the freshmen orientation for parents when Hayden entered Georgia Tech. Believe it or not, I did not cry during Hayden's honor ceremony for the IB

Diploma students a couple of nights before high school graduation. I did not cry at his graduation ceremony. At all these events I was happy and excited. But I had to leave the orientation sobbing when the dean of admissions read this preschool quote. It hit home—hard.

> A funny aside: The day we moved Hayden into his GT dorm, I came home very upset. As I mentioned in another chapter, he was just down the road a bit at Georgia Tech, but he was living somewhere else for the first time *ever*, so I was entitled to be upset, *okay*? (Insert giggle giggle!)
>
> Anyway, I went into William's room and lay down beside him on his bed, crying. He was patting my shoulder a bit and said very sweetly, "It's okay, Mom, all parents go through this, you'll be okay." And I responded, still crying, "No, no one loves their children like I do." William recoiled a little and said, very matter-of-factly, "Yes, they do."
>
> Later, after I stopped crying, this struck me as so funny! I have told this story to several of my mom friends through the years and we have all gotten a big laugh out of it. We *all* think no one could possibly love their child more than we love our own (insert giggle giggle).
>
> When William went off to college, Steve and I drove him two and a half hours away. We seemed to be okay after we hugged him and left him in his dorm room. We got to the car and he called me to tell us to wait up, he had left something in the car and was coming down. So, another goodbye. As we stood at the car and watched him walk, very slowly, up the hill back to the dorm, Steve just broke down. We drove the whole way back home with both Steve and I sniffling, barely speaking the whole way, just miserable that now both our boys were gone.

Most parents, when their last child leaves home (whether it's for college or for a job), have a range of emotions, but it seems that most of them center on being sad and even depressed that the house is empty and quiet. An empty nest—I tried to find out why it's called that. I, like most people, think that "empty nest" means we are very upset when our only or last child leaves home and there is no one left to take care of, to provide us excitement, or to be involved in any number of activities of theirs that kept us busy and engaged. Our house, our "nest," and our hearts are now *empty*.

We aren't necessarily ready yet or prepared to deal with this "nothingness," and our child leaving home can spiral some into depression, alcoholism, marital problems, and much more. In fact, in doing a little bit of research on this subject, there are articles from esteemed institutions, such as the Mayo Clinic, as well as tons of university research studies, discussing this anxiety-ridden phase for parents. It's not a medical diagnosis yet (I bet it will be at some time in the future since *all* feelings *must* be acknowledged, validated, and named), but it has been elevated to a title: Empty-Nest Syndrome. It's not just a colloquialism anymore.

But I'm a little confused. Don't birds push their babies out of the nest and hope they fly?

I don't think any of us, at least no parent I know (insert giggle giggle!), had this mentality! Of course, we don't want our adult children to live with us forever, but it's that feeling of really not wanting them to leave either that so many of us feel—the old catch-22.

Funny, Steve and I were almost sixty when Hayden moved to New York City. Since neither of our boys went out of state for college, this was a huge event for us even though neither of them had lived with us for several years. But Hayden packed up his stuff in a U-Haul and drove himself, with a wonderful friend, up to New York City and never looked back! We knew we were going to miss him not being in the same city as us, but we were so proud of his independent spirit. This is when you feel you have done a good job raising your kids—when they spread their wings and fly solo.

But, when William left for college and I knew I couldn't just get in the car and go see him, drop something off to him, or meet for dinner since he was almost three hours away, I was *very* sad—you could even say I was depressed—and I know Steve felt the same. Even though Steve and I rarely did this sort of thing with Hayden right down the road at GT, we still knew we *could*. Friends used to laugh at me when I would say excitedly, "Hayden's coming home this weekend!" They would say, "He's twenty minutes away!" But he was so busy with school and being a member of the GT crew team, we rarely ever saw him, it seemed.

But when William left and no one was at home to keep us otherwise involved, it was not a good situation for me. I would come home from the preschool around five or so and start crying. I told Steve one day when he caught me that we could just lock the door and get in our pajamas; *no one* would be coming in. I missed everything about our previous life.

That lasted for about a month. We started going to the gym every night and then eating out, a quick sandwich or salad, and then would come home to relax. With no more baseball game commitments—usually three or four times a week and all weekend—we went to a movie every Friday, started antiquing and art-collecting, and a number of other hobbies blossomed. Getting used to a clean house, hardly any laundry to do, no mountain of groceries to buy, and our time being our own, things were looking pretty good. Then came Christmas break. Oh my, William (and Hayden also, to some extent, since he had his own college apartment in Atlanta by this time) was coming home for over a month. About two weeks into it, Steve and I looked at each other and said, laughingly, "When are they ever going to leave?" (Insert giggle giggle!) They were rocking our empty-nest world!

See, we made it through and we were going to be okay. I never thought it would happen, but it did. Sometimes you just can't see it, but the light at the end of the tunnel, *for most anything*, is usually always there. During my saddest time right after William left, Steve said to me, "We were fine before we had them, and we are going to be fine without them." And you know what, that was more than true.

Both of them were "living their best life"—a very trendy phrase these days, and I hate trendy phrases—and Steve and I had started doing that too. Rediscovering, or maybe just looking differently at, your couplehood is a gift, and one that every couple should enjoy opening up when the time comes. You hear a lot about parents, after they have children, setting time just for themselves, having a designated date night, but let's be honest, that doesn't always happen, and again, if we are being honest, are any of us really interested in doing these things as we did before?

Of course, Steve and I did things with our friends or just by ourselves as we were raising our boys, even though this became less frequent as they/we became more and more involved in their activities. Having all grandparents in the same city *made* us do things without them just so each grandmother could get their grandkid fix (insert giggle giggle). But still, you are never the same couple as you were before you became parents—that is, until you become a couple again. It was a fabulous thing for Steve and me to discover this phase for ourselves, and then we got to rediscover ourselves all over again once I retired and we entered the *next phase* of our couplehood.

Back to the graduates. Obviously most of my experience is with preschoolers graduating into kindergarten, or kindergarten students graduating into their first step away from PPP into the "real world" of elementary school. Oh, if things were always this simple, while at the same time so monumental.

As parents of older children, boy, could we tell these preschool parents a thing or two about what the "graduating world" was going to look like ahead for them. But at PPP, we took this preschool rite of passage very seriously! For the preschoolers, we held a graduation ceremony at a nearby country club. Buffet dinner, graduation remarks, a celebration and presentation from the graduates complete with cap-and-gown procession, and tons of photos and tears. It was a spectacular and memorable night.

Sometimes this was the end of an era with a particular family, and that was always bittersweet for them and for us. Every year I said goodbye to a family I knew I may never see again. Families I had been intimately involved with for years—*poof!*—were gone.

This was one of the reasons, as we approached the 20th Anniversary of PPP, that it was so heartfelt and wonderful and "mystical" when, for some reason, all of us started running into so many of the old PPP families and alumni so randomly. *Why now?* we asked ourselves as this happened over and over again.

Through the years, PPP had two songs that held meaning for me that I passed along to the parents. These songs were either sung by the PPP graduates or were the backdrop for the video we made each year of all the fun and learning the students participated in during their pre-K year. If you want a good cry, look up these lyrics: Céline Dion's "Because You Loved Me" and Rascal Flatt's "My Wish." Both of these songs cover parents, teachers, and children wrapped up in the past, present, and future, and I looked out to the parents every year and saw tears flowing. I listened to both of these songs while I typed this paragraph and I still get goose bumps even though I've heard them a million times. I cannot think of two more prolific songs that touch the aspects of being a parent, letting go, and knowing that your child can look back and see the loving influence of parents and teachers in their life more than these two songs.

> *Shhh, a secret . . . if I get the chance to do a mother-son dance at either or both of my boys' weddings, I will be dancing with them to "My Wish." Feel free to borrow that song for yourself (insert giggle giggle).*

Let's talk for a moment about what happens after graduation with our children and, by association, to us.

For my preschool parents, the thought of what to do about kindergarten was a huge issue. What they knew was that their child was academically ahead of, and sometimes by a lot, other children entering kindergarten in the public, and even in most of the elite private schools in Atlanta. So, where to go from here? During our kindergarten open house each year, knowing that their child had already experienced kindergarten in PPP pre-K, the question each parent had to answer for their child was, should they continue to expand that academic gap by enrolling their child in PPP kindergarten, which operated in first-grade textbooks, or was it better to bite the bullet and have a possible stagnant year in public kindergarten, so that when their child entered first grade, they were more or less in line with their first-grade classmates?

PPP parents made a huge financial investment in the early-education phase for their child. How could they stop now? In the later years of PPP, I would joke in the kindergarten open house, "Just nine more payments," since most parents were excited (and you couldn't blame them) to enjoy free public kindergarten in the fabulous school system our North Fulton County community had. But I thought it was important to give them this nine-payment visual in order to capitalize on the investment they had already made in their child's education. To not do so, when you are now on the brink of actually realizing the benefit of their enriched preschool education as they enter "real" school, was hard for me to imagine that parents would ignore.

I never thought, and still don't, that a child should be reined in from learning. I would tell a parent, when they were concerned their child was academically too much ahead already, "Well, that ship has already sailed." I couldn't imagine that parents were happy when they went to public school registration, showing the teacher the writing, reading, and math samples their child had mastered, and the teacher would tell the parent they would keep their child busy with different work after the lesson for the other children was in progress. What? Learning in isolation after a background fostered in engaged learning? No way—not for my PREPPIES! (Insert giggle giggle!) I also didn't want the parents to think I thought public school was a bad choice for their child—both Hayden and William went to public schools, just not for kindergarten.

> An interesting aside: Throughout the years, the parents of PPP, as they wrestled with what academic path to take with their child, would lay the blame for this dilemma at my feet. The resounding mantra would be, "If you at least went through elementary school, we would *never* leave PPP!" William was in our very first kindergarten class and, as I stated in another chapter, he stayed at PPP for his first-grade year (obviously our *first* first-grade class). Families joked with me many times that they thought, as long as their child was younger than William, we would just continue to expand our elementary classes for him, thus benefitting their child (insert giggle giggle).

Just to clarify PPP's position on the kindergarten choice parents were faced with, and maybe one that any parent reading this chapter may be faced with: the inherent academic and maturity diversity that naturally exists in any kindergarten environment is vast. Children are funneled into the same kindergarten classes with a very wide range of preschool experiences. Remember my explanation of Hayden and William's very different "entering kindergarten skills diversity," since Hayden only went to one year in *total* of preschool before entering kindergarten—and that was only three days a week for four hours a day—versus William growing up at PPP for five years daily!

Children with reading and writing skills are sitting next to children who maybe can sing the alphabet song and that's it. Kindergarten teachers have no choice but to teach to the lowest educational factor—everyone needs to *leave* kindergarten with the ability to read and write, so the students *entering* kindergarten with these skills already, and some with even advanced skills in this area, are left to learn in isolation to a large extent, the "different busy work" teaching solution. This is not a good thought if you have a child with such a proud love-to-learn attitude to have to sit in boredom for an entire year. So what do you do?

It seems like it would stand to reason that I thought every PREPPIE should be in PPP kindergarten. Well, that's not so. I could see various reasons why students should go to other-style learning environments. It's not always about the ABCs of a school. It's about what a child *needs* to continue to develop a love of learning. Just like when a parent would present their child's accomplishments to us upon entering PPP and either want them to be placed forward *or* challenge us about how we were going to take their child to the next level, I would let them know there's a lot of development going on in a lot of areas for young children, not just one, not just academic. Sometimes a child may know how to write or read, for instance, but couldn't follow a three-step direction, didn't have the attention span or ability to focus through a teacher-directed lesson or circle time, or maybe they couldn't navigate the social structure in the classroom appropriately. These, and so many more areas of a young child's development, are just as important to address as academics as early as possible in their school career. Think about this if you have a highly academic child.

What are the areas that require more attention now, and the academics may need to take a back seat for a bit. Seems conflicting with my statement earlier about how a child's learning should never be reined in. Maybe. But there exist situations in three-, four-, and five-year-olds where the balance needs to be more aligned and the learning can still be given attention, just less accelerated, while other areas get the appropriate *needed* attention. As mentioned in the "Do You Treat Your Children the Same?" chapter, parents have to look at their child or children as *individual-style* learners and make the appropriate choices for each. In the later years of PPP, I would say to parents at PPP kindergarten open house jokingly (but maybe not) that if I heard one more parent make a kindergarten choice because their child wanted to ride the big school bus, I was going to scream (insert giggle giggle). But to be honest, sometimes we parents make choices for our children on a whole lot less.

I'll skip right over elementary, middle, and high school and go right to college. Why? Because once you have made your choice for your child for kindergarten, either public or private, the remainder of their educational path follows that choice almost without exception. That's why the kindergarten decision is so important for your child. But I will give the following observation and a bit of blanket advice.

It's so easy to stay involved in elementary school, because children are so young and parents want to *and* feel the need to still be in control. Middle school, not so much. Everyone takes a step back from their middle schooler in most every way. No one likes the middle school–age phase (insert giggle giggle!—but it's not really a giggling matter). This is when we parents start to loosen our grip and think it's okay because "it's time" to let go a little. We *think* it is our decision, but actually it's when we start to *lose* control, not give a little freedom. Middle school is when children just begin to get a taste of freedom. This is when we start to let them stay at home alone, go places alone, etc., but it's also where the problems start. Hormones are raging, and everyone, teachers included, just seems less involved with this volatile group.

But when our children get to high school, everyone steps back in with gusto! Booster clubs, everything from robotics club to football, are in full swing for parents. Teachers spend untold and unpaid amounts of time with high school students and events. We love being at the high school and participating in pre-event meals for the kids, fundraisers, being chaperones, or driving them to all sorts of events (when carpool was just fine in middle school). We blazon our kid's name on spirit wear and socialize almost exclusively with the parents of our high school kids.

Do you hear parents of high school kids talk about the "unsavory" or "problem" kids in high school? "Wow, Billy/Suzy was such a good friend of my child in elementary school. I wonder what happened to them." Well, the answer is, *middle school happened to them*, more times than not.

Parents—stay involved with your child during middle school when the roots of their choices, freedom, and decision-making are taking hold.

Who they were in elementary school does not matter. *Who* they are in middle school going into high school will.

So, college. If you thought being involved with your child's kindergarten choice was hard, that now seems easy when it comes to their college choice. We all live through our child's choice of colleges in the view of society. It would be great if this wasn't true, because it puts so much pressure on a child to feel their value is based on what college accepts them. Bah! Watching various social platform videos of parents standing over their child at the computer on acceptance day to see if they get the "fireworks display" of acceptance or the form letter breaks my heart. In the past, even in Hayden and William's college days, it was a letter in the mail—it looked the same whether it was acceptance or denial. There's something about this computer-generated visual that shakes the soul of a family. Notice I say *a family* and not *child* because remember, everything happens to the collective family, and college acceptance is a biggie in so many family and society ways.

I love hearing numerous high-profile, successful people talk about not being college graduates. I could give you a list of people and their accomplishments whom you maybe didn't realize were not college graduates or even college attendees. What? That from me, an owner of a preschool and a proponent of "Loving to Learn"! Well, there are many ways to learn, and once your child is going into adulthood, it's time to listen to your child or maybe open your eyes.

Not every child is going to get accepted to the best college. Not every child even wants to go to college. They may have other interests or talents that go untapped for four years as they try to make college fit (okay, almost no one graduates in four years anymore), which may mean even more time is taken—or wasted? I know, I know, an education is never a waste, but is that always true? I do not have the answer to that.

I did not go to college by choice, and most of the time, I don't feel one bit "dumber" because of it. I have wished many times in my life that I had some of the life experiences that college provides, but you know what, I had a totally different type of life experience in the working world, which I loved. I would have to guess it made me a pretty good business owner because of those experiences, which college may not have provided to me. Who knows? I saw a quote in a fashion magazine from some celebrity I tried to remember that said, "Own everything that's happened to you. Those experiences make you who you are today." I have told this same sentiment to my boys *many* times in their lives. Nothing—no experience, either good or bad—is ever a waste. In fact, some of the disappointments or bad things that happen to people, in so many instances, turn out to be the *best* thing, the most meaningful thing, that could have happened (as we have all read in a million motivational or self-help books). Go figure.

I know tons of adults my age and tons of adults my sons' ages who went to college and never did anything with their degree. Again, I'm not saying college is a waste—it isn't. But this is also a reality as well. I know tons of my girlfriends who went to college, married, and never had a job outside the home. Was college a waste for them? Of course not. All I'm saying is that college is not the "end all be all," and we shouldn't make our children feel so. Especially if they give it the "old college try" and it doesn't work for them.

So relax. Your child will find their way, just like you did. Our job as parents of our college-age child is to help them see their path for what it is and support that path for them. Sometimes that will mean supporting your child's efforts, and stress, in seeking as many acceptances to as many colleges as possible. Or it may mean helping your child look outside the box to see how their interests and talents can be best moved forward. Maybe it's a four-year degree, a two-year degree, a technical college, culinary school, broadcasting school, apprenticeships, or any of a huge variety of careers that exist. I said to numerous PPP parents through the years, "There's a job for that?" It's true—there's a job for whatever *that* turns out to be!

> A funny aside: Hayden was a high-honor graduate from Georgia Tech in one of their most difficult colleges—the

Architectural College. When he interned during his senior year, it was for a luxury-brand magazine in Atlanta. He found his passion, and it wasn't building construction! Steve would laugh as he would proudly tell people that Hayden was an honor graduate of GT and was selling magazine ads (insert giggle giggle)!

But you know what? Hayden would have been miserable in a job using his degree. He made a six-figure income acquiring customers and handling advertising budgets, and that would have never happened right out of college in building construction. He was involved in everything "happening" in Atlanta, which led him to a job in a high-paced TV market, then to New York with an iconic magazine, and then on to managing corporate clients and traveling around the world in his current job.

Does this mean his college years or degree were wasted with studying and excelling in a degree he's never once used? Obviously not. It just ended up taking a very different, and perfectly tailored, path than the one he pursued in college.

William didn't enjoy school, but he excelled in baseball. He didn't see the necessity of a lot of the classes he had to take as ever having a purpose in his life—and a *lot* of people feel the same way, if we're being honest and, like Hayden, never utilize their actual degree. He will now be "playing" out his passion for baseball as a professional umpire, hopefully one day being in the MLB in a different way than being a player.

There's not a degree for that in college. If there had been, he could have pursued that and been an honor graduate as well, no doubt. He wishes he had been umpiring all along instead of pursuing other career paths. But his love of baseball has led him now to what was meant to be, just like Hayden's journey.

Was college a waste for William? Again, obviously

> not. Nothing is ever a waste, and his college baseball experience certainly contributes to his abilities as an umpire. But again, based on what William may ultimately do, like lots of other people, myself included, a four-year college degree may not be necessary.

These are just to illustrate observations that may come into play with your child. *Be open to them.*

So, like William told me that day as I was crying when Hayden started college, *Every parent goes through this "college thing" one way or the other*, whether your child goes to college or not. It's not college, necessarily, it's losing the grip on our child as they become an adult. It's no easier for one of us than the other. We all express our Empty-Nest Syndrome in our own way. We all go through the steps to find our new normal in different ways. But we all do find it. Let your child find their way too.

For parents, whether it's with a lot of upheaval and distress or with a lot of soul searching and reconnection to our "prior" selves, we all find that *we were just fine before we had them and we will be just fine without them*. For our children, it's whether they can comfortably find their future selves and be happy. When *that* happens, then we are *all* happy!

CHAPTER 12
YOU CAN'T MAKE THIS UP!

This is another trendy phrase that I hate to hear people say (but, like all trendy phrases, while being extremely overused, they are glaringly correct nevertheless). Over the years at PPP, my team and I could not believe some of the extraordinary coincidences that happened, pretty much daily! We would randomly talk about something that had happened with a particular parent, and they would walk in. We would mention a past PPP alumnus or parent we hadn't heard from in years, and they would call. We would come up with an idea at one school and the other school would call with the same idea on the same day. We would sometimes say we were living in an "Alexa" bubble—"the cloud" must be hovering over us—the internet gods were spying on us! There was no other plausible reason or explanation for all these coincidences.

This soon began to spill over into my private life when I no longer had a professional life. Since I had a little time on my hands, I started jotting down some of the most outrageous of these coincidences. It soon became evident that this sort of thing happens to a lot of people.

Here goes, interesting or not (insert giggle giggle!):

- I was reading a book, *The 10th Kingdom*. There is a portion of the book where the characters are moving from one dimension to another. A group of trolls from one dimension step through the "looking glass" into modern-day Central Park.

During their stay, they come across a CD player and, of course, they have no idea what it is. Pushing buttons, it finally starts playing a CD and the Bee Gees (my favorite group) come on singing "Night Fever." Once they go back to their dimension, with the CD player, they tell their friends it's a strange thing that, in the other dimension, there is a sickness that only occurs on Saturday nights (insert giggle giggle). So . . . I have about two hundred songs on my phone, only two Bee Gee songs. I read this particular passage in the novel, later that day went for a run, pulled up my song playlist, shuffled the songs, and started running. The *first* song that came on was the Bee Gees "Night Fever"! I'm not kidding.

- I went to the local small pharmacy that Steve uses. It's one of those "compound pharmacies," so it's small. On that particular day, one of the two pharmacists had their six-month-old daughter there with her. They were sort of shuffling her around between the two of them, putting her in her car seat, sitting her in her swing, etc., so I asked if I could hold her. She was adorable and was very engaging with me, just laughing and cooing. The pharmacist said, "Boy, she really likes you. I've never seen her act like that with a stranger."

  I said, "Well, I love kids! I owned a preschool for twenty-five years and just retired a couple months ago." As I handed her back, I said, "What's her name?" She told me. It was the *same name* as the company that had just purchased my preschool!

- A story was recently in the news about a wife who was convicted of killing her husband by poisoning him with eye drops she put in his water over a period of time. *What?!* I had never heard of that! That night, I was reading my book (an Agatha Christie book) and *a person was killed with eye drops!* That's not all. A day or so later, I was watching a favorite news show that has a panel of four to five people who talk about politics in an entertaining manner. They started "fussing" about an issue (in a joking way) and one of the panelists says, "You better watch out, I'll put *eye drops* in your coffee." Who ever heard of this? Not me, but now I'd heard about it three times in two days!

- I write about Slender Man in the chapter on technology. I really don't know where that came from—it just jumped into my mind from reading about it many years ago. I was currently reading Stephen King's *The Outsider*. The night I wrote the chapter with Slender Man noted, Steve and I were in bed reading, and a character in the book compared the outsider to Slender Man. Not only that, but a couple of days later, William noticed the book on the counter. He picked it up and sort of laughed—he said, "Are you reading this? I *just* finished the first season of the TV series last night." *What?!* I didn't even know there was a miniseries made from this book and William had no idea I was reading the book. He said that he just "came across" it searching around for something to watch! Two crazy coincidences . . .

- A friend of mine was looking for a doctor to address a condition that she needed diagnosed. I was telling Steve about it and he said, "She should go to Dr. ________, he's an authority on that and has written books and speaks about that issue." This is Steve's doctor. The next morning, I am reading a national magazine and Dr. ______ was noted in an article about that issue!

- I was watching TV and a commercial came on about the supplement turmeric. I began wondering if this supplement would be beneficial for me, so I picked up my phone and typed in the search bar, "benefits of . . ." Before I could type anything further, up pops "benefits of turmeric." Of *all* the things one could be searching for the benefits of, I wouldn't think *turmeric* would be particularly high on this list—but there it was. That "Alexa" cloud bubble again . . .? Just *who* is listening? Scary.

- I was reading the book *The Gilded Hour*. One night, I finished the book but I was not sleepy yet, so my only choice was to read the author's note at the end of the book (which I usually never read). This section was about four to five pages long and I thought that would be just about right to get me sleepy. The author references an orphanage (which is a prominent theme in the book) that was located in New York City at the intersection of Great Jones Street and Lafayette. *Just that afternoon,* I had watched *Law & Order SVU* and they were called to a situation at the intersection of Great Jones Street and Lafayette! I am not kidding! I had, of course, never heard of this intersection before.

- I am now reading the book *Bygones* by LaVyrle Spencer. One of the characters in the book is having a baby and in the delivery room the nurse

(I believe) says she thinks it's going to be a baby boy. The mother says, "If it is, we are going to be in trouble because we haven't thought of any boy names yet. But if it's a girl, it'll be Natalie." *What?!* I said that *exact* sentence myself many times prior to William's birth, and it's been told over and over, through the years, about how we named William after his Uncle Bill hours after he was born because we were so sure he was a girl and his name was going to be Natalie. (Remember this from another chapter I wrote for this book about a year ago! And I'm just now reading *Bygones*.) Unbelievable! I mean, the *exact* sentence, word for word!

- Okay, last one, and bear with me . . . It is March 21, 2020, and the coronavirus has shut down the entire world. Steve and I have been arguing if all the very drastic measures were necessary and if it's way too much to shut down the entire economy. I was on an outside run (all fitness clubs along with other businesses are closed) and on my two-hundred-song playlist plays Barbra Streisand's "The Way We Were." The lyrics are, to me, now eerily about the way our world, prior to COVID-19, used to be instead of the way we are now and will we ever be the same again—instead of about a lost relationship, as this song is really about. I became overcome with emotion and had to sit for a minute and have a good cry before I could resume my run, so desperate is our world at the moment, and this song hit that issue hard! Later that night, Steve decided we would take a break from the horrible news and watch Charles Dickens' *The Tale of Two Cities*. There is a central character in the book, Dr. Manette, who is imprisoned in the Bastille in

France for sixteen years. Upon his release he is decrepit and insane. I had never read or seen *The Tale of Two Cities* and had never heard of Dr. Manette in any form. So bear in mind these two separate and random things. I pick out a new book to read from our upstairs library during the afternoon, *Society Rules* by Julian Fellows (of *Downton Abbey* fame). Reading it in bed this same night, on the first few pages the main character of the book receives a letter from a long-ago friend. As he thinks about getting this letter out of the blue, he compares it to the song "The Way We Were"! A few pages later, as he goes to visit this long-ago friend and the friend comes into the room, very ill and old before his time, this same main character compares his long-ago friend *to Dr. Manette!* Who, of course, if Steve and I had not randomly watched that movie *that night*, I would have just thought he was referencing a random doctor of their younger days since I had never heard of Dr. Manette before today—and the '70s song "The Way We Were." Who would have thought that would be mentioned too!

- Okay, this is *really* the last one—I swear (insert giggle giggle)! Steve and I recently attended a college game out of town that William was umpiring. The concession stand had funnel cake fries on the menu. Who ever heard of such? That night at the hotel, we were watching a TV show and a scene was in a diner with a sign above a booth showing FUNNEL CAKE FRIES! Unbelievable! At the next day's game, I got me some (insert giggle giggle)!

You can't make this stuff up!

Another thing "you can't make up" is all the different ways people view or use or communicate facts. I once wrote an article about fun back-to-school facts. I started the article by stating "the fact" that eating eight grams of chocolate has been shown to boost brain power due to flavanols in the chocolate. But is it *true* that, by eating chocolate, you will make a better grade on a test? See what I mean? Something can be proven but may not necessarily translate into being "true."

What makes something a fact? If you run an internet search on that phrase, you get such a convoluted explanation of fact versus truth—believe me, you will be more confused about what the truth is than ever. Sometimes when Steve and I are watching the news and we switch between conservative shows and liberal shows, you will hear the same "fact" presented in a totally different and opposing way. It will make you nuts! I've said to Steve more than once, "There must be political facts that can't be disputed or spun to fit either party's agenda." Right? But I can't find an example of that.

Okay, here's a taste of reality versus facts, or maybe perception versus reality: When William was a bar manager in a trendy Atlanta bar, he had the opportunity of seeing many celebrities come in and out. One night, a world champion boxer, or mixed-martial artist, or some sort of featherweight prize-fighter person (I won't name him) came into the bar, dressed in pants and a blazer. William laughed at himself telling us this story because he said that if he saw this person in a bar, and some sort of dispute might "happen," he (William) thought he could "take him" based on the way this guy looked in his street clothes (smaller than William). He laughed at himself because he said, boy, would he have been wrong in his *perception* of this guy if he had not known *who* he was! William said, "He would have whipped my a**, and that's a fact!"

Here's another: When Hayden was eighteen, his Irish dance group had the chance to audition and then go on to perform on one of the very popular TV talent shows which I will not name. It was a huge honor and very exciting. The show was being filmed in Miami and I flew down just for the taping and then right back. When I got there, Hayden showed me the legal document they all had to sign. It stated that the producers of the show could take any portion of anything that happened during the taping and edit it in any way they wanted, into perpetuity. As in, they could take a facial expression, an answer to a question, etc. and dub it to any response or situation they wanted, totally out of context, and there was nothing (legally) you could do about it. *What?!* This was scary to me, but Hayden, being eighteen, had already signed it. Then, before the show started, a comedian came out to warm us up and to get footage, again to be dubbed into the final show production, to show the audience's reaction to the performances. They had us actually stand up and scream, wave our hands, and clap excitedly. They had us scrunch up our faces in disgust at a very gross joke, etc.—you get the picture. So next time you see one of these types of shows, or maybe any type of show that has a live audience, don't believe the reactions you are seeing to be the *reality* of reactions going on at that time. It's only what the producers are trying to make you think you are seeing. It's just not a fact, and definitely not the "reality" of the TV show.

Again, if you look at the internet explanation about what makes something a *fact* and what makes something the *truth*, you can easily see how the same thing can be viewed completely different. It would seem to be a fact that fire is hot, therefore if you touch it, you will get burned. How can that fact be argued? However, there are people who can walk on fiery coals and not get burned. So, is it a fact that fire will burn you, or merely that it is *true* that fire is hot? And what about when we can swipe our finger through a candle flame and not get burned? I haven't done that since I was a kid (insert giggle giggle). Fire is hot—but it doesn't always burn? Which is it?

There were some other interesting "facts" in my article that seem questionable as being "true." As I am rereading what I wrote, and of course I found these "facts" on the internet—I didn't research them myself, obviously—I am now seeing that some of the fun facts (and that's what they were represented as in my article), I really don't believe are *true*. For instance, I don't think it's true that the average child will wear down in use, approximately, 730 crayons. That's just too many! I know, I know, it says "average" and "approximately," which is how we all get away with quoting to each other a lot of facts as truth.

Short chapter, maybe not very useful, but just gave me a little break from some of the other hard-hitting chapters (insert giggle giggle!), which is why I inserted it near the middle of the book to give you a little break, even though I wrote it dead last. So wait—it's a *fact* that it's short and useless information, but *true* that I wrote it last, so it isn't a *fact* that it gave me a break—and that's the *truth* (insert giggle giggle)!

Like I said, *what makes something true* is very confusing and usually in the eye of the beholder—and *that's a fact*!

CHAPTER 13
OUR MILLENNIALS AND MILLENNIALS IN THE WORKPLACE

The most favorite article I wrote through the years was an article inspired by a situation that happened with my millennial, William. This article centered around years of elite travel and college baseball coming to an unexpected and heartbreaking end for him (and us) and how we all dealt with it. While millennials seem to have the image of being entitled and self-absorbed, as so often happens with a lot of stereotypes, the opposite is most often the truth. I weave the actual story of this baseball game throughout this chapter as it pertains to how parents so often treat their millennial in a protective way, wanting everything in their child's life to be without strife and wanting them to be the beneficiary of whatever positive results their child envisions for themselves. If this is not to be, then we parents feel the need to step in and "fix it" for them, or maybe to justify or expose an injustice where one may not be warranted.

While writing this chapter and reflecting on so much written and expressed in today's society about millennials, I would like for parents to search ourselves on how we treat *our* millennial within the family structure compared to how we treat or expect certain behaviors from "other" millennials in our work-life sphere. I think many of us expect more from "other" millennials in our outside dealings while making possible excuses for our own millennial—again, let's be honest with ourselves, parents. I wrote in another chapter that it is sometimes comical how glaringly obvious the misbehavior of others seems to us while we are making excuses for our own behavior (or misbehavior). As this discrepancy relates to parent–millennial circumstances, it's often not the fault of the millennial, even though it is their "responsibility" to deal with, fair or not. So here goes . . .

The news cycle was intrigued a while back with a federal investigation titled "Operation Varsity Blues," whereby numerous parents all over the world committed various nefarious deeds, including paying high-dollar amounts to bribe school administrators and athletic directors, paying to have SAT scores altered, forging athletic résumés, and, in fact, photoshopping their child's face on an athletic achievement of someone else in order to get their child accepted to elite colleges. I mean, isn't this what good parents do for their children—help remove the barriers to their success? If you have any doubt, just read my chapter in this book entitled, "What Kind of Parent Are You?" Helping to remove barriers for your child's chance at succeeding seems to be the defense of some of these parents involved in Operation Varsity Blues. And I confess, I am struggling with myself with this answer if I *truly* search my soul. I ask you all to do the same.

In my article, I espouse this same sentiment by admitting that my husband and I would (and I *quote)* "do anything, and I mean anything" to have changed the outcome for my son in his heartbroken disappointment of his team losing their chance to participate in the NAIA College Baseball World Series. I mean, that's important stuff, right? And at that moment in time, we *would have done* anything to have changed this outcome for him.

Here's the deal. The parental justification for our fantasy of what we would be capable of doing to change this particular disappointing outcome for our son: His team was every bit as good as the team that beat them in that one fateful game (in fact, his team was even better than the other team based on their season statistics and accomplishments). *If* there was some way that we could have changed the outcome of that one game, we wouldn't be doing so for a team that was undeserving, a team that wouldn't have made a good showing, a team that, throughout the season, was thought to have a better-than-good shot of ultimately *winning* the World Series based on their season record!

See where I'm going? See how a parent can justify their behavior? This may very well have been part of the thought process of these parents caught up in Operation Varsity Blues. The point is, they have good kids. These kids would probably have done well at these colleges, no matter *how* they got accepted. The children who get into colleges due to legacy status, or maybe the donation of a building to a college, certainly tips the scales in their child's favor, right?

As any of us know who have had kids search out their college choice, it's almost comical to see some of the kids who get accepted to a certain college while others get rejected. Many parents have asked themselves, *How could this happen?* It sometimes feels as though it's just a toss-up and the luck of the draw, and not really based on the very best choice, especially if it's *your* child who is adversely affected. So what's the problem in helping the process for your *deserving* child if you are able? What/who would it hurt? This is how Steve and I felt in our fantasy about changing the outcome for William and his very deserving baseball team.

> Two parent–millennial asides: Hayden was in an Irish dance competition in New Jersey in his later years of competing. He came in first place in this competition, and the trophy was almost waist high!
>
> At the airport returning home to Atlanta, this *huge* trophy received a lot of attention. One man said to Hayden, "I don't know what you did, dude, but it must have been something great!" (Insert giggle giggle!) The only problem was that we had to have his name engraved on this trophy and bring it back for the next year's competition.
>
> So, it's now the following year, time for the

competition, and Hayden was really sick; however, we decided instead of sending the trophy back (at considerable cost), we would just go ahead and go and hope he started to feel better and, of course, maybe win again.

The day of the competition, he was feeling only marginally better, but here we go. When it was his turn, he got up there and danced beautifully; no one would have guessed how bad he felt. Digging deep as always, Hayden doesn't shy from a challenge. However, toward the very end of the dance, his competitor (they dance two at a time) fell. In all other competitions we've ever been in or seen, this is just too bad for the dancer involved, *but* one of the judges stopped the almost-finished dance. Unheard of!

He told the boys to relax during the next set of competitors and come back and redo. That was like less than ten minutes! Hayden was in *no shape* for that. I was furious. Should I make a scene? Should I exert my/Hayden's rights? Recognize the millennial parent in me? While Irish dance competitions are huge, it's still a small community, especially for older (and especially male) dancers, so I didn't want Hayden to be tainted in the eyes of judges and competitors he would see in the future.

So, Hayden and I decided he would just have to bite the bullet and re-dance. He didn't win and we never went back to that competition, and I *never* forgot that injustice to my child.

The same type of thing occurred for William when he was around twelve. On opening day of baseball season, there were various events going on in celebration of the day. One of the events was a Homerun Derby. The competition went on for the posted two-hour time frame with a ton of competitors, with

> William in the lead! The competition was brought to a halt after the last participant in line had their turn, and we were holding our breath. If he could hold on to this lead through this last competitor, the trophy he would win was (also) about waist high!
>
> Just as the final kid finished and the competition was declared over, all of a sudden here came another competitor, breathlessly running up. His father asked if he could get in even though time was up. The teenager in charge said okay to this adult. What do you know? This "after the deadline" participant ended up winning, hitting just one more home run than William did. I was furious.
>
> Don't poke the bear when you are dealing with a mother—it will not end well.

But back to the article on William's college game. Almost six years later as I am rereading this published article and writing this chapter, it seems almost (and I stress *almost*) trivial now. But at that time, as I spoke with my son the following day, I couldn't imagine that this was not the most important thing going on. I even said to him, jokingly, that I couldn't imagine everyone in the community was not feeling this same unimaginable loss on this day. I mean, most of the parents on the team already had airline tickets and hotels booked to travel to Idaho for the World Series, that's how sure of our "deserving" team we were! But was I really expressing a serious sentiment as his mother? Dramatic, yes. Specific to me and Steve as parents, no. Parents these days always think what's specific about their child is the most important thing in the world to everyone, or at least to a lot of people.

But the story *about* the game was not the point of my article. It was my son's ultimate and surprising reaction to his disappointment. It was about William knowing that a disappointment for *him* was harder on his dad and me than it was on himself that touched me. The fact that he thought that next morning to call and check on his dad and me *before* I had the chance to call and see how he was doing was beyond words to me. He was the one who should have felt cheated, mad, and, in fact, entitled to this win, right? He was the millennial and had been raised to expect certain outcomes, and if not, parents should fix it, right? But no. William was calm and accepting of this loss, blaming no one, and ready to move on. Steve and I had to do the same.

I am trying to figure out where to go from here in this chapter about millennials, because truly this could be an entire book. I have watched, for almost thirty years, Steve and I, parents of my boys' friends, and the parents enrolled in my preschool raise our children. I have told numerous parents that my generation, the very tail end of the baby boomers, is the first generation that did not raise our children in the same way we were raised. Why is that?

My parents weren't as uninvolved as a lot of parents of their generation as far as "leaving their child to their own devices." My parents were somewhat similar to my style of parenting, being involved with me and my brothers, but not quite as much in control as parents want to be now. However, most parents of my parents' generation didn't dote on their child very much. The catchphrase of my parents' generation was something more along the lines of "if you get in trouble at school, that's *nothing* compared to the trouble you are going to be in when you get home!" Corporal punishment (some of you may not even know what that means) was still acceptable at the school level—and then you got another swat on the fanny by your parents when you got home, no questions asked. Today, parents first look to the authorities or the "system" to be at fault, not their child, and boy, I can include myself in various situations in that category.

It's no wonder millennials have the bad rap that they have of being so self-absorbed. It's their parents who are self-absorbed, living vicariously through their children's accomplishments, feelings, and on and on. We can't keep our noses out of it! (Insert giggle giggle!) Things happen *to* the collective family, not just to the child. Sometimes the child doesn't even realize something has happened *to* them! We parents most often *create* the "to" situation!

> An insightful aside: My sixteen-year-old niece worked after school at a neighborhood yogurt parlor. There was an array of fresh fruits, candy, and other toppings for the yogurt, self-serve style. Obviously a big part of her job was monitoring this self-serve buffet. It had to be maintained in a clean manner, replenished as necessary, and most importantly, made sure people did not put their hands in the toppings or otherwise contaminate the offerings.
>
> While monitoring this one day, a little girl, probably around six or seven years of age, reached in to get some of the cookie/candy pieces with her hands. She wanted a little taste while she was waiting for her mom to finish at the yogurt dispenser. Of course, very sweetly, my niece told the little girl not to touch the topping container. This should have, and could have, been the end of it—the little girl pulling back her hand and maybe lesson learned from my young niece to not do something like this.
>
> However, the mom hurried over—you would think to make sure her child understood the social infraction of etiquette. But no. Instead she said to my niece, "Oh, it's okay," and my niece didn't know how to really back up against this adult, so her supervisor stepped in and said, "No, it's not okay. We will have to throw out the whole container if it's touched."
>
> To which the mom said, "Well, I don't want anyone talking to my child like that!" *What?!* Now what lesson do you think was learned from this mother to her child?

Of course, I could give you thousands of examples of this type of parenting from my dealings with parents in the preschool as well as observations at the ballpark, school, mall, really almost anywhere there is a parent-and-child interaction with the public. And, full disclosure again, I am guilty of this behavior myself, and more than once, I can assure you. It's "believe your child" over all else. It's "let your child hear you push back on their behalf" to any authority necessary. You know a fond saying in the day-care industry is, "We'll believe only half of what your child tells us about you if you do the same about us!" But that's just a *haha*—neither party ascribes to this ethos. Both sides want to believe all! This is discussed more in the "You Have to Pick Your Battles" chapter, but it is important to bring up now about the raising of millennials.

A couple of years ago, I ran across an online video of motivational speaker Simon Sinek. If you have a chance, check out his video on millennials in the workplace. It's about fifteen minutes of jaw-dropping, eye-opening common sense. You will see yourself and your child in most everything he is saying (insert giggle giggle). The premise really is that the "problem with millennials" is not their fault, but the product of the way they were raised. In fact, he actually says "through no fault of their own" about a hundred times as he is weaving the thread of the way millennials act from a young age through their adult years, *through no fault of their own*.

The desire of parents to "empower" their child has overtaken common sense and reasoning. The "speak out and make yourself heard" and "embrace your power" ideology has been given—and I emphasize, *given*—as opposed to earned, to children at way too young an age. I have personally been told by parents at the preschool that they have told their child (three and four years old!) to speak out against a teacher, not to "take it"—*whatever "it" is*. I have had scheduled meetings with both a mother and father engaging me to do something about a situation that borders on the absurd of something their three- or four-year-old child has come home and said about something that happened at the school. When calling the teacher into the discussion, such a rational explanation was given that most times the parents had a good laugh at themselves and all was good (remember the reciprocal "believe half" concept);

however, there was that occasional parent who looked beyond reason and wanted validation of their child being a victim and the necessary retribution. This "stack up, don't back up" philosophy follows these children from school into the workforce.

When I attended the parent orientation at Georgia Tech, the parents were told it is against federal law (and they cited the statute) to discuss a student with a parent without the student's consent/involvement, even though the school knows the parents may be footing the bill; however, the student must be treated and recognized as a legal adult. They then launched into examples about parents calling teachers or administrators about everything from a child's roommate problem to grades and class scheduling. They also (maybe passively aggressively so) advised us that this was a new phenomenon, one that college administrators of the past had never dealt with. We were encouraged to let our *adult* child handle these matters for themselves in preparation for the real world. But our kids *want* our involvement. Their brains were patterned from an early age to "speak up," then get your parent involved too! This "parent handling" even spilled over to several adults I hired to work at the preschool, and when a problem arose, their parent wanted to get involved—no thanks. I was very quick to tell the few parents who called about a problem their adult child was having at work that I would not be discussing any employee issue with them, period.

> A funny aside: Have you heard about that Australian (I believe) high school that reportedly put a voicemail to parents on their answering machine about pressing certain numbers to get the person you need—as in "Press 1 to lie about why your child is absent today. Press 2 to make an excuse about why your child didn't do their schoolwork. Press 3 to complain about what we do. Press 4 to request another teacher for the third time this year. Press 5 if you want us to raise your child." This went on for ten different items! Hilarious!

> But unfortunately, most of us are guilty as charged (my hand is raised) of at least one, if not multiple, of these items on behalf of our child.

Another wonderful resource I referred parents to many times is any book authored by Madelyn Swift. I first came across her in a seminar hosted by the National Association for the Education of Young Children (NAEYC). Like Mr. Sinek, her approach is practical and full of common sense. As parents, sometimes practical and common sense are the hardest paths to take. It seems that we sometimes search for the most complicated and hard-to-balance solution to a perceived issue involving our child. I have referred many times to two of her books and shared them with my preschool parents with success. *Getting It Right with Children* and *Teach Your Children Well* are guidelines on giving yourself a look at how easy it might be/could be to raise your child well *if* you apply common-sense principles and rules instead of seeking a more complex child-rearing philosophy.

Letting life dictate how we respond to a child's mistakes instead of trying to sway, alter, or even completely change the practical outcome is the most positive and impactful way to parent. Yes, I think it might start out as being the hardest way to parent, based on my own meddling in my children's life experiences, but starting out that way and sticking to what we know in our hearts to be right, *instead of wanting something to be right that isn't,* would save ourselves and our child a lot of heartache ahead.

The real world is coming. Is your child prepared to face it without you? Statistics are showing that with millennials, this is more and more not the case. Parents are figuring into almost every decision this generation of children is making. Even millennials who are successful in their own right still feel it necessary to bring their parents into their decision-making process. When Steve and I married, that was the end of our parents knowing pretty much anything pertaining to our married life, bills and expenses, house purchasing, vacation plans, etc., and we married at the young ages of twenty and twenty-one! For my generation, once you were out on your own, *you were on your own*, period. However, just today I heard a popular radio economist say that parents are spending twice as much on their adult children (millennials) than they are saving for their *own* retirement. Again, parents, we are a funny breed!

> A funny aside: We set up Hayden and William's first student bank accounts—linked, of course, to our bank account—when they graduated high school. In fact, both of them have a framed deposit slip from that *very first* deposit into their *very first* bank account as a high school graduation gift from us in the amount of their graduation year. For Hayden, $2,008, for William $2,011. You can steal this idea if you want (insert giggle giggle).
>
> As of this writing in 2019, those same accounts still exist for them, linked *to* and open *to* my inquiring mind. Neither one of them seems concerned about this intrusion. From time to time both of them will make a sarcastic remark about my snooping but really it's not a serious concern to either of them. And of course, I'm sure when the boys marry this will certainly change, but for now, it seems just fine to them—or maybe the joke's on us and they have *secret* bank accounts (insert a big giggle giggle).
>
> UPDATE: I have just discovered (in fact, just from general conversation) that *both boys* have an account that is not tied to me at all! Money flowing in and out of these accounts—shutting me out (insert giggle giggle)!

It's a sad fact in the psychology world that there is now a phrase that is referred to and counseled to millennials as a "quarter-life crisis." We, of a certain age, know about the "midlife crisis." This typically occurs maybe around the age of fifty in past generations. But some of our children are reaching *their* life crisis at twenty-five. Things are just not turning out the way they planned. They aren't fulfilled. They don't have a work-life balance—which is almost treated as some sort of medical condition for millennials. They aren't treated "special" at work or in their personal life.

In other words, in most ways they are still relying on their parents for validation of their worth. Millennials are marrying later and later, with some proudly stating they are "self-coupled." What does that even mean? Many millennials are deciding not to have children or are putting off becoming parents into their late thirties and forties. And most are *content* with this whole situation.

> A funny aside: Before Steve and I had children, we hosted a young girl in our home from Barcelona, Spain, during her senior year of high school. It was a delightful experience and we have maintained a relationship with her and her entire family for now over thirty years. In Spain, it was typical for young men and women (at that time in the 1980s) to not move outside their parents' home until they got married or, of course, if they had a job that made it inconvenient to live at their childhood home. It was very strange to her that my younger brother, who was in his twenties and single at the time, lived twenty minutes or so from my parents in an apartment on his own. She just didn't and couldn't understand this, no matter what we said. Why would he be paying that kind of money, having to buy his own groceries, be alone, etc., when he had a perfectly nice room at my parents' house that he actually moved out of?! Well, it seems to be a good and logical question, and one it now seems young people in the United States have come to embrace—this "European" way of thinking and living. How convenient just to continue living at home and continue to be taken care of as the "child" you were while having the

freedom of being an "adult" all at the same time—maybe millennials are outsmarting us *instead of* having a crisis . . .? (Insert giggle giggle!)

As a business owner, I attended several seminars on how to manage millennials. As a baby boomer, as well as some employees of PPP being from the Greatest Generation, we had a hard time with these millennials. One of the seminars I attended addressed how the top Fortune 500 companies in the country, with, of course, the smartest business minds around, were adjusting their whole way of doing business, from the human-resources perspective, to *accommodate* the "needs" of millennials. The work-life balance I mentioned earlier is now a very real concern to these companies and one they take very seriously in a competitive job market in order to get the best of the best in young talent. I have discussed and commented on "the real world is coming for these millennials—will they be ready?" But instead, the *real world*, at least to some extent, is in the position of "getting ready" for these millennials! Again, they have outsmarted us!

An aside: One of my long-term directors at PPP is currently employed by a company that operates an on-site day-care center for a very large company. It's an interesting aside within this aside on how the workforce has changed. When I was working in the corporate world, no one cared what you did with your child for day care; that was not the "business" of the corporation. Now, a very large percentage of the most successful corporations, all over the country, have on-site childcare for their employees that is not only convenient and state of the art, but either free or at a substantial savings when compared to an off-site option. This is a very interesting perk, as well as a corporate commentary, for this workplace generation.

But back to the original aside. I recently had lunch

> with her, and I could not believe the environment she worked at! Of course, the day-care facility is brand new and state of the art, just gorgeous and innovative in every way. However, the actual corporation's environment is beyond words! It looks like a city unto itself. Beautiful buildings, quads of architecture, and everything that anyone would possibly need for a work-life balance *all in one place*! This "workplace" has a beautiful building on "campus" that houses *nothing* but a restaurant, coffee shop, salad bar, exercise-gym facility, and a bar-type area with arcade and pool table (and maybe other service and entertainment venues I don't know about). They have Friday cookouts and festival-like events just for the employees and their families.
>
> I told her it was hard to believe any actual work goes on at such a social-friendly environment! However, the school of thought these days is that that is *precisely* how to get the *most* out of the millennial workforce. Go figure.

For me and my generation, the school of thought was: You come to work. You get paid for the quality of that work. You take pride in a day's work. You work until things are done and not until then do you go home. Why was I having to give (it was suggested) a monetary bonus to the employees who were not late to work for a week or that didn't call out? That was outrageous to me—a product of the baby boomer, overachiever, and pleaser generation. You get paid to come to work—paid *extra* as a thank-you for *actually* coming to work. Ridiculous. Of course, I saw the necessity and the benefit, not only to me but to my staff, of providing a pleasing work environment and to also show my gratitude to my staff and faculty in numerous ways; but to create a work environment that also satisfied their social needs or to reward anyone "just for coming to work," I couldn't imagine. It seemed I had to draw a line . . . somewhere. But *where* is that line for millennials?

> An interesting work aside: William had a baseball coach who had a philosophy about being on time for practice, really for being accountable as part of a team. I later used a form of this philosophy in faculty meetings for years. I called it "Catching the Ball."
>
> It went something like this: Practice started at 2:00 p.m. At 2:00 p.m. the coach was standing on home plate ready to start practice by taking infield (which means hitting the ball to a position player). If at 2:00 p.m., he hit the ball to your position and you were not there to catch it, you ran ten laps and very possibly didn't play the next game. You couldn't be walking toward the field, in the dugout putting on your cleats, in the bathroom, whatever. Practice started at 2:00, so that meant whatever time it took for you to get yourself ready to be at your position, ready to "catch the ball," then that's how long you needed to give yourself. For some people, this might mean thirty minutes prior to practice, for others it may be five minutes—whatever, personally, you needed.
>
> I tried to instill this in my faculty—we even simulated some mornings walking into a classroom and tossing a ball. I would tell them, "You can't be pulling into the parking lot or walking into the building at your start time. You have to be all settled and standing ready in your classroom to greet your students and parents. You have to be ready to catch the ball."

As in most things in a work environment, the rule, procedure, philosophy works for a while, then everyone just forgets about it, but I would resurrect "Catching the Ball" from time to time. But even beyond this example, most millennials work in flex time these days. Whatever time they get to work is acceptable. So many millennials work from home, and you can imagine what a flex work environment *that* creates for them; some have never had the responsibility of showing up and being accountable at an actual office at a certain time. For my type of business, however, where teacher-student ratios were paramount, some of the millennials we employed could not adjust to this "old style" of work ethic of actually showing up on time, every day. It just didn't register with their millennial-trained brain. And don't even get me started on millennials not working on their birthday (insert sarcastic giggle giggle).

> A foot-in-the-mouth aside: I won't say which one of Hayden's jobs, since I don't want any of his past companies thinking this about him (insert giggle giggle), but here goes.
>
> One day a mom came into PPP in the middle of the day, just popped in to look at the monitors for her child because she was "in the area." She was in outside sales for a huge company and her time was her own, which we talked about. I started bragging about Hayden's job and telling her he had the same type of job experience and how great that he, as well, could do all sorts of "non-job errands, etc." I even expanded, *as moms can do*, about some of those errand-type things he enjoyed doing during the work day and how lucky he was, leaving out, however, that so many evenings of his week revolved around company business.
>
> She said, "Does he still work at __________?" Yes, he did, and then she said, "I haven't talked to (Hayden's boss) in a while, but we are social media friends because we went to high school together."
>
> OMG! I broke out in a sweat! Me and my big, bragging mouth! Was she going to tell Hayden's boss what I said . . . which might have even been exaggerated (*as moms also do about their child*)? OMG, I was going to get Hayden fired! I couldn't breathe until she left, and I called Hayden to confess what I had done/said. He just laughed and laughed. He knew his company and his boss knew

> how his days went and how successful he was in customer acquisition and service and he was totally not worried. Whew . . . but I learned a very valuable lesson.

But back to my millennial, William, as the chapter started. It's Halloween 2019 and William is leaving with a group of friends for an out-of-town football weekend trip. As I'm typing this chapter, he's leaving and it's all I can do not to stop typing and pack up a few car snacks, including some Halloween candy, for him and his friends. He's twenty-six . . . *Okay,* I know, and you know, and *they* know (after some eye rolling and maybe embarrassment in front of his friends) that they would really enjoy these treats several hours down the road. I'm just saying . . .

But back to the seriousness.

Are *you* getting *your* child ready to "Catch the Ball"? Or is your child, like William did to Steve and me, trying to get *you* ready for something? Maybe for them to grow up? Will we let them? I talk about the "real world" coming for our children and if they will be ready for it in another chapter. When I see some of the ways Hayden and William have persevered through challenges and disappointments in their short lives, I can see, like so many other millennials I know, that they *are* ready for the real world. Maybe it's not in the same time frame or situational conditions we were made to acknowledge or adhere to when we were coming of age, and maybe the style of what it means to be accountable in today's work-life balance is different, but who can say which way is better?

Like Ralph Waldo Emerson so wisely tells us, "Life is a journey, not a destination."

As I am getting back to writing due to a break with Thanksgiving and Christmas events, it's now New Year's Day 2020 and William is getting ready to embark on a very exciting chapter in his life. He's going to Florida to attend a six-week elite umpire school. I, of course, unsolicited, have two sacks of groceries all ready for him to take, including a Ziploc bag of detergent pods—what's wrong with me?! (Insert giggle giggle!)

CHAPTER 14
YOU HAVE TO PICK YOUR BATTLES

The published article I wrote, of the same name, was due to the need I saw to address why parents are seen so often giving in to the demands of their child, or maybe just not wanting to take the time and effort necessary to "pick" the right battles with their child. And as always, I am including myself in any type of perceived parenting deficiency . . . and maybe *especially* this particular one (insert giggle giggle).

Sometimes giving in to my kids was a *certainty* from the beginning of the "battle"—they knew it and I knew it. We were just going through the motions in order to make me feel good as the parent, that I tried to say no, and if I'm being honest, sometimes a parent says no knowing all along that they are ultimately going to say yes, and maybe our kids will like us more because we changed our mind in their favor. You've seen the glee kids get when this happens, and instead of us feeling defeated as parents, we feel good . . . again, parents, we are a funny breed. Do you see yourself in this scenario? I do. We never *actually* changed our mind, we were going to say yes all along . . . just do the dance.

"Well, you just have to pick your battles." Who of us parents have not used that phrase more than a few times? But if we are being truthful with ourselves, *why* do we say that? *When* do we say that? Most certainly, from my experience with using it myself or watching others use it, it's when we are in the midst of losing a battle with our child and we are embarrassed about it; we don't know how to turn this loss into a win *or* how to "save face" in public. I've even seen teachers use that phrase when it just doesn't seem worth the effort to enforce a classroom rule. I've seen parents use it when they know they are ultimately going to give in to their child. When these situations are about important things like rules, then this is a huge problem.

I wrote in another chapter about brain research as it pertains to young children, that children will search for patterns that have been ingrained in their brain from the earliest of ages. Have you seen that child who always seems to misbehave? Have you noticed the child who is always calm? It is more than probable that that is exactly what their home life is like and they will search for that common denominator in most aspects and interactions of their life. The child who arrives at school like a tornado—you can bet his morning started out like that, and in fact, you can usually just look at the parent who dropped him off and tell *their* morning was chaotic. Usually they are just as out of sorts as the child is and will flippantly say to the teacher, "Good luck with them today!" To which the teacher may respond, in their head, "So what's different about today?"

From time to time during the owning of PPP, I had an incredible speaker lead professional development sessions for the faculty. On several occasions I had him hold sessions for the parents in the evening to give advice on situational discipline and to field questions that ran the full gamut of family life. I provided free childcare to the parents since I thought it was *that* important for parents to attend. Bob Lancer could be considered "a child whisperer." As teachers, we would sit and listen to his calm revelations of what causes havoc in the classrooms and what our responsibility was for that. As parents, and even in our adult relationships, we listened as he shed light on missed mental and physical cues of a problem that we may not be paying attention to. Sometimes just meeting a person where they are is all it takes to diffuse a conflict or a provocation.

> A funny aside: Bob had a formula I heard in various seminars of his. It was as simple (insert giggle giggle!)

> as "Never lose your poise." He told us that when you lose your poise, you lose your power, in *all* situations. As a parent, I am pretty high volume, as is my husband. We yell in our household—either in regular banter or when discussions escalate; sometimes it's hard to tell the difference (insert giggle giggle). "Get to your room," "How many times do I have to tell you," the old "I'm going to count to three" form of discipline. These and many other phrases were yelled at/to my children routinely.
>
> After one of the sessions with Bob, I practiced (for a time) the Poise/Power method. His premise was to always mean what you are saying to your child so that when the need comes to discipline them, you can calmly communicate to them the discipline and they will respond because they know you mean it and will not back down, or have to resort to yelling to them the discipline. This quiet poise in the face of a tense situation was so out of character for me that it would almost scare my boys! It was like something had possessed me—who are you and what have you done with my mother? (Insert giggle giggle!) As they got a little older and I would Poise/Power them, they would roll their eyes and say, "Have you been to that man again?" The point really being that their brains were already coded from an early age to not respond *until* I yelled—in most situations, not all, thank goodness.

Walk around any school. Do you see some classrooms out of control and some classrooms calm? Is this because the children in one classroom are "better" than the children in the other classroom? I would propose not. I would submit that you can relate the behavior of the children to the behavior of the adult in charge, either teacher or parent. From time to time I would have to call a teacher into my office and remind them to keep their demeanor in check in the classroom. Raising your voice, counting to three, threatening things they knew they couldn't follow through on were not good choices for classroom management, nor were these effective parent–child discipline tools. Contrast that to the classrooms (teachers) who started the year with a calm demeanor, showing the children that they *would* follow through from the start with the classroom rules. These teachers rarely had to discipline at all throughout the year. The children, some of whom were unruly in previous classrooms, miraculously behaved in this type of classroom environment. Their behavior was recoded due to a calmer and logical follow-through of consequence/result from the adult in charge.

What's more is, from time to time we would hear from the parent that the climate of the home had indeed changed with the child's "now" calmer school behavior. Since the parent didn't have to yell and discipline the child due to what they heard about when picking up the child from school, everyone's quality of life improved. This then spilled over to the morning routine not being so provocative, which meant a calmer child was delivered to school each day—cycle continuing, voilà!

Sometimes I would have to counsel a parent, when we got to a stage of partnering in behavior management that had escalated to my involvement, to *not* start the child's morning off by reminding them of their bad behavior. Try to recode their brain to not recall bad behavior before it even occurs. If anything, a young child should be reminded to have a happy day, not to dull their brain first thing in the morning with sour thoughts of how bad their day would/could be. This continuing negative mantra was definitely *not* the way to change behavior. "Don't hit your friends," "Don't bite," "Don't push in line," was just reinforcing in their young brains to recall and default to this type of behavior when they became frustrated during the day. We even heard this validated in professional development classes that as soon as you say to a child, "Don't," all they actually hear, all their brain recognizes, is the *behavior*, not the "don't." Make sense?

An aside: Some parents wanted detail by detail each and every day about their child from whatever teacher was in the classroom at pickup. I advised my faculty that any problem that rose to the level of a parent's "need to know" should be handled by the lead teacher before she left for the day, either by a phone call or waiting around for a private discussion. I instructed the assistant teachers that they should be engaged with the students, so conversations of this nature would not be appropriate around the students in the classroom setting nor as other parents would be continually coming in and possibly overhearing.

The reasoning for this was, in a preschool environment, misbehaving (to use that term loosely) is expected to a degree. It's one way children learn appropriate behavior. If we approached the parents of every child who pushed a child, didn't respond appropriately to a teacher, cut in line, talked when they shouldn't, we would be doing nothing but having these types of negative parent interactions every day! Not what we wanted nor what a parent wanted to hear after a busy day.

However, we didn't shirk our duty to partner with the parents on appropriate behavior management or try to lock them out of what was going on with their child. Most child-development experts will tell you that preschool children will not connect a punishment at night with something that happened during the day. All this negative information might do is destroy a pleasant evening for everyone while not really being productive behavior management for the child. The teachers should be competent and trusted to handle the issue at the time and move on. When things started to become a pattern of inappropriate behavior or harmed another child, even first offense, the parent

> was always made aware and strategies were put in place, with updates provided, maybe on a daily basis. Again, once this was explained to the parent—who might have said to us at some point, "Why didn't I know about this before?"—it made so much sense to them and they were thankful to have been spared a lot of distress at home that was not necessary.

Back to the losing battle and ultimately how we might have ended up with aspects of the millennial culture. Here's just a simple example of a parent losing a battle and setting a child up for a chaotic school day: At PPP we provided breakfast from 6:30 a.m. to 8:30 a.m., when the school day began. We would have a variety of cereals, fresh fruit, milk and juice, and something extra like bagels, pancakes, french toast, fruit bars, pastries, and other breakfast snack items. Some parents would get their child a bowl of cereal, a bowl with fruit, a bowl with a bagel or whatever, milk *and* juice, and—wait for it—sometimes there would be a bowl with a bagel with cream cheese and an *additional* bowl with a bagel with jelly along with all the mentioned cereal and fruit bowls! All the bowls would be crowded around the child, nothing right in front of the child within easy reach. Obviously too many choices *and* too much food.

Consequently, the child ended up sitting in front of all this chaos not eating, thus not getting their morning nourishment, and eventually the food was thrown in the trash. No matter how the teachers tried to comfort a parent by telling them they would certainly give their child as much food as they wanted as they finished each phase, the parent couldn't deny the child's desires at the time. So what the parent thought and felt, as they rushed out the school doors, that they had provided their child a hefty and hearty breakfast, ended up being just the opposite.

Because a child's demands are met, and a child doesn't have the intellect or maturity to realize when their demands are unrealistic, the child is left with chaos they don't have the skills to handle. This truth deals with so many other areas in parenting our children far more important than this example.

After the teachers telling me how this morning routine was going for a lot of the children, I had to make a decision based on what we felt was best for the child rather than what looked like a high-end customer-service item for the *parent's benefit*. As a business owner, I didn't want to appear to my customers to be cutting corners or trying to save money. But, I finally acquiesced to the teachers and said I would try it their way.

We reduced the breakfast offerings. We went from multiple cereals to one "sweet" cereal and one "healthier" option, a fruit, and milk and water. On Friday, we had a treat—back to the pancakes, french toast, fruit bars, etc. Again, voilà! Everyone became re-coded to this new procedure and loved it! "Fun Friday" breakfast started to be a thing that everyone looked forward to and enjoyed. Some of the parents even took the time on Friday morning to sit and have breakfast *with* their child! The other days of the week the students ate a hearty and healthy, but simple, breakfast and their school day became more productive instead of starting out chaotic, hungry, and grumpy.

See, parents don't always realize that sometimes what they think is the best for the child really ends up being detrimental. Again, trying to make something right that isn't, forcing a desired but sometimes unrealistic outcome. How many times as a parent can we truly look at ourselves and say that? I know that's been my fate more than a few times—some things of a very minor nature and some not so much. "Picking battles" is a tricky calculation.

I'm going to give a couple more examples, not to berate parents but to let each of us see ourselves, maybe a little or a lot, in variations of these examples and learn from them, laugh at them, or share with others by example more appropriate ways to interact with our children.

We had a policy, Monday through Thursday, that the preschool children were required to wear a "uniform" consisting of black or khaki bottoms and a red, black, gray, or pink PPP-logoed top (either T-shirt or sweatshirt). It was very "option oriented" and kid-friendly, and what we were trying to accomplish was having the students be in comfortable, inexpensive clothing each day. On Friday the students could wear clothing of their choice. Boy, we didn't know what we were getting ourselves into when children got to make their own choice, because in so many cases, this choice seemed to be *totally* child directed (if you get my drift).

We ultimately had to set boundaries on the "of their choice" clothing. Children would come dressed in costumes (because they wanted to), or other clothing choices that were prohibitive of a productive preschool-child day. Boots, princess slippers, expensive clothing that the teachers were told to be sure not to let the child get dirty or ruin, just to name a few. So when a child would arrive on a uniform day out of uniform, the parent would look at us and actually say, "Well, you have to pick your battles." *Well, this was a battle to pick.*

Wearing the uniform was a *school rule*. If you aren't enforcing a school rule to your child, what *are* you enforcing? What message did this send to the child? When presented with this situation, we would politely tell the parent they could not leave their child at the school out of uniform. This would cause havoc with other parents who maybe *did* "pick that battle" that particular morning, or maybe had to stay up late or get up early in order to wash/dry a school uniform because they were all dirty, and never mind the four-year-old girl who got upset because Suzy was in pink pants on a Wednesday and why did she have to wear black or khaki! *Whew!* No, a *parent* had to be taught that a school rule was a school rule. You can imagine this was not a pleasant task for us to tell a parent, who was hurrying to work or other functions, that they would have to go home and get their child's uniform or purchase a new one. But this was definitely a battle *we* were forced to *pick* and to *win*.

Just one more example, I swear! We had coffee service for the parents each morning. At various times I had adult breakfast bars or muffins for the parents. Of course, as soon as this ended up being for the children instead of the parents, *because the child wanted it,* I had to stop giving the parents treats. Again, simply telling the child at the start that this was not for them, instead of giving in and then trying to backtrack later, was more of a problem for all of us than it was worth to provide the parent a quick breakfast for their car ride. And funny enough, the parents were happy when I stopped providing this to them so that they *didn't have to* "pick this battle," even though they missed the treat for themselves. Parents—we are a funny breed!

Examples of our parental shortcomings aside, what *is* important is that children *thrive* with rules and boundaries. Just go back to my example of the differences in classrooms earlier discussed—happy children with rules and expectations known and met. If a child cannot count on the adults in their lives to provide good choices that result in a stable and calm day, who can they count on? Themselves, that's who! Hey, news flash—they are happy to set the rules and make their own choices, *and what* they *think is a good choice oftentimes results in chaos for themselves and the ones around them.*

> A not-so-funny aside: It's a couple of days after Halloween. I am reminded of a late-night comedian's annual event of having parents send in a video to his show of them telling their children the morning after Halloween that they, the parents, ate all the candy. What ensues is a mix of emotions. Some children cry, some children are very empathetic and tell their parents that it's okay, and some children absolutely disrespect their parents on a level that you know can't be an uncommon occurrence in that household. Screaming at their parents, throwing things at their parents, and even kicking or striking their parents!
>
> My suspicion that this is a common-place occurrence is validated, not because the child is doing it, but by the reaction of the parents—or should I say their *non-reaction* to this level of behavior from their child.

For all my shortcomings as a parent, for letting my children rule in more things than I should have, I cannot imagine under any circumstances either of my boys hitting or throwing things at me, ever, for any reason. I have a sense of humor like anyone else and I am very leery of what is now called "virtue signaling," so I am not saying I haven't viewed these Halloween videos and laughed at them. However, it does signal a much larger problem than a child being upset that their parent ate their candy. It signals that children have become more and more empowered to take matters into their own hands on a level we should be concerned about. These Halloween "funny" videos showcase that truth in firework clarity.

Now a funny aside: So as not to appear that I am so virtuous as to be above taunting my children, here's how it would go: Sometimes when I needed a form of discipline I would make up something I was going to do for them *until* they messed up. For instance, "We were going to go to McDonald's tonight for dinner, but not now because you [*insert the infraction*]." Boy, did these types of things get to them. It worked so much better than telling them that when we got home they would have to go to their room—I mean, what child's room isn't a wonderland these days? By using this form of discipline, under certain circumstances, the child feels immediately impacted in a real way and the parent and family can go about their normal, "planned" evening since you were never planning on going out to eat, the circus, an arcade, make milkshakes after dinner, or whatever you choose to use. Mission accomplished. Feel free to use this if you would like—it worked like magic (insert giggle giggle).

I would like to also highlight a couple of situations in society of "Picking a Battle" adult to adult. These examples stray away from a parent–child standpoint and focus on social norms and practices that a lot of us ignore, scoff at, or just blatantly demand as our right to "win" as adults. Children cannot be expected to be clear on what battle to pick if parents act in an entitled manner. More on entitlement later . . .

As I stated earlier, it was hard from a business standpoint to push back against a parent, our customer. However, it was necessary to do so since we felt it was a point of honoring the parents (customers) that *were* abiding by the rules. I think this was very much appreciated by our customers.

So here goes. I just returned from the gym. As any of you who belong to a gym or club know, there are rules, and just like at a school or office environment, these rules exist for all and for good reasons. Among many of the rules of the gym, there are two that I see broken all the time: talking on your cell phone while exercising and not wiping down the equipment after you use it. Talking on your cell is just annoying to the other exercisers, but not disinfecting the equipment can have unhealthy consequences, thus the importance of this rule. While in the middle of the coronavirus scare, and now after, I am still seeing people get off equipment and not sanitizing. It has *always* been my practice to disinfect any equipment that I use *before* I use it as well as after. The school of thought I practice, and I have told Hayden and William since they were old enough to realize what I was talking about (wink wink), is to never leave your health or your future in the hands of someone else. I'll just leave it at that.

The other situation I have firsthand observed on several occasions is a very large grocery store chain refunding money to customers for any type of item purchased (or not) from their store. To my amazement, when once I was behind a customer at this grocery store and they were returning several items (a large jar of exotic-type olives that had ten or so olives swimming in the juice and a bakery cake that only had about two slices remaining) and got her full monetary refund. When it was my turn at the customer service desk, I could not help but inquire about this situation. The agent advised me that it was the policy of this grocery chain to not challenge a customer on any refund, no matter how egregious the request.

Obviously we are customers of the gym and customers of the grocery chain. However, I believe that when a rule exists, for instance at the gym as I mentioned, it is the responsibility of the gym or club personnel to politely approach the customer to adhere to these rules that govern all (or if they don't want to enforce the rules, then *they* should be ready to disinfect each and every piece of equipment as they see people leave it). In the case of the grocery store, I believe it is the responsibility of the customer service agent to diplomatically let this person know that you can't just bring back things that you ate the majority of and expect your money back! A logical, reasonable person must understand that. But wait, I guess not, if they are taking the time to actually do something as crazy as this. The grocery agent told me they *even* take back items that have another grocery chain's logo on it—unbelievable. These are just two examples of battles to pick with us adults who should know better.

But back to children, since adult behavior—specifically when adults are customers—may be too late to address (insert giggle giggle). To borrow from Bob Lancer and Madelyn Swift: keep your poise—not only with your children but in all your relationships—*and* parent with integrity and, above all else, common sense. As parents we know what's right and wrong. We know what type of child we want to raise and how we want society to view our child. But first of all, we must model appropriate right and wrong behavior to our children.

Changing our minds constantly—even when it's in their favor—does not give our children a sense of continuity and security that we actually know what we are doing, that we are confident in ourselves as parents. And that, my friends, is our Achilles' heel, and our children know it.

Let's pick the right battles, and more importantly persevere so our children are truly *winners*. If we can do this, we *all* win.

CHAPTER 15
OUR TECHNO-SAVVY KIDS! NOT JUST FOR GEEKS ANYMORE!

What do you think about technology with our kids? Since my boys were pretty much grown up before the technology boom, I don't have a lot of firsthand experience in dealing with young children as it pertains to this incredible phenomenon. I am very thankful for that. When Hayden and William were growing up, a Game Boy was about as "tech" as they got. I remember one year for Christmas, we got them each a portable DVD player that they could use individually to watch a movie. They were in heaven.

Nowadays you see so many young children hooked up to a tablet or to their parents' phone—or even their own phone!—mindlessly roaming around games and other content while in the car, at home, or in social situations. I was on a run the other day and a mother pushing a child in a stroller was coming toward me. On this gorgeous day, the child (a toddler) was looking at a device instead of looking around at nature—so sad.

I hate to look around a restaurant and see a couple or a group of people all looking at their phones instead of communicating with each other. Restaurants are now sending a message to your phone, suggesting diplomatically to turn it off when you are eating—how sad is that? I mention motivational speaker Simon Sinek in the chapter on "Parents and Millennials" and I urge you to view some of his videos. He had an interesting observation about being on your phone in a restaurant. He said that even those of us who make a point of not having our phones out, which is good, *will* whip them out as soon as our companion goes to the bathroom. He commented that people are missing out on just looking around and finding wonder in what's going on around them. Maybe you will see something interesting. Maybe something you see will spark a thought or an idea, and he says this is not happening. I think he calls it a loss of innovations, since we are not open to this thought process because of our phones. Maybe you will see a fashionable outfit and will want to copy it—I do that . . . even mannequins in store windows (insert giggle giggle). But if you have your face in your phone instead of experiencing the world around you, this doesn't happen. Interesting and so right.

Do you recall the Pokémon-finding social media thing a few years ago? PPP was a Pokémon spot (or whatever they called it). I didn't know too much about it but enough to know I was proud that we had that "honor" (insert giggle giggle). At least the PPP parents and kids thought it was cool! Anyway, Steve had no idea what was going on with this game but came face to face with it one day as we were shopping at an outside shopping mall near our home. Groups of people were walking around, laughing, and following their phones—almost like zombies. Steve noticed this and said, "What in the world is going on?" It looked like some sort of orchestrated event that we were not privy to! I didn't know what was going on either, but then all of a sudden it hit me! They were looking for Pokémon! I explained it to Steve and he said, "This is nuts." It did look like something in a movie, people looked possessed; it looked like a form of mind control. Was it? Hmm . . .

It's interesting that so many popular cars have tablet technology for movie watching and game playing for young children. Recently, I was behind a huge SUV on the highway that was streaming a college football game on a huge screen built into the outside of the car! Is that legal? I was so distracted. So many parents search out the best SUV for their young family that has tablets already built into the back of the front seat. I think it's probably a standard feature for SUVs these days. This was not how this technology started—having one screen flip down for everyone to watch together in the back seat, which probably would have at least led to discussing what they were watching or laughing together, even that would be better than what's going on now. But no, now each child has their own choice of viewing with individual seat capability, plugged into a headset, totally isolated from each other.

This wasn't a thing when Hayden and William were growing up. I drove Hayden back and forth, forty-five minutes each way, to the private school he attended during his middle school years. We either talked the whole time *or* he had to sit and listen to me problem-solve business issues with my admin team. To this day he will make comments about something going on with him in the workplace and say, "I learned about that because of all the time I spent in the car listening to you."

I've already written about William gaining a love of music, which he still has to this day, specifically for the songs of my and Steve's generation because he and Steve listened to these songs so much when they were driving to school or sporting events through the years. It's wonderful to see him enjoy our albums on a turntable stereo in his room.

Hayden and William are both "Rush Babies," listening to a lot of talk radio while in the car with either Steve or I, whether they wanted to or not (insert giggle giggle). These types of parent–child interactions, really generational give-and-take radio-listening situations, sadly, are a thing of the past. Eating around the dinner table is a thing of the past and now car-ride interactions are too . . . sad.

Do kids even say anymore, "Are we there yet?" They are so happily plugged in, I don't think they are really concerned anymore about the length of a car ride, and I propose that's pretty much why this technology was inspired and even demanded. The frustration management I discuss in another chapter—that our culture is so engrossed in trying to minimize for our children—rears its ugly head in almost all aspects of family life. My goodness, a child shouldn't be bored while in the car for ten hours or ten minutes! Always cautious about not "virtue signaling," I admitted in the first paragraph about Steve and me getting the boys a handheld device they could view movies of their choice on. No doubt, from this point forward when we went on a trip, these devices were an integral part of their car ride. I'm sure Steve and I didn't mind the peace and quiet (insert giggle giggle!), but by this time they were almost teenagers, and you know what can ensue in the back seat of a car for any length of time between brothers.

But how could we, as parents, predict what was ahead for our children?

We now have terms such as "cyberbullying" and "going viral." The choice of the word "viral" is a very interesting comment on the infectious way information spreads and the havoc that anything known as "viral" can cause. I don't think this word was chosen by happenstance. We have teens doing dangerous things due to following, in cult fashion, certain bloggers or make-believe people. What about that Slender Man nonsense a few years ago? Children were committing crimes because they were trying to be like, or please, Slender Man. Scary stuff. There was just a recent criminal case about a young girl who goaded her boyfriend into committing suicide from text messages sent back and forth.

My favorite show, *Law & Order SVU*, had a show plucked right out of the headlines about a mom, using an alias, who cyberbullied a rival classmate of her daughter's to suicide. Pedophiles also troll and stalk our children, gaining their trust and abusing unsuspecting teens. At PPP, we had cameras installed in our classrooms from the day we opened in 1995. These cameras were way ahead of the market's technology in other childcare centers at the time (color monitors in real time instead of black and white that moved like robotic viewing). It was the best "reality show" on TV, I would remark to parents!

The parents would sometimes ask if they could access the

monitors through their computers at home or at work, and for a time we did have a disc they could install that would allow them to call us and gain access through our acknowledging their computer, but that quickly became obsolete and it just went back to being a system they could look at in our lobby. So many of our tech-savvy parents would tell us that internet viewing was just not safe, even password protected. I mean, if the government and other huge corporations' computer systems could be hacked (in some cases by teenagers no less), what would prevent a breach in our little preschool technology by the pedophile world from happening?

When computers first started being prevalent in children's usage, parents were warned not to let your child have a computer in their room. By eliminating the privacy component, you believed you had eliminated the danger component. But that's not so easy these days. Almost every school requires computer-generated schoolwork to be completed online or submitted electronically by a deadline to the teacher via the computer, thus it's "better" for a child to have the peace and quiet necessary to do this in the privacy of their room. At least, that's the argument the child puts forth and parents go along with. Parents can set safeguards, but kids find ways around that, don't they? My generation quips, "If I can't figure out how to use my phone, computer, cable TV, and so on, I just wait for my ten-year-old grandchild to visit!" It's amazing how "wired" young children's brains are these days in their understanding of technology—mind-boggling.

The American Academy of Pediatrics recommends no screen time for children under two, except for video chat. What? Parents actually have to be advised about *limited* screen time for a baby?! Children often resort to temper tantrums when a device is taken away from them, and of course, as I discuss in several chapters, this behavior results in a parent giving in to them to keep the peace, and the manipulation skills of a child are rewarded in yet *another* way.

Doctors warn that children of such a young age do not learn valuable self-soothing techniques when they are bored or have other strong emotions, so to the screen we stick them to make them happy. Isn't this what we all want, to make our child happy at all times? A more dangerous way to look at this scenario is, do we give our children the availability of so much screen time to make our child happy *or* to make *us* happy so we don't have to interact with our child as much? Parents need to take a long look at that possibility the next time they hand their child a tablet or a smartphone. I'm just putting that out there to keep things honest between us parents. Keeping it real, as they say.

However, I did come across one study that cited drug use, drinking, car accidents, and sexually active teen behavior statistics are all down. Obviously this is good news, but it seems to be a byproduct of the lack of social communication and interaction of teens, which is *not* a good thing. Can't we accomplish keeping these statistics low without sacrificing our children's ability to connect with each other? Depression, feelings of isolation, lack of sleep, and general unhappiness that everything in your life doesn't measure up to the glamour of others is also a byproduct of too much reliance on the screen. And all of these negative and harmful areas of concern for our youth were driven up even higher throughout the two years of schools being locked down during the COVID pandemic.

The term "influencer" is now a thriving and very lucrative career choice. Almost any company you can think of funnels money, and a lot of it, to influencers, from home renovations to makeup to pet products to where to shop, home décor, fashion, and health concerns, in order to get these influencers to push their product to consumers. If companies aren't utilizing this new phenomenon, they are losing a huge market share.

In researching, I saw a study that two out of three teenagers and young adults own a smartphone. "About as complete a market saturation as possible for a product," and that study was done in 2015! No doubt it's three out of three now in 2022—you even see homeless people with cell phones and it appears, from news reports, that we are handing out cell phones to people crossing our borders into our country. Talk about total market saturation of a product. Again, a business would be stupid not to take advantage of this advertising vehicle.

You can find almost anything you need to know on various internet platforms. It can be a beautiful thing or it can be a nightmare. I reference Operation Varsity Blues in various chapters throughout this book. One of the fallouts, among many, was one of the young girls, who benefitted from her parents allegedly buying her way into college, was dropped from various contracts she had secured from beauty outlets as their influencer when this scam was exposed. She is a beautiful, twenty-something girl, and her knowledge about makeup and fashion is beyond words (insert giggle giggle). No really, it sounds funny but it's true. She can influence the purchase of *any* product she uses, thus boosting the profitability of huge fashion and beauty-product corporations. And she's not the only one.

You don't have to be a celebrity to influence. You just have to be smart and knowledgeable about what you are selling, and the "hits" and "followers" fall into line. It's genius. (Okay, anyone who knows me is giggling themselves silly because they know I have no idea what I'm talking about . . . insert huge giggle giggle! But I'm sounding pretty good, right?)

> A funny aside: I once asked an adorable little girl at PPP, I think around four years old, where she got a beautiful princess necklace she wore to school one day. I expected her to say something like, "From my mommy." She responded, without hesitation, "Amazon."

Simon Sinek states that if you are grabbing your cell phone in the morning before you greet your family, that's an issue. I do that—I didn't realize it was an issue until I read this and thought about it. So many of us depend on our phones for everything from the weather of the day, what time it is, our alarm to wake us, our calendar of appointments, health features, and who is trying to reach us via text or email, personally and professionally. I hate, on Sunday afternoons, when the new update on my phone tells me the average amount of time I spend daily on my phone. *Yikes!*

Have you seen the commercial about how all of us wait anxiously and stressfully for the little text bubbles to be replaced by someone's reply? This commercial has one of the most prolific and celebrated movie directors of all time in high stress while waiting for *another* extremely popular actor's response. I mean, talk about influential! And of course, the obsession with texting, even the most mundane and non-urgent of messages, has led to countless automobile accidents and deaths for all age groups. States have had to outlaw the use of phones in our hands for any type of communication while driving. Weren't we smart enough to figure that out on our own? Evidently not.

Now what about technology in education? I once had a kindergarten teacher state very emphatically in the kindergarten open house, when asked about technology with our students, that she would never dream of teaching the students with SMART Boards or any other form of technology. Especially for kindergarten students, PPP's philosophy was that the teacher–student engagement was paramount to continuing to solidify the "Loving to Learn" ethos of PPP. It was horrific for us to think about such young children learning in such an artificial manner. When explained in this way, it made 100 percent sense to the parents, and I bet they looked at SMART Board learning, which was all the craze, in a different way from then on.

The last couple of years of my owning PPP, we did, however, implement a thirty-minute rotation a couple of times a week (similar to the students' exposure to the other Specials of PPP) of STEM-based tablet instruction. I think this satisfied the portion of parents who thought our lack of technology-based learning may be putting their child behind, since this was how public schools were trending. They didn't want technology-style learning to be a shock to their child when they entered public school. I agreed.

It's interesting that students can now be totally homeschooled, with or without their parent. Homeschooling has evolved from a parent sitting down at the kitchen table teaching their child, to children now using the internet to learn at home with a wide range of teachers, even globally. Interestingly, William umpired a high school baseball game a year or so ago and it was a homeschool-affiliated team against a public school team (just thought I would throw that tidbit in on the evolution of homeschooling).

Many school districts have the capacity of internet-learning technology if there is a snow day or other reasons for the school to be closed. In the "olden days," kids would have a day off from learning if there was snow, you know, to play in the snow . . . but no longer. It was interesting to watch schools at all levels adapt to home-based learning during COVID-19. Systems put into place during this time are still being utilized now, two years later, and disputes between parents, teachers, and school boards are ongoing. Pundits are now saying that the COVID-19 situation will forever change the landscape of the way we educate our children, especially the crazy expensive college tuitions, and further, that college campus life could be a thing of the past. Scary thought, huh?

But aside from all the emotions of this, how far behind are our children, especially our young or at-risk children, going to fall in development, and not just academic? I can't get my "educator" mind around children learning exclusively by sitting in front of a computer. It gives me a pit in my stomach, so I can't even begin to imagine what parents are feeling. So sad.

I have evolved over the years, of course, to seeing the reality and the value of the internet in education and, in fact, the value of the internet contributing to the success of a business. A huge political issue these days—when *isn't* there a huge political issue these days?—is the accessibility of the internet to children in rural areas or lower-income areas that don't have this educational enhancement available to them.

I was in a meeting several years ago with a congressional representative in Georgia and fellow GCCA board members, discussing issues with him concerning the childcare industry. He had a bill currently in front of the Georgia legislature for the expansion of broadband internet to all parts of Georgia for, mainly, educational reasons but, of course, would be of broad spectrum value to everyone. The funding of this internet expansion was tied to approval, with his possible backing, of passing a gambling law in Georgia, as in casinos or racetracks or something like that, which could possibly affect funding for Georgia pre-K, something like this . . . it was sort of hard for me to follow.

As of this writing this legislation hasn't gone anywhere yet. The devil is always in the details. And again, editing this chapter months after the original writing, these same areas and these same children have been left out of months of learning without the availability of the internet once schools closed all over the country in March 2020, and it looks like this situation will continue for these children into the new school year and beyond.

As for adults, it was interesting to watch the incredible difference from the early years of PPP to the later years of PPP of a majority of the parents transitioning from a workplace to a home-based work environment. We can get food delivered, groceries delivered, medicines delivered, shop for any and everything, video-chat a doctor, as well as work and be educated while never leaving our house. I mean, there's nothing, seemingly, that can't be accomplished through the internet! I laughed when telling Steve (during the COVID-19 crisis) that we received advisement from our dental group that they are now offering "tele-dentistry"! What?!

But where will all this convenient isolation ultimately lead us or the generations to come?

I recently saw a commercial where a parent in the future was explaining to his son, while touring a museum and seeing a wallet displayed, what a wallet and all the plastic cards contained in the wallet were used for "in the past." The child was perplexed about this accumulation of stuff that people used to have to carry around to identify themselves or to be able to purchase things, since in this future time, you just used your fingerprint and any information necessary to be accessed about you was stored there. Future, huh? No, stuff like this is happening *right now*! The commercial was influencing any of us who aren't hip yet with this technology how behind the times we are. What, already?

> A funny aside: Several years ago, Steve and I were entering a Disney property in Florida, I think it was Epcot, and it was required to give your fingerprint to enter. We declined this requirement and a green-coated Disney representative had to come over and question us. It appears the innocent age of Mickey Mouse is officially over . . .

In conclusion, going "viral," being an "influencer" or being "influenced," "sharing" our lives, and enjoying information we may never have been able to access before is never going to go away. There is so much good—even great—about the internet and the value it brings to our lives. But for me, I think I'm just going to stick with my day planner and my wallet—hey, it's a Louis Vuitton wallet. How's that for "influencing"? (Insert giggle giggle!)

CHAPTER 16
ARE OUR KIDS SAFE IN OUR SCHOOLS?

Nothing is as scary as losing the feeling of control over the safety of your child. As you know, my boys are men now and their safety is still a concern for me. They *never* left the house (and still don't) without me saying, "Be careful." Hayden lives in New York City, and whenever I hear of something going on there, I'll text him immediately. He sometimes laughs because he has no idea those things are going on since he's not involved, and nowhere near it, but I just need to be sure. When the boys were living at home and I heard a siren, I would quickly text them just to be sure it had nothing to do with them. I'm sure you get the picture, and I'm sure a lot of you are the same (insert giggle giggle).

But what about when we send our children to school? Unlike car situations, we don't think that they'll be in any danger, do we? Well, maybe now we do.

Steve and I take a holiday trip to New York City every December. We took the boys with us from the time they were eight years old or so up into their twenties. In 2012 we took our first trip alone to NYC after so many fabulous trips as a family. After hours of walking and shopping, we stopped at a crowded, noisy bar to have a cocktail, and on the TV was the aftermath of the Sandy Hook Elementary School shooting. I saw the headline running at the bottom that twenty-six people had been shot, twenty of them children. I don't want to say I dismissed it, but I didn't think it was something that had happened here in the United States, so even though it was horrendous, I didn't feel as affected as if these were American children. I am sad to admit that out loud. Something this horrendous must be in a country without the morals, sophistication, or sanctity of children that we have in the United States. This is what I thought. All of a sudden it became clear that it *was* in the United States. Steve and I just sat there in disbelief and sorrow. Little did we, and the country, know that school shootings were going to continue. Weren't Columbine and Virginia Tech just an anomaly?

Obviously being an owner of a preschool, safety in all forms for the children in our care was always paramount. We had small group sizes. We had a much lower teacher-student ratio than prescribed by the state of Georgia as appropriate. We had dedicated teachers who took the safety of their students very seriously and always let us know about anything that needed attention on the playground or classroom before it became a safety issue. What we couldn't protect against was the unknown. What we couldn't predict was the crazy person out there who is determined to cause chaos and destruction.

Each year the teachers were required by the state of Georgia to obtain ten hours of professional development training. Since the teachers of PPP were so tenured, it was extremely hard to continue to find classes that were of benefit for the group to take. We joked so often that most all of us could teach a professional development course on just about any subject (insert giggle giggle). After years of training drudgery, we discovered a wonderful specialist who designed and provided courses *specific to PPP* that we all looked forward to taking.

> A funny aside: My brother David and his wife, Stacy, got tickets for my nieces, Emma and Leah, and themselves and a friend of Emma's to see Taylor Swift as a Christmas gift one year. The concert wasn't until August or something crazy like that, so the girls looked forward to it for a long time!
>
> Since the tickets were purchased so far in advance,

you guessed it, my brother had a work event come up out of town and could not go to the concert. Enter Aunt Kay to use his ticket. Well, I didn't really want to go—weeknight, downtown Atlanta, crowds, and whatever excuse I could come up with. So, it was decided that the mom of Emma's friend would use the ticket. But Aunt Kay wasn't done with this concert. I was asked by David and Stacy (and I was happy to do it) to go pick up the girls at their school and meet Stacy at a parking lot right off the highway so she could just come straight from work, get them from me, and get right back on the highway.

Emma's friend and her mom were going to meet at this convenient parking lot as well. Stacy arrived prior to them, so I left. On the way to the concert, Stacy was saying how much she appreciated my picking up the girls so that it was easier to jump on the highway and head downtown, saving a lot of time. This mom, also a good friend of David and Stacy, said, "So does your sister-in-law live or work near here?" Stacy replied that I owned a preschool nearby so it was easy for me to help out. She replied, "What preschool does she own?" Stacy said, "PPP," and this mom responded excitedly, "You mean *Kay*?"

Stacy about ran off the road! Yes, this was our favorite trainer! These two families had been close friends since their girls were in kindergarten, and she had been our trainer for several years and knew of PPP for years prior to that. But never had these worlds collided until now. What a story! You can't make this up (insert giggle giggle)!

Back to school safety. Since the training topics were based on PPP needs, our needs soon reflected the concerns of our parents and teachers around intruder safety, and so a training session was born. For several hours, we roleplayed, solution-brainstormed, and came up with a safety program to fit the environment of PPP in case of a dangerous situation that could result in possible harm to the children. The teachers were told that the "code" we came up with should not be shared with anyone outside of the PPP faculty. The code phrase we agreed on was something we thought would be logical to an intruder for us to say through our intercom system as a way of appeasement and acquiescence to the intruder, but was obviously designed to bide time and cause an alert to the faculty, allowing time for help to be called and possibly get the students in a safe situation. This system would work both ways in the event of a front office breach or if someone came in the building through the playground into a back classroom.

We hear so much, batted around in a political sense, about today's children having to go through intruder exercises. Where to hide in the classroom, locking and securing the door, escaping through a window—it's a lot for a child to absorb, for sure. We trained our teachers to act calmly but purposefully during this exercise, just like when we conducted fire drills, so that the children would not be unduly upset. In comparison to children of earlier generations having to hide under desks to shield themselves from possible air-raid bombings, this had to have been just as traumatic and as necessary as today's intruder training exercises. The trick to *anything* presented to children that is unpleasant is the *way* it's presented. When trusted adults act without drama, this calms a child and, instead of scaring them, can actually make them feel prepared, more in control, and safer.

As I have mentioned in various chapters, PPP is in an affluent suburb community of Atlanta. But, as we were soon to understand, that meant nothing if someone was bound on destruction of any sort. So what do parents do? How do they drop their child off at any school without worrying about their safety? We've heard over and over, and we said it ourselves to PPP parents, "If someone wants to get in your building, they are going to get in." Without building a fortress around your school or even your home, without doing away with windows in the building, without eliminating a free-space playground, how are schools ever going to be "safe"? Of course, this has become (as everything these days) a huge political football. Teachers carrying concealed guns, banning guns, policemen patrolling schools, and metal detectors that everyone walks through are just a few things that have been offered up as possible solutions. But again, as we saw in other mass shootings before and since Sandy Hook, none of these things worked or would have/may have worked. So, again, what's the answer?

A wonderful PPP family (that ended up having three children go through PPP from the Infant Suite through kindergarten) came for their initial tour. The mom, as so often happened, toured various schools, weeded it down to a couple, then Dad came to help make the final choice. So, this dad came on his lunch hour one day to PPP alone. He told us his wife was very excited about PPP, just loved everything about it, and was looking forward to enrolling their first child in the PPP Infant Suite. But she was concerned about safety, not just at PPP but at the other preschools she toured as well. He then launched into what she had told him about the various safety measures to keep children from being abducted or harmed, and he asked me what he should think about all that.

So, I went into what measures we had in place to keep our students safe, and he stopped me and said, "No, I'm not talking about that. What I'm talking about is, if all you day-care centers have to have such measures to keep someone from coming in and taking my kid or killing my kid, I think I'll just keep him at home, thank you very much." Wow, did that put a different spin on things! Usually, I could explain our security measures and the parents would either think they were fabulous, adequate, or maybe make a suggestion. Never had I had a parent say, what really is obvious, that if someone wants to get in, they are going to get in and you really can't keep my child safe, no matter what you have as your marketing spiel to make me think otherwise. Wow!

A common thread with parents about our security system was

why we didn't have a parent code pad to enter the building instead of the PPP staff "buzzing" people in from the lobby into the school proper through the locked door. Some parents felt that this would be a safer system. I explained that, unlike other day-care centers, at PPP we were either up front in person to have our eyes on each and every parent coming in, or, if we had to leave the front desk, the locked security door would prevent anyone (even parents) from entering the school and everyone would have to wait in the lobby for authorized entrance until we returned. I further explained that if we gave a code to parents, then that would give us license to leave the front lobby unmanned for any number of reasons and for any amount of time, and anyone could get in *by a well-meaning parent*. Further, I gave an example that everyone could relate to of "piggy-back entry" into any building in our everyday experience from apartments, dorms, or office buildings. You don't close the door in someone's face—you let them in, maybe even hold the door open for them! We bolstered this argument from our knowledge of parents coming to PPP from other day-care centers and verifying this system as happening daily as well as my affiliation with so many directors at GCCA that had this parent code pad system. I told parents that this system, I felt, gave the parents a false sense of security since the administration would have no idea who was in the building or who had left the building if they were not up front like we were.

We once had a parent send a letter to the parents in his child's classroom eliciting their joining him in demanding from us that we "beef up" our security measures. I believe an armed guard was mentioned. Nothing had happened at our school or in the community to scare this parent into this suggestion of action on our part; it was just a generalized concern (and that he owned a security company that might be engaged to provide this service could have come into play). Steve and I were on a cruise at the time and this was communicated to me one morning as I checked emails. Several parents had brought this letter to the attention of my admin team, and the parents were not in agreement with this suggestion by this parent. The letter stated that he (the parent) was not comfortable leaving his child at PPP. Steve and I responded to this parent that we would *never* leave *our* child anywhere *we* thought was unsafe, and therefore he should consider very carefully his child's continued enrollment at PPP. This family surprisingly . . . (?) continued their enrollment at PPP.

Again, being more honest with PPP parents in the later years, I would tell them that unfortunately we had to "protect" children from one parent to the other parent due to court-ordered restraining orders. We had to "protect" children from divorced parents picking up on days they were not authorized to do so. Parents whom we had had years of wonderful relationships with, we were now in the awkward position of having to tell them that they could not enter our building to pick up their child. We had several situations where I had to call a parent to tell them of this breach by the other parent and the police would have to be called. Imagine! What if, using the parent code pad system, a well-meaning parent, recognizing another parent, let them in not knowing this would cause a legal issue if no administrative person was up front to intervene? So, to tell a parent concerned about safety that the chances were far greater of *them* letting in an unauthorized *parent* over an *intruder* was not out of the realm of possibility. I owned PPP for twenty-five years and was involved with thousands of preschools and day-care centers through the Georgia Child Care Association, and *never* did I hear of a "random" abduction or a shooting, knocking on wood as I say this.

Of course, nothing (as we have seen) is foolproof. I thought we had a good system, or I wouldn't have had it. But, like anyone or anything else, it wasn't without flaws. We would prop the security door open during the busy drop-off and pickup times. We would prop the door open if we were having a full-school event. Of course, during these prop-open situations, we were always up front, supervising and keeping a visual on who was entering the building, and this just seemed to fit the very social and family-oriented community feeling that PPP successfully fostered with our faculty and parents, and thankfully—luckily—never presented a problem. Again, you get sucked into a possible false sense of security and procedures, of any sort, fall aside.

I say "luckily" nothing ever happened, but I don't think we were "lucky." I mean, things weren't happening all around us and we were just escaping it. I still maintain the chances of something happening, then or now, are very small—in fact, practically non-existent. Sadly, I'm sure the administration and parents of the Sandy Hook community thought the same thing.

So what's the answer? Homeschool? Guns in schools? Better mental healthcare for any would-be criminal? Tougher gun laws? Fortress-structured schools? I could go on with possible and improbable proposals. Prayer for the country and for our children is certainly a proposal as well. Other than that, I, like everyone else, whether anyone wants to admit it or not, do not have the answer on how to ensure our children's safety at school. I wish we did.

CHAPTER 17
SOCIAL MEDIA IN TODAY'S WORKPLACE

This will no doubt be my shortest or maybe the least valuable chapter, but we'll see as it develops. I am technologically challenged and proud of it. I wore as a badge of honor, and still do, that I didn't have a social media presence of any sort until creating a website after writing this book—early 2022! I told my boys I was not going to learn how to text. If they wanted me, they could call me. Of course, that didn't last long and now I'm a champion texter, known for my full command of emojis!

> A funny aside: I once heard a radio host talk about how texting had set the human race back thousands of years. Instead of communicating with words, we were now communicating in hieroglyphics! He was so right! I know I sometimes use symbols as my full response when texting—no words at all (insert giggle giggle)! Before I realized I could use emojis in emails, I would type to my admin team a sentence and then actually *type* the words "insert smiley face emoji" or "insert red dancing girl emoji." That's where the "insert giggle giggle!" comes from in this book—a tribute to my early days of non-techiness.

One of the first things the acquisition company did at PPP was to launch a social media page. Not only did the acquisition company want it, but my administrative staff had wanted one for years. It was bad enough that I had held out for *years* without even a company website, an unheard-of practice in the business world at the time. This was also a sore subject with my younger administrative staff—they lobbied for a website hard. My pushback was that I wanted to tell prospective parents about PPP in person, not on the internet. That seemed to work well until the world started passing me by, so I had to acquiesce to a website. Wow! That website "give-in" on my part changed the landscape of our prospective parent base.

The best story I can tell you about our website is that we had an email inquiry and ultimate enrollment in our Scholars Summer Camp program from a family in China. Having families contact us from all over the world was starting to become commonplace, and it was totally knocking my socks off! To think our little PPP business was reaching people all over the world and they were actually sitting around their homes discussing enrolling at PPP when they moved to the United States, actually saying those words, was an astonishing realization.

But back to this particular enrollment. This family arrived at PPP the morning of starting the four weeks of summer camp they had chosen for their son based on the calendar activities posted on our website. Their son was twelve years old, which was at the very top of our age group range. Neither he nor his parents had very good English skills, just barely enough to communicate. Before the end of the first week it was obvious to the parents, as well as to us, that PPP was not a good fit for their son. So I sat down with the parents to discuss their options.

Through various ways of communication, it came to light that this family came all the way to the United States from China for the *sole purpose* of attending PPP summer camp! Unlike other families from all over the world that attended PPP due to living here for various portions of the year, this family was staying in a hotel for four weeks *just so their son could attend PPP summer camp*! I was blown away, I couldn't believe it, it was almost impossible to grasp! Now what could I do for them? This child was extremely intelligent and not really into some of the field trips and activities we were doing, even though they had chosen the specific weeks' activities. So, I helped them find a science/robotics camp at Georgia Tech, and before the end of the first week at GT, they let me know their son was enjoying it very much. As a rule, since our camp always operated at capacity, we did not offer any type of refund once camp weeks were committed; but I refunded *all* their money, even the week they attended, and was happy to do so. The fact that someone thought enough of PPP to specifically travel from the other side of the world to attend was payment enough.

As laughable as our website actually was—and believe me, it was so low-tech it was a joke—we were told many times how appealing it was from the parents coming in for tours. Huh? It had real photos of students, teachers, and PPP events, not gloss stock photos, and I think that made it appealing to parents. It was "real," and parents got that same feeling when they came into PPP and met everyone. This was what I was afraid we were going to lose, the "real" feeling, if we had a website. But by keeping the website so low-tech, it worked, which is why I would never change it. Just finally *having* a website made my admin staff happy, and I was happy it didn't seem to change the personal parent connection that was important to me.

> A funny aside: I once had a parent come in for a tour. She was overcome with joy that she had *finally* found us! She said *everyone* in her "Mommy and Me" monthly play group came to PPP. *They all loved PPP. Their kids were so smart because they came to PPP. They couldn't say enough good things about PPP.* She went to the trusted internet search one day to find "PPP" . . . but there was no PPP. She was frantic. Where was *the* "PPP"?! She had to wait a whole month to get back to this loosely associated group to find out what "PPP" stood for. *Whew* (insert giggle giggle)! She ended up being a mom we enjoyed for many years with her lovely children.

But the website fight wasn't anything compared to what was coming next: social media, and my teachers' involvement in it. In various seminars we attended, as social media was becoming a very prevalent thing in the business world, we, like other companies, had to come to grips with how to handle it. Some seminar speakers advised to have a no-social-media policy in your staff handbook. I couldn't figure out how to do this. How could you tell an adult they were prohibited from having a social media presence? Then there was the advice to prohibit your teachers from accepting parents as "friends" or followers. We were advised to not even allow teachers to give out their email addresses or to ask for a parent's email.

But just like me, as I discussed in the chapter about starting PPP, some of our teachers were mothers of young children who were classmates and playmates of our parent clientele, and therefore their child was invited to parties, sleepovers, playdates, etc. The children may have been on the same Little League or soccer, ballet, or swim teams. We even had a teacher who was a coach on her son's basketball team that had various PPP students on it as well! How could I possibly prohibit them from being "involved" with each other?

We also allowed our teachers to babysit our students and some were even hired as tutors. We had nothing to do with this relationship and I will say that it never presented a problem. Parents were thrilled to have access to these wonderful ladies and I looked at it as yet another service I provided, yet didn't actually "provide." So here again, how could I not allow teachers to give out their email or phone number to parents?

I will admit that I never came up with the solution that fit my business model as it related to social media; however, I have cautioned my own two boys to be very, very careful about social media and how it could affect them in the workplace long term.

It is widely known that the first thing prospective employers do is check an applicant's social media profiles to see what pops up. We were also guilty of doing this for applicants and even for some parents after they toured PPP, in certain situations. It was amazing (and scary) what you could find out about people, which made me even more concerned about my own teachers' social media presence.

Thankfully, as mentioned, it was never a problem for my business, but since I have retired, it has kept me up at night thinking about all the things that could have happened in this realm when you are dealing with employees who take care of other people's children. I was so very protective of my families, of my teachers, and the privacy of both, as well as my business privacy and exposure concerns, and the fact that I was so uninvolved in technology that I didn't even know what to be afraid of or how many different ways social media could be used, it just added to my insecurities in this area. My staff assured me that some of my fears of exposure for PPP were unfounded, but you hear stories of breaches in one way or the other, so I was just never willing to take the chance. I used to tell my staff, "I won't know where 'the line' is until the line gets crossed!"

When the "new" PPP launched a social media page, this took the place of my beloved "baby": the PPP PRESS. When we started PPP in 1995, we put to press the first of the monthly publications of the PPP PRESS. Each and every month for the next twenty-three years, the parents were treated to all the news and announcements of PPP, accompanied with fun photos of everything going on and upcoming at PPP. From the cut-and-paste days to the luxury of pulling photos from the internet or off our camera, this was a labor of love on my part. We consulted these old newsletters to help us plan upcoming events as well as look up old students and photos we knew we had captured in a newsletter. Though a lot of my memories and personal papers were tossed away in an upstairs storage cleanup without asking me first, which was heartbreaking and in my opinion rude, I at least have the notebooks of old PPP PRESS newsletters, which I will always cherish.

Funny aside: We had a hilarious parent many years ago

> who always kept us on our toes on a variety of issues with very blunt and sarcastic, but very funny, remarks and insights. One day she came in with newsletter in hand and said to me and my director at the time, "Okay, girls, y'all are cute and all, but you ladies are in the newsletters way too much!" We looked at each other and said, "Really?" We had no idea we put photos of ourselves around the school and with the students in the newsletter that much, so we started looking through back issues. We couldn't believe it! We were very prominently represented in most of the monthly newsletters and just didn't realize it. We had a huge laugh and watched that very closely from then on!

For me, nothing will ever take the place of paper and pen. My admin team through the years would laugh and laugh at me for my calendar desk blotters that they eventually refused to buy for me; sometimes I joked with them, "Who is really the boss around here?" (Insert giggle giggle!) I could visualize where I had written some phone number or someone's name down, on what calendar month, and in what color pen.

I still use a day planner instead of noting dates on my phone. I recently went to refill my day planner for 2022 and could not find a refill for it. When I went up to the counter to ask the young associate if they could order one for me, she looked at me like I was a crazy person. She didn't even really know what I was talking about, and this was one of the big box office supply stores. She suggested I look to the internet. What? Come on, this isn't *that* old school that it's been relegated to internet sites to acquire!

> A funny aside: I have kept a box of my day planners for probably the last thirty years. It chronicles a lot of important things that have happened in my life, personal and professional, and in our family's life. Years ago, as teenagers, Hayden said that someday he and

> William would probably fight over who would get these day planners. William said, "Hayden, if it comes to a fight, I'm sure I'll win and get them!" Hayden responded, "William, I didn't mean a fistfight." In their different ways, I know both boys know that there are a lot of special things memorialized in these calendars and one day they will want to look through them.

So, that's about it in regard to technology and social media. I know I am sometimes missing out on interesting family news or photos. Hayden will sneak a screenshot to me of a sweet post William made about me or Steve or a photo William posts that I would otherwise never know about—William rarely posts, so when he does something like this, it makes it extra special. People tell me all the time how clever and interesting Hayden's social media posts and photos are and how they look forward to "living through him," so I know I am missing out on a lot of interesting stuff concerning him.

Update: The world has been quarantined since March 2020 and it's now August. Hayden kept a daily blog on a situation going on with a neighbor's patio furniture. As stated, I don't have any social media, so I missed out on it, but I have heard from family and some of my friends that it was hysterical beyond words. One friend of Hayden's said it helped her get through the boredom of the quarantine.

And as the last example to illustrate even further how social media has shown us what a small world it really is and how we are all connected, just listen to this! A mom at PPP had a friend she went to college with years ago go on a mission trip to Africa. This friend, of course, took tons of photos of her trip and posted them on her social media page. My PPP mom told me that one day she had a little extra time and she decided to scroll through these hundreds of photos of this mission trip of her friend to some country in Africa. Wait . . . was that a PPP T-shirt on a child in this African village?! Yes, it was! This college friend had *no* idea that PPP was where a long-ago college friend's children went to. She was merely taking a photo of an adorable child in this village.

My PPP mom couldn't believe it and brought the photo in for me to see. How did this happen? Did someone here in Georgia maybe give their child's outgrown PPP tees to a charity organization, which then ended up in this African village and on this child on a day that this unrelated person to PPP happened to be on a mission trip and took a random photo and happened to be a college friend of a PPP mom, who ultimately saw this social media photo? Whew! Is that crazy or what! As a PPP community we all started thinking how great it would be to try and get in touch with this child and possibly help him in some way. Unfortunately, this wonderful idea never got off the ground, but it was still something a lot of us thought about from time to time, how really we *all* are connected in this small world.

But even with all this connectivity and fun keeping up with friends and family, I am still happy overall not to be tied to my computer looking at social media content. Can you just imagine (now that you may know me a little bit, giggle giggle) how much time I would spend investigating, watching, posting, and commenting on various platforms now that I am retired!

> Okay . . . last funny aside: When my best friend Felicia turned sixty a few months after my retirement, her kids threw her a birthday party. They contacted a few of her closest friends and asked us to send a *couple* of photos of us with Felicia to include in a family memory gift book for her. Well . . . I pulled out my old photos of us in high school, wedding photos of us, us with our babies, and then old yearbook photos of Felicia as a majorette, and the two of us in beauty pageants and senior superlatives. Her poor daughters were inundated with photos and commentary from me (insert giggle giggle). I bet they said to each other, "Hey Kay, make your *own* Kay/Felicia memory book!" See how obsessive I can be?

But here Steve and I are still, in 2022, holding our own without a social media presence and maybe missing out on a lot of things going on around us. Oh well . . . what's that saying? "Ignorance is bliss." (Insert giggle giggle!)

CHAPTER 18
ARE *YOU* A VICTIM? WHAT ARE *YOU* ENTITLED TO?

I had several conversations with parents over the years that started with, "Last night my child told me . . ." and then enter almost every possible scenario you can imagine. I once sat down with a dad in my office to hear him out on how he thought his pre-K daughter had been *harassed* by another four-year-old classmate. I had to caution more than one parent not to use the word "bullying" to characterize an interaction their toddler or preschool child was involved in. I had to tell parents over the years that I could not reveal the name of another child they were questioning the behavior of in order for them to approach that child's parent (or even that child, heaven forbid!) on behalf of their own child.

To my dismay and discomfort, I, on several occasions, had to tell a parent that an incident they felt their child had been a "victim of" was actually initiated by their child. Sometimes this might involve a physical injury, minor or maybe not-so-minor, their child was the recipient of. This is not so easy a needle to thread when you have a parent with a child who has a bump on their head or a bite mark.

This was *never* the first position I took when discussing with a parent their concern. When this discussion did occur, or escalate, I was pushed to this point with a parent due to their insistence that I or the teachers take some drastic measure to "do something" about this situation their child was involved in, sometimes more than once. Again, not so easy to tell a parent of a one-year-old that their child has the second or third bite mark on their arm because they were constantly taking things away from the other children and the location of the bite mark indicates that and is backed up by the teachers in the classroom. To a toddler, biting in frustration, over really anything, is just the same as the toddler who pushes and manhandles other toddlers to get their way. The only difference is that in one situation a physical mark is apparent, and in the other case, most often, there is no *identifiable* or *visible* injury. However, again to my dismay, over the years I had to disenroll a biter while not disenrolling the toddler who was too physical with classmates.

> A funny aside: When we first opened PPP and were trying, obviously, to deal with all sorts of issues we had never been exposed to before, we had a biting issue in the TII classroom, William's class. Having to call various parents to tell them that their child had been bitten in our very new preschool was a hard call to make. Steve and I (sort of) joked to each other, "Why can't this biter just bite William? Then we wouldn't have to call anyone!" (Insert giggle giggle!)

This was not the fun part of my job and I'm sure it was not fun for the parents involved either. But let's put all this into a preschooler's perspective.

Parents wanted to engage their child on what happened during the day, and we obviously encouraged that. Preschoolers, as a demographic group, however, really don't know how to or maybe don't want to engage in this way, and if you are like me and have boys, this lack of wanting to talk about their day and answer a hundred questions lasts into adulthood (insert giggle giggle). In fact, we also advised parents that things the teacher might tell them at pickup that occurred during the day may only be for information, not for any action on their part. In most cases it was not necessary to discuss the situation with their child or discipline their child over it, since the child may not even remember or correlate the evening discussion or punishment with something that occurred during the day, as discussed in another chapter. But as the type of parents in the present-day era I have already discussed, myself included, we want to know *all* and be involved in *all* that affects our child. Beyond that, we think everyone *else* wants to be overly involved with our child. (Insert giggle giggle!)

Sometimes my staff and I would giggle when a parent would arrive for pickup and look at us and say, "So how was Suzy today?" or "Where is Billy now?" We had many activity rooms in addition to the classrooms, and obviously could not keep up with where one child out of two hundred children may be at any random pickup time. Nor did we know specifically how their child's day had gone or how much lunch they ate, or if they successfully potty-trained during the day, if they napped, or a host of other questions that were sort of thrown at us about a specific child by a parent as they breezed into the lobby for pickup.

We were, however, very involved in the overall classroom functions, and loads of times this would result in sharing all sorts of fun information with a parent about their child at pickup. This was very important to us, as well as to the parents, and helped foster trust and overall customer service. You could just see the parents glow when they were met with this kind of banter from us in the lobby. As we all know, *kids can say the darndest things* and this was always fun to relate to parents. In fact, we often wished we kept notes and compiled things we heard ourselves while visiting the classrooms or things the teachers relayed to us, just priceless comments. One of my favorite "kid sayings" occurred when an adorable three-year-old boy ran up to the lobby ahead of his parent coming from the classroom, and as he looked at the colored monitors displayed in the lobby, he said to us, "So, where am I?" He knew that his mom had told him she could watch him in these monitors, and so he wanted to see himself too! Adorable.

> A funny aside: One of our funniest and "only the facts" type moms gave us a hilarious story we told over and over through the years. One of my front desk assistants at the time gave this mom a call to let her know that her child, who was having difficulty potty training, had finally poo-pooed on the potty. Expecting a yelp of joy from this mom, she instead said in the humorously sarcastic way that she had, "Are you really calling me at work to tell me that? Y'all have never called me before, so I thought there must be blood!" No, we just wanted to share—or overshare maybe? (Insert giggle giggle!)

In the absence of a preschool child being able to articulate the hundreds of mundane yet pleasant, fun, or learning experiences they had during a typical preschool day, sometimes the conversation with their parent would default to more nefarious tracks. This was due to nothing more on the part of the parents, I believe, than just trying to connect with their child's day. It may go something like this: "Who did you play with today?" "Were they nice to you?" Which—*ah-ha*—might just elicit the preschooler to say, "No, they wouldn't share," or "No, they wouldn't let me get on the swing," and on and on. Now we have the attention of the parent, and more importantly, the child has the attention of the parent.

We, parents, are not satisfied until we know each and every infraction perpetrated on our child and if it's from an adult or a preschool classmate and *why*?! Then the questions might go to, "Did you tell the teacher?" "What did she do (or say)?" Oftentimes the "infraction" was so innocuous that the teacher either was not told or did nothing to mediate a benign incident. There was more than one instance where a parent would approach us with a concern about a behavior from a classmate of their child, and the teacher or one of the front office team advised the parent that the child mentioned (accused) was on vacation for the week.

Remember, when I said in another chapter, "If you believe half of what your child says about us, we will believe half of what your child says about you." I'm not sure either side ever adhered to this edict. We even had an instance where we were put in a position to *prove* to a dad that the child, whom *his* child "swears" hit her, was not in attendance that day or even that week. But months later when something else happened with his child that he had a concern about, he circled back to that previous incident involving that same child like it was *never a fact* that that incident *never happened.*

I was once approached in group form with a group spokesperson wanting me to disenroll a child that the teacher nor I saw as being a problem. This group cited the "fact" that this child had already been disenrolled from another school for similar behavior, and I had to let them know this child was born while his older sibling was attending PPP. Their "fact" was wrong and their mob behavior unjustified. All this is just to represent how eager parents are to believe their child, to root out anything that may adversely affect their child, and to ensure that their child's school or society experience is optimized, *even if it's unjustified and at the expense of others.*

But to what degree, in all of this, do we pattern in our child a mentality that victimhood elicits the most attention from the parent, in fact from society? In today's twenty-four-hour news cycle, do victims, perceived or true, not get the most attention? Wouldn't it be great to have the news or social platforms concentrate more on stories of positive social interactions that happen constantly? Not newsworthy, right? Instead, they cover, sometimes ad nauseam, perceived slights and alleged infractions of all sorts of things before evidence, context, or statements from all involved are discussed or even marginally investigated, sometimes *creating* a mob reaction as presented above.

Of course, no parent wants their child to actually *be* a victim, of anything. But sometimes, at the preschool, we wondered if this was really true, as weird as that actually sounds. As parents, do we sometimes enjoy our "parent power" of being able to take up for our child? What about just ensuring that our child is given attention—sort of the "squeaky wheel gets the most oil" philosophy? What about showing those in "authority" that *we* are really in ultimate control when it comes to our child? What about just feeling like a good parent because we are acutely aware of everything and anything going on with our child and aren't afraid to confront any issues we see? At PPP we often commented to each other that it seemed some parents didn't see themselves as "good parents" unless they were rectifying or bringing attention to some injustice to their child, perceived or real. Do any of us see ourselves? I do.

I didn't intend to bring into this chapter the disgraceful way our political discourse has created all sorts of division and issues, but since it involves a child, I'll go there. Recently, the media incorrectly reported on a *child* initiating a provocative act against an *adult* "protected" class (which also agreed with the media's political narrative). This incident, as reported, was completely out of context and eventually proved completely untrue *as reported*. This child was harangued on TV, even in a personal interview; even some TV personalities said they wanted to do physical harm to this child! Ultimately this child's family settled an unprecedented lawsuit with various news outlets for damages in the millions of dollars for this shameful behavior on the part of the media. All because we are engrossed these days, and enamored, of victims (and certainly if the "victim" situation pushes forward an already ascribed "agenda" of some sort).

I would propose, in fact, there is a segment of society that wants to be a victim, and we see this more and more with our young people. *It's trendy, it's deemed righteous, and it's attention getting—how much more attractive could it get?*

When one of my sons graduated from high school, the principal gave a very funny, yet soberly correct, social comment on how things had drastically changed for our young people from "his time." He related that when he was a teenager, *any* form of confession of one's feelings, any slights, and any feelings of inadequacy, embarrassment, or failure was completely hidden from the public at large. For today's kids, he went on, all of these things are "shared" on various social media platforms. It may seem that this is healthy—this being in touch with our feelings—but is it? There seems to some degree that young kids these days may see that being a victim gives them some sort of social status and attention. Do they imagine or make up forms of victimhood just to have something to "share"? It seems to be true in many cases, but then what happens when fantasy becomes the truth?

Sometimes we see, in social platforms or in actuality, a person concoct a situation which accuses or catches someone else up in the web of victimhood they are wanting to weave, mostly for attention, but sometimes for profit. A recent issue that has been interesting to watch develop is a popular TV actor allegedly heading up a scheme involving two other acquaintances to perpetrate a violent incident against himself but blaming a political party's rhetoric as the culprit by prompting a hate crime. It not only satisfied this actor's political agenda, but it gave him a period of popularity and attention, which is valuable to people in the acting business. How quickly it turned into unflattering notoriety and legal issues that he never considered or thought possible. I mean, it was just a "pretend" attack on *himself*—no one was really hurt—so what was really the harm? But look at the damage to real victims that his attention-getting subterfuge had and will cause. Tsk-tsk . . .

The issue of victimhood sometimes dovetails into the subject of entitlement, which I discuss in more detail in the customer service/entitlement chapter. If you listen to Simon Sinek discuss millennials, this is not their fault. Again, it is, as he so humorously and accurately states numerous times, "through no fault of their own." One obviously can only conclude that the "fault" lies with us parents—raise your hands, parents! I am guilty as charged. Children are told, and parents demonstrate in various ways, that they are special and possibly exempt from certain norms. Our children see us not shying away from taking up for them for any and all perceived or actual slights. If we are not there to do this for them, well, they've learned from the masters how to do it themselves.

Entitlement—it's a loaded word these days. It can either mean that a person or group is entitled to special or different treatment due to explained disadvantages, or it can mean, in a derogatory fashion, that a person or group *feels* they are entitled to special or different treatment for no explained reason, just because they want it to be so.

An example: We had a wonderful tradition of having available to all the students a "travel treat" in the afternoon when they departed with their parent. The housekeeping staff prepared these small snacks, enclosed in a small container with a lid. Sometimes it would be an assortment of cereals, crackers, butter cookies, pretzels, so on. This was a treat—a small one at that—and wasn't intended as any sustenance for the child. Numerous times we were asked by a parent, as their child expressed displeasure of the snacks offered, if we would go to the kitchen and get what their child wanted. Yes, ma'am, that's true. I always taught my boys, as we would go to fast-food restaurants and they got a toy, which again, would have nothing to do with the meal, that "you get what you get." I've been present at numerous fast-food places when a parent went up to the counter and asked for a trade of a toy, even after it was already opened! I'm guilty of a lot of things, but I can say I tried to instill in my boys that I would not go to bat for them on things like this—things that were just because they wanted it and no other reason.

None of this is to represent malicious intent on any of our parts as parents. We just want to be the best parent. *The guidebook that is so often touted as missing for parents leaves us with only the examples to follow of parenting in the particular times that we live in.* With exceptions, of course, but widely to be accepted as a "good parent," you follow these examples. It was incredibly refreshing whenever we would witness parents actually stand up to their kids—isn't that a crazy twist on how this interaction should go?

However, for so many of us, this is sometimes the way it does go. What have we done wrong? To see parents, and there were many, who would say to their child, "Choose a travel treat or let's go without one, period." What a seemingly small but hugely important social and authority-laden lesson this was to these children. The next day, the child didn't whine about the snacks, they just chose one, or not. The next time a societal norm is presented, this child stands a better chance of acting appropriately simply by virtue of learning the lesson of not getting the choice of snack they wanted—first-world problems, I believe millennials say.

When children we have made to feel special and entitled act so, we wonder why. A child cannot distinguish from how they've been programmed to expect special or entitled treatment to when it might be embarrassing to us as parents when they act on this.

I was struck several years ago when I heard the story of an NFL player who made his young son give back a trophy he received as being part of a team that didn't have any accomplishments that year (in the competitive sense). That seems weird, doesn't it—getting a trophy for nothing. I think all of us can agree that this doesn't make any sense. But wait . . . like I've pointed out in other chapters, what seems logical in parenting has gotten so off track these days by the "social police" that we turn our backs on what we know is not logical, because to do so would not be "politically parenting acceptable"—not going along with the crowd of a particular period of generational parenting, the "every child's a winner" approach.

These days children get rewarded by parents and institutions for doing nothing, and that's what children now expect and what parents expect as well. It's the feeling of no child, no matter what the age, should be made to feel that their effort (or maybe their lack of effort) should not be recognized and celebrated. They tried—or wait . . . maybe they didn't? It doesn't matter which, both are rewarded, and the child's self-esteem is protected. No wonder millennials get to the workforce and don't understand what's going on. No wonder they are having a crisis at a young age and seeking their parents' approval and guidance. It's the parents who told them to expect recognition and reward, no matter the level of effort or achievement, so back to the parents is where they default to and we (parents) continue to validate these feelings.

To hear this NFL dad explain how he explained to his son the pride he will feel when he actually *deserves* a trophy and how hard work will make him strive to deserve a trophy—making hard work the reward and not the actual trophy—was so incredible. I wanted to reach through the TV and hug this man. I know I wouldn't have had the intelligence, integrity, or nerve to buck this parenting system of "everyone's a winner" mentality. I'm being honest.

Like most of you, I would hug my child and say "great job" no matter what. Steve did have this type of honesty with our boys (even though I would flash him the evil eye . . . insert giggle giggle). Steve would offer valuable advice and critiques instead of blind praise. The boys valued his praise so much more when it was given, and his approval, I'm sure, always had so much more meaning to them than mine.

Yesterday, I was watching a "house-flip show" on one of the popular DIY channels. A mother and son were trying to flip (and make a profit) on a million-dollar home. It was extremely important that every single day, each and every single expenditure be watched closely in order to make this a successful venture, since the profit margin would be so small. The (millennial) son would very frequently not show up for the day's work until after 12:00 p.m., sometimes even 2:00 p.m.! When the host of the show, in his frustration, confronted this young man, the young man said he just felt so overwhelmed by everything going on and expected of him that he just decided not to confront it at all, just to stay in bed.

Was the mom mad and frustrated at her son? No. In fact she was (like a lot of us moms) making excuses and trying to elicit sympathy for her son's behavior to this show's host, but he was having none of it. He didn't see anything special or any entitlement this young man had to not be responsible for his behavior and told him so, in no uncertain terms. Not surprisingly, this was the first time this child (adult) had been talked to in this way and he really didn't know how to take it. But, by the end of the show, this child (adult) had turned things around and was an extremely important part of the financial success of the project.

Could it be that he just didn't realize that, at some point, he would be held accountable for his behavior's consequences *instead of* being entitled to his behavior? And how much do you think his "self-esteem" was elevated due to turning around his behavior and being successful *instead of* his bad behavior (and self-esteem) being protected, as parents so often mistakenly try to do for their child? Interesting.

Bottom line: all our children are special—but only to us or our family. I'm not typing some huge revelation. We've been told this time and time again by society, yet while a lot of us nod our head and agree with this premise in theory, we keep instilling in our children that *they* are special. Further, we empower them to stand up to anyone or anything that treats them otherwise as not being fair.

Even scarier for our society, we accuse the offender of having possible legal exposure for *not* treating them so. It's true. People have lost jobs or lost the respect of their peers or society for not recognizing a perceived victim or having to tread so lightly so as not to offend anyone. I mention the straightforward clarity of Madelyn Swift in other chapters. I believe she said at a seminar I attended phrases like, "If you don't want to be called a thief, don't steal. If you don't want to be called a liar, don't lie." So, in the above example, "If you don't want to be called lazy, get to work." These days we can't call things legitimately what they are. How did we let things get this far off track?

Never let your child think they are anything other than special to you. Children depend on that unconditional love; in fact, they are *entitled* to it. I know my boys have that secure and unwavering knowledge. It doesn't mean I can't be disappointed in something they do or don't do, but they know I love them as we work through that issue. But otherwise, help your child realize just how special they are by helping them to see, to understand, to know, and to act in a manner that shows they have to earn and prove their worth to society by their deeds, by their integrity, by their understanding of others, and by their own humility.

When we have raised our children to live in this way, then we can truly say how *special* they are and that they are *entitled* to respect.

CHAPTER 19
YOU CAN LEAD A HORSE TO WATER . . .

Showing my age, but a lot of readers, and certainly the young parents of PPP when I put out this particular article, may not have ever heard this phrase or know what this old adage refers to. Well, it refers to all sorts of things that you can hope for or "think might can happen" if only you could lead someone to your way of thinking . . . but alas, it's usually not to be so.

For instance, making a child eat. How many of us parents have tried and tried unsuccessfully for that end result of our child eating a good meal? We think we are doing everything right. We plan a good meal, a meal we think our child likes. But they don't like it. We get up from *our* meal and fix them something else, one that they say they want. And in my experience, maybe they will or maybe they won't eat that one. So, we continue to cajole, promise a great dessert if only a few bites of anything are taken. We negotiate, we maybe even offer or prepare a third choice, and ultimately we lose anyway.

Let's delve into this phenomenon a little. In several chapters, I discuss how young children learn, from us well-meaning adults, cues on manipulation. It's really very clever of children at their very young age, toddlers even, to learn how they can garner and keep our attention and, in fact, make us "do" things. Eating is one of these things, unfortunately—potty training being another. Have you ever chased—yes, I am saying chased!—your child through your home, spoon in hand, wanting them to eat "just one more bite"? I have, more than once.

I have mentioned that both Hayden and William had premature births. Hayden only weighed a little over four pounds when born and his sucking reflex had not kicked in yet. William was just barely over five pounds and started off hardier than Hayden. We had to leave Hayden at the hospital for an additional week after I was discharged a week after giving birth. It was very hard to do—I kept thinking, "Who leaves their baby at a hospital and just goes home?" Post-pregnancy hormones are a b*tch!

When we finally got Hayden home, eating was a *big* problem. I never planned on breastfeeding, but when my pediatrician came into my hospital room the day after Hayden's birth, he told me it was not an option, Hayden needed my nourishment. So, onto the breast pump I went and onto the breastfeeding class at the hospital with a doll to practice latching techniques with when everyone else had their actual baby—another "kick in the belly" for me! I had to do a combination of breastfeeding and then supplement with a few ounces from a bottle. Hayden couldn't try latching for too long because of the calories that expended for him. It was just an eating mess! And don't even get me started with the process of "drying up" my milk production (that I didn't want to have in the first place) when it was time to go back to work! We were told by the doctors to stick his heel with a pin or pinch him to make him eat so he would not fall back asleep or be disinterested. *Who does that to their newborn baby?* I lamented.

Anyway . . . appointment after appointment at the pediatrician showed them checking the box "Failure to Thrive." That's an *actual* printed phrase on a baby's growth form—how callous and disheartening for a mother to think her baby is not thriving. It sounded like a death sentence to me! Once, I asked them to please not check that box. Hayden was growing, just not very fast, and did not present on the printed growth chart until he was in kindergarten. I told Felicia once that I would prefer them to tell me he had some sort of illness that they could give me a medicine for rather than to keep on with this illusive "non-diagnosis." There was no cure or really anything I or anyone could do to make him eat more. As he became older, I would do anything to coax him to eat—he had our undivided attention at meals. I would chase him down the hall with a spoon of peanut butter or pudding, with him gleefully running ahead of me. I would do anything for that golden "one more bite"!

My pediatrician one day laughed at me when I related this story to him. He asked sincerely what good I thought "one more bite" was actually going to do. An eye-opening question! Funny, just this week I saw a commercial for a boxed macaroni and cheese product that showed a mom chasing her child down the hall with a spoon and the child laughing ahead of her. Of course, once she made the macaroni dish, the child ate contented at the table. So see, this chasing is really a thing! Another commercial portrays a child being "potato paid" with french fries for every bite of broccoli she eats, with a smug look on her face. See, it's a documented societal behavior, memorialized in commercials, to help guide parents on how to get their children to eat, and maybe more to a point, it illustrates how a child uses food to their benefit to manipulate a parent's behavior. As you can see, we are *not* dealing with hungry kids here. Get my point, parents?

I have shared that chasing story and my doctor's reaction to it to so many parents at PPP over the years who had this same problem with their child eating. We have giggled together because his point was so obvious—one more bite . . . why? In the early years of PPP, questions during an enrollment tour centered on the teachers' qualifications, activities for the students, things like that. In the later years of PPP, almost every parent tour centered on food. Allergies children had, concern for organic choices, healthy snack questions, or what we would do to supplement a meal or a snack if their child didn't eat what we were serving. We were challenged very frequently by parents to allow them to bring their child's lunch and snacks.

At PPP we had a company that catered our meals each day for lunch. The catering company's sole business was school lunch service all over Atlanta. They were licensed and had dieticians to design a healthy, calorie-rich, child-pleasing lunch for children in appropriate portions and following USDA requirements for a balanced and healthy meal for children. They also offered a gluten-free meal, a vegetarian meal, as well as dairy-free and other allergen-free meals. This huge array of meal offerings, however, did not address all the eating questions and concerns we had from parents. I had to, more than once, tell a parent that we did not "cater" to picky eaters. They would say, "But my child is a picky eater," and I would reply, "We have a whole building of picky eaters." (Insert giggle giggle!)

I will say that we did have many children who *loved* our meals, and William was one of them. He, like many other children through the years, would eat things at PPP that he wouldn't touch at home—Sloppy Joes for example. We had numerous parents ask us about a certain recipe or brand of food item we were serving that their child loved. Funny enough, when they made this at home, their child was not interested. This led me to the conclusion, and right I think it was, that these children, William included, *knew* that the teachers were not going to, nor were they able to, fix something else other than what our kitchen staff brought into the classroom. Even at their young age, the children realized that it was eat this or nothing, so they chose to eat. That's the key right there: *the choice of the child to either eat or not.*

So let's explore that a little more. Eating is more than getting necessary nutrition. It's a national pastime. Eating can be a joyous activity *or* a source of huge anxiety. As a society, we associate all sorts of human nature and connectedness with eating—family memories, friendships, business success, and community activities—all including food. We also have so many different philosophies and tenets about food and food choices. When I was young, most everything I ate was prepared by my mother; we had little store-bought food choices. She made biscuits with lard, she made cookies for our snacks with butter or Crisco, we drank Kool-Aid by the gallon during the day and sweet tea with dinner at night, and we had fried food almost without exception every night. And we were healthy.

If I described this type of diet to the young parents in the later years of PPP, they would be horrified! I would sometimes feel like I was leading a parent astray when I would listen to what they wanted their child to eat in a day, and I would advise, as diplomatically as I could, that I didn't feel they were giving their child a balance. In my research during these years on food requirements for young children, children *need* carbs and sugar. It's fuel for their growing bodies and brains. However, like so many things in life, any of us can find an expert to validate our views on just about anything, so I, as well as these parents, could validate our food theory to each other.

Myself and some of our teachers would cringe for a child when they were not able to participate in "Cooking with Literature" or a classroom birthday-party treat because their parent wouldn't allow them to eat certain (what they saw as) unhealthy foods. There were times when I had to explain to a parent, and I had to be very cautious with this, that in our society food is "king" in a lot of situations, and especially for children who don't understand or who have not chosen for themselves a restrictive diet, they are looked at in a suspicious (if you will) way by their classmates. Why can't they eat what everyone else is eating?

We would see a particular child, maybe, not be included in other ways during the day and we felt their non-inclusion in the classroom way of eating contributed to this, dare I say, ostracism. We would try to explain to a parent that a cupcake or cookie here and there or whatever the teacher had chosen as the weekly "Cooking with Literature" item (which usually *was* a healthy snack item, but sometimes it might be something more "fun" related) would not disrupt an otherwise sugar-free or "healthy" diet for their child. Then maybe this is when I would try to describe to them the way they were shining an unfavorable spotlight on their child to the other children. Fair or not, children just operate this way, and I felt an obligation to alert the parent on what was being brought to my attention by the teacher.

When there was a child who truly had an allergy and legitimately couldn't eat everything the other children ate, we felt bad for them that this was not a choice their parent made for them, it was a medical necessity, but still could have the same unintended societal consequences. It was so appreciated and good for the child when these situations were handled by a parent to go to great lengths to provide the same food items for their child in a form safe for them. We partnered with the parent in any way possible to have this situation turn out in the best way possible for their child. In the later years of PPP, it became a lot easier for parents to provide this accommodation thanks to Whole Foods, Sprouts, and even the larger grocery chains, having rows and rows of gluten-free and other allergen-free food choices that looked just like what the other children were being served . . . even cupcakes (insert giggle giggle).

It was also interesting to us that in the early years of PPP, we used peanut butter not only as a great food choice for the students but even in arts and craft projects (you may remember the peanut butter pinecones with bird seed), but in the later years of PPP, peanuts and peanut butter were deadly to a lot of children. What happened to create such a peanut allergy in the United States, we wondered. Then there were the parents who would put down that their child was "allergic" to something in order for us to provide an alternative (what they felt was a more healthy option or, in the extreme, to allow the parent to bring their child's lunch). Sometimes it later came to light that their child was really *not* allergic—it was just parental preference or that they were really just "giving in to" their picky eater by bringing the child's desired lunch.

This subterfuge would surface when a parent would forget or maybe didn't have time to prepare their child's lunch, and we would be told to "go ahead and give them, *just for today*" something that we had been told, and indeed had documented, that they couldn't eat. In these cases, I would have to say to the parent that we were not able to do this since it was documented as an allergy. Sometimes parents would start off by declaring a food allergy on the enrollment form just to take it off their child's form later when it became burdensome to continue to bring in their child's food. This was eye-opening to many things about parenting styles.

As I said, I would do anything and prepare anything for Hayden when he was a toddler and preschooler in order to get him to eat—again guilty of much of what I present in this chapter and in my article. At PPP, in the later food-conscious years, we would even have grandparents come up to the school and either remove their grandchild from the classroom to feed them something different (since we would not allow that within the classroom setting), or they would sit in the classroom and spoon-feed their toddler or young preschooler the school-supplied lunch to make sure they ate. We very much discouraged both of these situations due to a) hoping to introduce the child to more of a variety of things to eat, and b) not allowing a child to learn to feed themselves during that developmental phase was not in the child's best interest.

We had more than a few students in our Toddler I class have to have professional medical therapies and intervention to learn to manipulate their tongue for solid foods due to missing that appropriate developmental phase while in the Infant Suite of learning to eat solid foods—again, most often by parental choice. I once had a parent who wanted me to commit, before he enrolled his four-year-old daughter, to ensuring the teachers would spoon-feed her because that was what she was used to at home. Before I could really think ahead and stop myself from what I was about to say, I told him, in no uncertain terms (I think I even wagged my finger at him—insert giggle giggle!), "That needs to stop *today*." He enrolled, and months later he came up to me and thanked me for that straight talk.

> An interesting aside: We had a delightful little girl in our Infant Suite who was the third of her siblings to start as an infant at PPP and grow through the preschool. With this third child, the parents decided to follow the food model of serving the child whatever the family ate. The mom had found a book on this method

> and decided to give it a try. Voilà, it was a huge success! Not only did this baby adapt and develop wonderful eating habits, but the family didn't have to spend the money (and time) on baby food. While this was not the reason they decided to feed the baby in this manner, in my experience with my boys, this would have been a huge benefit (insert giggle giggle).
>
> Our Infant Suite caregiver would sometimes be a little scared of this baby possibly choking on some of the items brought in, but there was never even a small incidence where this was a possibility. Of course, this mom, in her research into this feeding method, knew what was appropriate and in what stages certain foods were to be presented. This little girl would gnaw on whatever was put before her until it was the consistency for her to swallow and it just worked. We were all amazed to be honest. To watch her get the meaty part of a tomato and shed the skin—incredible!

In my published article, I discussed how unhealthy the adult behaviors I describe are for the child, even though as parents we think we are doing this *for the health* of the child. My pediatrician, as well as numerous dieticians, rejects these ways of feeding a child for many reasons. The vicious cycle of eating/not-eating for a child sets up all sorts of manipulative behaviors and a lot of unnecessary angst for a parent, as well as for the child. I describe in the article, and above, that not allowing eating choices and behaviors to naturally evolve can even result in physical deficiencies for young children to miss important development stages. I offer the advice in the article to parents to stand firm and not to give in to the "rescue" food method since this continues the cycle of a child not eating a healthy and fulfilling meal, which we are so desperately trying to accomplish. Unfortunately, this is advice that most of us *cannot* follow—again, myself included. Who can resist a child saying that they are hungry?! Not me, apparently . . .

> An interesting observation: Isn't it a funny thing that we can so easily see the right things that someone *else* should do? What seems to be glaringly obvious as right to do when it involves someone *other than ourselves or our children,* in any number of situations, is almost comical. We can always justify why we do the things we do while not seeing that same justification in someone else's decisions. Boy, could I write a whole book on that, and I could insert this paragraph in every chapter of this book!

But back to eating—as a child grows, this non-eating behavior and manipulation can turn into all sorts of issues, and not just eating issues. Children who have used food to manipulate their parents, or parents who have used food in a way to manipulate or control their child, such scenarios can possibly manifest in all manners of inappropriate behaviors. Children may become overeaters, children may sneak or hoard "inappropriate" food in their room or book bag, they may turn to drugs for the satisfaction they can't find in food, or children may not have that feeling of control any longer, if they *want* to eat, so to stay in control they become bulimic or anorexic. These may seem like extreme examples but are well-documented behaviors. Another possibility is that a child will continue to use these manipulative skills, honed in their young years, in other ways as they get older that have nothing to do with food. As well, you may see parents continue to try and control or manipulate their child in other ways as they get older, as they once could with food, when their child was young and helpless. Again, a vicious cycle.

Like I said, food is more than nutrition or even a society's way to connect with each other. Food is somewhat of an obsession for a large portion of society. Food, indeed, is at the very root of not only how we are able to live and thrive (there's that word again!), but also, in so many ways, the way society views us. Therefore, it stands to reason that the importance of food, not just as our sustenance but at the heart of our personality, is important to everyone.

As parents of young children, it is up to us to establish early eating patterns that not only are healthy for the body but also healthy for the mind. We need to not put such an importance on the *act* of eating and what *may or may not occur* if *we please whoever is in our eating sphere.* But again, this is precisely the cycle a lot of us find ourselves in. Doctors will tell you that your child will not starve. They will eat when they are hungry. As much as we may want this to be on "our" schedule, at "our" command, what we *want* them to eat, and even how *much* we want them to eat, we cannot make them do any of these things. The more we try, the more problems this causes for everyone. In the case of a pattern of manipulation skills learned, *by the parent as well as the child,* it would be better to just go ahead and prepare the child's desired food choice (french fries, for example, instead of broccoli) in the first place rather than to "force" a behavior on a child for a reward. Neither the child nor the parent wins in this scenario.

> I'll leave this chapter with a funny aside: In our household, William is not our picky eater, but he is an interesting eater. He likes almost any type of food, and like I mentioned, he liked the food served every day at PPP. He's commanding in stature and has the body of an athlete; however, he eats in small spurts. I used to joke with him that I didn't want him to spend the night away from us (which he would have done almost every night, he was so social!) because that mom would not know he *needed* to eat every few minutes (insert giggle giggle).
>
> This is what he does: He sits down for a meal and eats a small portion of it and he's done. However, in just a bit, he needs to eat again; he's *hungry*. When he was young and we would go to a restaurant, he used to hate me asking him, multiple times, "Are you

done?" He "rested" a lot during a meal and then would just stop. Even his college baseball coach, when the baseball team was on a trip and they ate at a nice restaurant instead of all the fast food, told Steve and I that William ordered a big steak and ate only a few bites of it. He said this surprised him.

In our family we call this "Wiggy Leftovers," and we all love to finish the "Wiggy Leftovers." In fact, we'll fight (insert giggle giggle!) over his leftovers because, for some reason, they appear so appetizing! We laugh that these leftovers are sometimes the best part of our *own* meal (insert giggle giggle). We also can be seen at any given time wearing William's clothes. Don't ask . . .

So, as I started, "You can lead a horse to water, *but you can't make him drink.*" That's how the old saying goes, and like so many old sayings, this one has endured the test of time for very sound reasons. In fact, taking into account my own behavior and my years of observing parents (and grandparents) at PPP, this saying has never been more relevant to the times as it is now.

Food continues to be an interesting family and societal dynamic and struggle. This is so interesting. We *all* need food, so what's the big deal? Go figure!

(Okay, so you don't think we are totally weird, William has really comfortable athletic swag! Insert giggle giggle.)

CHAPTER 20
HOW DOES CUSTOMER ENTITLEMENT DRIVE CUSTOMER SERVICE?

Will this chapter be more about children or parents? It will be hard to tell and indeed to separate. As a service provider, where did we see our obligation and desire for the ultimate customer service experience affect the way we treated our customers? How did we ultimately see our obligation steer us to help our customers overcome "frustration management" in themselves, and more importantly in their children, as applied to their entitlement to customer service? So, let's see where it goes.

Entitlement: "the belief that one is *inherently* deserving of privileges or special treatment; the fact of having a right to something" (Oxford Languages).

When should entitlement come into play? Sitting here contemplating this chapter, I really can't think of a particular situation where someone is automatically "entitled" to special (redundant) treatment. Can you? Is entitlement expected and reserved for the powerful or for the powerless?

Just yesterday I heard a radio talk show host discuss entitlement as it relates to politics and business. He was saying that in all instances, impartial components of competency should be all that is considered in hiring a person, electing an official, or admission into educational institutions. It should never be due to whatever basis you want to put forth for who might be "entitled" to a special condition, either to create an environment of diversity, to right a perceived wrong, or maybe to level the playing field, and I would have to guess also just because someone is powerful and expects their position of power to continue. He gave several examples of instances in politics, business, and education where "entitlement conditions" were expected and used and how that ultimately (but not surprisingly) failed. It made perfect sense and, in fact, seemed ludicrous to use an "entitlement" model to make any sort of important decision. Don't we all want to be secure in the premise that we earned what we have, not that it was unauthentically "given" to us and that everyone knows or suspects that, *but even worse,* that this is the impression, when in fact we actually worked hard, earned, and *deserved* it?

At an educational seminar I attended many years ago, I was mesmerized by the common sense of Madelyn Swift, which I have mentioned in other chapters. If my memory serves me, she walked out on the stage and immediately opened up with the question, "How many of you think your child is special?" The majority of us raised our hands, smiles on our faces, secure that we were giving her the correct answer as dedicated and loving moms, teachers, and caregivers. She smiled and said, quite profoundly, "Well, they aren't." She spent the first segment of her seminar outlining the very obvious and common-sense reality that treating (or even thinking) that your own child or your students are special or entitled is extremely detrimental to those involved *as well as* to those who get "left out" of an entitlement environment or way of thinking and acting.

Citing both these people above, with their examples, makes it seem so logical and made so much sense to me at the time. But is it really that simple?

I have outlined in various other chapters that PPP was a very high-end private preschool. We sought the niche of providing the ultimate educational experience for young children coupled with ultimate customer service to the parent, at a high price. A "Ritz Carlton" experience versus a "Motel X" experience, if you will. We had a variety of very high-profile celebrities enroll their children at

PPP. A majority of our parent base were very affluent. North Fulton County is replete with "McMansions," with some of the highest real estate values in the country. Parents at the top of their business field and a host of celebrities and professional athletes lived within our preschool sphere, and most chose PPP for their children. We also had a segment of our families who could afford to enroll their child at PPP, but only if they scrimped in other monthly expenses. Bringing your child to PPP, with both these types of clientele and the price we charged, gave an entitled mentality to a lot of parents. For affluent parents who had learned to expect "special" (entitled) treatment, or the parents who could barely afford PPP wanting to get "what they paid for" (what they were *entitled* to), as well as all those financially "in between," the expectations and the end result were the same. See how it's not so logical or simple?

I often tried to illustrate in staff meetings to the teachers and administrators that if you have saved for years to be able to stay at a pricey resort property, you would expect, and rightly so, the most over-the-top attention to customer service that you have fantasized in your mind you were going to get—that you are "entitled" to. That's the type of customer relations I wanted to have for the parents at PPP no matter what their expectations were or what level of economic status they were at. I wanted to always "wow" them, and I implemented all types of activities in the customer service realm, both for the parents and for the students, to make sure this goal was achieved.

However, it came to light in the later years of PPP that maybe this was not the best way to approach a child-care environment. Maybe it was a good strategy for running a hotel, where people come and go without influence given or received, but maybe not what's best when you are partnering with parents in raising their children, and in fact, helping to show them how to be a better parent—partnering to "raise their child," "helping them to be a better parent." Is that too presumptuous? Well, maybe or maybe not.

Parents sought our advice and our help in forming their child's personalities and behaviors due to the amount of time we spent with their child and the trust they had in our experience. Conversely, parents also used us as a source to blame when things went awry. Sometimes I would have to remind a teacher that we weren't the child's parent, nor were we responsible for their upbringing. But was that true? Didn't parents hold us accountable to a degree about how their child was turning out? Didn't we get praise as well as blame on how a child behaved? The answer to both of these questions is yes. Obviously we *loved* getting emails, notes, and verbal praise from parents on the influence we had in their child's success. Adversely, we rejected a parent's feelings that we were to blame for their child's unacceptable behavior or perceived personality faults.

The teachers felt on a daily basis this dual obligation/perception. If you are a dedicated teacher of young children, not just someone doing a job until something better comes along, you *live* this obligation. You feel the satisfaction of success and you feel the agony of failure when you don't reach a child. You cannot separate the education phase with the child-rearing component of your job. Most parents did not separate these two components either. Due to any number of reasons, some parents had (and teachers as well) to influence a child's behavior, we would see a lot of "giving in" to a child's desires, as I have outlined in other chapters.

"Frustration management" skills for young children are currently at an all-time low. We used this phrase to parents a good bit. We saw children unable to handle any type of frustration. Parents, and sometimes teachers, worked very hard to limit any type of frustration for these young children. Both parents and teachers would try various manipulations of situations to stay ahead of frustrations in order to keep the peace, home or school related. Sometimes, the parents' (and child's) feeling of entitlement could dovetail to unrealistic expectations and sometimes their inappropriate behavior.

PPP teachers and the administration team attended professional development sessions that addressed this new-day "frustration management dance" in order to have a peaceful classroom setting.

If your students were unruly, look first to yourself. The classroom may be too overstimulating or not stimulating enough. The schedule may be too full or too boring. The expectations may be too high or there may be none at all.

One of the most popular seminar hosts at the annual NAEYC conference would have the group in stitches demonstrating how we expect students to sit "crisscross applesauce" for twenty to thirty minutes in circle time and being frustrated ourselves when we have to constantly admonish these students for "fidgeting." He would say, "Have *you* ever had to sit that long crisscross applesauce? It's very uncomfortable." How right he was! Other seminar hosts would give examples of letting the children leave circle time when they felt bored, overwhelmed, disinterested, or maybe if they were misbehaving. The premise being that children should not have to sit there when they could be exploring other interests, *or* if they were taking away from the learning environment for the other children. While seemingly logical on the face of this demonstration, the teachers in the classroom see nothing but chaos if you let the students dictate when they feel disinterested in the group learning session going on and are free to get up and roam—behavior the child or parent may think they are entitled to. So what's the answer?

When I was a child, you did what the group was doing. You weren't empowered, or entitled, to get up from a teacher-directed activity and just decide you wanted to do something different and *further* than was deemed as okay or "developmentally appropriate," as we so often hear the "experts" espouse now. We would hear the experts at seminars advise us to "manage" the behavior of an unruly child by allowing them the *privilege* of being the teacher's helper, give them other important tasks to curtail their unruly behavior *or* to prevent it from happening in the first place, again "managing" their frustration *before they got frustrated*. But teachers viewed this as rewarding bad behavior or not giving a favored task to the "deserving" child who followed the rules. How is this fair? How does the unruly child recognize that their behavior is not acceptable and is not to be condoned or rewarded, thus learning to aspire to better outcomes due to better behavior? How do you square this circle?

Teachers were asked, when in discussions with parents on an unacceptable behavior, "So what was going on when this occurred?" In the later years of PPP, when we felt more the pull of being a legitimate "expert," if you will, on child development more than in the early years of having more a philosophy of blind customer service, we would respond to the parent, "That's not really important to what was going on—the behavior is not acceptable under any circumstance." What some parents were sometimes trying to tell us is that unacceptable behavior would turn into acceptable or justified, in their view, if their child was not treated in an "entitled" way—a way that they felt they were "paying for," or in a way that they didn't want their child to feel slighted. As mentioned in another chapter, some parents had empowered their child to "not take it" from anyone, adults included. Sometimes this was the actual reason for the unacceptable behavior from, actually, both parent and child.

We once had posted, in our conference room, an 1890 quote from Mahatma Gandhi on our employee board: *"A customer is the most important visitor on our premises. He is not dependent on us. We are dependent on him. He is not an interruption of our work. He is the purpose of it. He is not an outsider of our business. He is a part of it. We are not doing him a favor by serving him. He is doing us a favor by giving us the opportunity to do so."*

I lived by these words without even knowing this quote existed. However, as PPP gained the reputation of excellence in education as well as customer service in the community, something else started to be just as important to me. Instead of blind obedience and acquiescence to the customer, be it the parent or the child, it became important to be a legitimate voice to parents on the ethos of PPP values and attention to being the best we could be in our obligation to providing excellence in customer relations as well as education. We felt that being transparent in this desire and being able to back up our decisions, instead of kowtowing to the customer, would actually translate into *better* customer service and elevate our reputation, and more importantly benefit the child. This became what we felt the parents were "paying for" and were "entitled" to expect.

Just a small *business* example: In the early years of PPP, if a parent questioned a charge on their bill, I would, as a courtesy and in the spirit of elite customer service (and I would specify that to them), just take the charge off. I thought this was the best way to handle it to make a parent happy as well as save me time of investigation and explanation. In the later years, I became more aware of showing the legitimacy of a PPP decision to elevate our reputation to the customer base rather than simply appeasing a parent. So in this type of situation, if a customer thought they were overcharged for lunches or diapers, if they thought they didn't attend a holiday camp, or had been overcharged a prorated amount for starting in the middle of a month, I would take whatever time necessary to research the concern to either "prove" PPP was correct, or, just as importantly, to admit that we were indeed in error. It seemed to me that parents would more appreciate knowing we weren't taking advantage of them rather than feeling good that something was just removed because they questioned it. Early on, I thought customers loved this feeling of "getting their way." But the later years made it unimaginable to me that any parent would think we were "gouging" them monetarily or trying to take advantage of them in *any* way. My philosophy changed over the years, which changed my behavior. But what about my parent base? Did their idea of "the customer always being right" or what they thought they were entitled to change? Which, as a customer, are you more impressed with or do you desire? Is it being right at any cost, *or* feeling confident that a company or institution you have put your trust in is living up to that trust and integrity, *especially* if it involves your child . . . or your money?

We had a parent ask us to drizzle a child's medicine over a popsicle so that the child would take the medicine (not kidding).

We had a parent ask us to change their two-year-old's socks when they came in from playing just in case their feet were sweaty. Early years, I would tell the teacher just to do it—not in the later years. We watched as a parent removed whatever color of marshmallow bits from Lucky Charms cereal their child didn't like on *a particular day* and we quickly moved in to tell the parent to please not do that because that wasn't in the best, long-term interest of the child. This is not to say in any way that we became sanctimonious. Believe me, our customer service obligation remained a privilege to us. It was just that it became as important to us to act with integrity and be genuine in our relationships with the parents. I can honestly say that, in almost all cases, the parents genuinely appreciated our *appropriate* intervention, advice, and guidance and recognized the spirit in which it was given.

> A funny aside: I had a parent come up to the front desk one afternoon and say, "Boy, did Ms. _____ just put me in my place!" Of course, I immediately broke out in a sweat! How dare a teacher of mine put a parent (a customer) "in their place"! So, I said, as calmly as I could, "What happened?" She said, "Well, I walked in the classroom and all the kids were behaving perfectly. I asked Ms. ____, 'How do you do it? I can't even get my *one* child to behave!'" This parent then said that Ms. ____ calmly responded, "It's easy. I just say no." This parent then said to me, "Boy, did that shut me up!" And then she laughed at how easy that is (or should be) for a parent to do (insert giggle giggle). She was not at all insulted. She was glad for the straight talk given by someone she trusted.
>
> An interesting aside: Very early in the PPP years, a mother arrived at PPP to drop off her child. She was very flustered and came right up to my director at the front desk as other parents were also in the lobby

dropping off and looking at the classroom monitors located in that area. This mom went on to describe that she and her husband were *furious* that their one-to-two-year-old son had come home from PPP with a diaper on that had a pink banner of cartoon characters on the top of the diaper. She said, in no uncertain terms, that if this *ever* happened again, they would *not* be returning to PPP.

My director listened to her and apologized for this *gross error* (insert sarcastic giggle giggle!) and told this parent that she would assure that this *egregious act* (insert another sarcastic giggle giggle!) would never happen again. The mother left, somewhat placated for her bluster that she had prevailed on behalf of her child in this issue. Immediately another mother (who had heard the entire exchange) turned around from watching her child on the lobby monitors and looked at my director and said, "Oh my god, how in the world did you keep your cool? I would have told that mom to get the h*** out of here and take her son and his pink diaper with her!"

My fabulous director just laughed and said, "Kay frowns on us cussing out the parents." We told this story over and over through the years at PPP—it was a funny commentary on the reactions of *both* of these parents.

Early years, this was our behavior toward the parents—say and do whatever we felt they needed from us to feel heard and appeased. Later years, I believe we would have heard the parent out, but then we would have told the parent, diplomatically of course, that this was the diaper we were sent by our supplier and there was no detriment to their child in any way by having a diaper on that had a blue, pink, or no banner at all, and we would be using these diapers for *all* children until the supply was gone. In an effort to further validate as well as help solve their concern, we would offer to allow them to bring in their own diapers for their son until these pink diapers were all used, and, of course, during this time there would not be a diaper charge on their account. In my mind this would have satisfied the legitimacy of PPP not doing something wrong or harmful toward this child, *as this parent was accusing us of*, as well as providing the parent the choice of handling their concern on their own if they thought their one-year-old son was being "harmed" by wearing a pink-bannered diaper. This response would show the parent that their concern as a customer was equally as important to us as the trust they placed in us to care appropriately for their child.

It's a fine line to walk when that time arrives in the life of your business when you become as concerned about being viewed by your customers as operating with integrity while balancing the customer's desire to be heard and appeased, and probably agreed with, if you really want the truth of the matter. I know we've all heard (and if you are the customer, and we *all are* at some time, you believe it) that "the customer is always right." I submit that maybe these two opposing views might be governed by what type of business you are engaged in and how high the stakes may be if you bend to the customer's will instead of standing your ground. In the case of being held responsible and accountable for how a child is "turning out" by a parent, as well as by yourself (if you are the dedicated professional I spoke of earlier), then you must lean toward what you feel (or know) is the better option for the child's well-being, whether this is congruent to the parent's view or not.

In the later years of PPP, we were okay with a parent disenrolling if they felt we were not meeting their expectations. In the earlier years, I or we may not have been as confident in our actions or beliefs, but after being involved in thousands of children and parents going through the preschool, there were few situations we hadn't seen before and had experience with either being right or wrong in the way we handled it, thus learning from these situations. With diligent and compassionate discussions, we could at least shed light to the parent on our point of view and its possible correctness.

Sometimes this was not the outcome, and the disagreement may or may not lead to disenrollment, either initiated by the parent *or* by us. Sometimes these discussions would end in compromise.

As I said in several chapters about various situations, either side of an argument can usually provide expert or experience documentation to bolster their opinion or their side of an argument. The key to being a business owner of any type of business is, if in dispute with a customer, *never* adopt a righteous attitude. That is a dealbreaker and only makes both of you dig in deeper, whether you ultimately see the other's side or not. In all but a handful of situations, I always gave myself wiggle room in an argument for the parent to keep or gain the upper hand. I believe no one is "entitled" to receive treatment from another based on their desire only, but both sides, presenting their case for certain treatment that might be out of the norm, should be heard out and a solution hopefully agreed to by both parties.

Entitlement. I believed during my years of owning PPP that everyone was *entitled* to their opinion. I believed that everyone was *entitled* to be heard in a compassionate and open way. I believed that children were *entitled* to have a dedicated teacher and positive role model involved in their lives at PPP on a daily basis. I believed that everyone was *entitled* to be treated in a fair and integrity-driven way.

This is not the way I led off this chapter with the definition of "entitlement." In the way that I am now using "entitlement," it's not as a privilege or special treatment—it was the way I tried to handle each and every situation presented, from child related to parent (customer) related to employee related. I truly felt that all were *entitled* to this relationship with me. It was not reserved for the celebrities of PPP, or the most involved parents of PPP, or the longest-tenured teachers at PPP. It was reserved and could be expected by everyone, therefore not making this special, but *expected* as a given.

I hope I had a high percentage of success in this form of *entitlement.*

CHAPTER 21
HOT FUN IN THE SUMMERTIME!

At PPP, Summer Camp was over the *top*! We started planning the following year's Summer Camp as we were experiencing the current Summer Camp, making notes of what was awesome and what didn't live up to expectations. Remember the story in the "Social Media" chapter of the family from China who traveled to the United States for the *sole* reason of enrolling their child in PPP Summer Camp for four weeks? PPP Summer Camp had legit worldwide cred (insert giggle giggle).

The campers of PPP went on numerous field trips throughout the summer to some of the most coveted venues Atlanta and the southeastern part of the United States have to offer. Most summers we advertised a schedule of over fifty field trips.

While on campus we had various companies come in for arts and crafts activities, STEM projects, and the very popular, camo-outfitted, weekly Sc.A.T. (Scholar Athletes in Training) Boot Camp, where the campers enjoyed off-site athletic feats with professional athletic trainers and celebrity NFL "PPP family" appearances from Chad Hall, Matthew Stafford, and Jared Cook to work out and motivate the campers. Almost every teacher at PPP wanted to be a Summer Camp counselor, returning to their classrooms when the school year started. We had many parents who wanted to chaperone many of these trips. I mean, what a lineup we had for these fortunate campers each summer, and the adults, parents and teachers alike, didn't want to be left out! Who could blame them? Hayden's *very first job* was as a PPP Junior Camp Counselor when he was nineteen years old. He became a kid again, experiencing so many of the same field trips he loved when *he* was a Scholar. Everyone wanted to be in "Mr. Hayden's group." William, of course, used his baseball skills several summers as a baseball coach for the PREPPIES with several of his high school baseball buddies, and returned as a college baseball player to "sign autographs" for our summer campers.

> A funny aside: One of the high school baseball guys who helped William coach the summer baseball camp called up to the front office through the intercom and said he needed an incident report. I went back to the gym where the baseball drills were being held to see what had happened. One of the campers had a small red mark on their arm. As this coach was moving his (plastic) bat, this child had run up to give him a leg hug and was accidentally hit. It was very minor—really nothing at all—but I looked at the young coach and said, "You know you just hit Chipper Jones' son with a bat." Boy, the look on his face (insert giggle giggle)!

We called our school-age students SCHOLARS, and being a ROCK (eight years or older) or a STAR (five to eight years old) in Scholars Summer Camp was a coveted position within the PPP hierarchy. ROCK STARS all!

> A funny aside: One of the first of two infants we enrolled when we opened PPP in 1995 was a precious little girl and a wonderful mom and dad whom we enjoyed so much. When this little girl was four years old and a dedicated PREPPIE (insert giggle giggle!), the family moved into the Brookhaven area of the city, away from PPP.
>
> One night while the little girl was telling her parents about something cool that was going on with the

school-age students at her new school, she kept calling them SCHOLARS. Her mom finally interrupted her and said, "Sweetie, you know those kids are called Rangers, they aren't called SCHOLARS." The little girl stopped her excited story and got such a sad look on her face and responded, "You mean I'll *never* be a SCHOLAR?"

The mom called me the next day and told me this sweet story. We both understood that for this little girl, as with most all the PREPPIES, being a SCHOLAR was just the ultimate coolness!

Funny enough, that was the last time I heard from this mom, *until* she heard somehow, fifteen or so years later, about our 20th Anniversary and called me with congratulations and photos of this gorgeous and accomplished PREPPIE of so many years ago. Mystical!

But there's always "an aside," isn't there, and summer camp is no exception. Summer camp was certainly a "HOT" button topic within the community as well as through the state of Georgia's regulatory agency, BFTS (Bright from the Start). As a board member of the Georgia Child Care Association (GCCA), we were smack in the middle of the summer camp fray. In a nutshell, this is what the controversy was about: for-profit companies/institutions would open (what I liked to call) "pop-up" summer camps in order to capture a percentage of the financial boon that happens during the summer months of camp. No doubt, both working and non-working parents have the desire to provide a fun summer camp for their school-age child. PPP, as an established preschool just like all other day-care centers or home-based licensed centers, was governed under strict, numerous, and rigorous regulations. Background checks, educational requirements, group size, teacher-to-student ratio requirements, teacher credentials, transportation requirements, outside space requirements, and a host of other safety-based regulations are, again, rigorous and multiple, and yes, onerous. It's sometimes a burden not only to be aware of all the regulations, but to abide by them and still run a seamless and profitable business. But then here came summer camp, and the state of Georgia allowed just anyone to start taking care of children ("our most vulnerable," as they are routinely called by the government). *And that is just not understandable, safe, right, or fair.*

Various citywide newspapers as well as television news outlets, on several occasions over different years, tried to shed light on and indeed expose this unsafe summer camp practice. As an industry advocate, GCCA tried to show the state officials how this summer camp practice was, most importantly, unsafe for children, but also, as an unintended consequence, damaging to the financial well-being of year-round day-care centers. It was fascinating to me that the state of Georgia would allow such a situation to exist. It was just as frustrating that parents who would hold our feet to the fire over the most minor of issues would remove their child from PPP for the summer to place them in an unlicensed, unregulated summer camp with huge group sizes and teenagers supervising their child *all day*! I would just have to grin, tell them that we would miss their child in our fun summer camp, and we would see them back in the fall—obligated to hold a spot for them for three months.

I would share links with the parents of PPP from the newspaper as well as TV stations' exposé on the unsafe practice of enrolling your child in an unlicensed, unregulated camp. I would include within this email my insights as to the real *and* potential problems associated with enrolling their child in these types of camps. Of course, this could have been, and I am sure was, seen by some as self-serving, and I can't say with all honesty that it wasn't. I didn't want to lose a segment of students to other summer camps, not only for financial reasons but for a variety of reasons. Not only was I concerned about the children's safety, but I was angry at the unfairness of entrepreneurs taking advantage of the summer camp market without being responsible for any of the regulations.

My argument, straight at the state of Georgia through GCCA, was that it was unacceptable for someone to come up with a financial business model that saw them creating a business for three months of the year to take care of children (our most vulnerable) without being subject to any rules or regulations. All that was required by the state regulatory agency was for these "people/companies" to file an exemption from the rules and regulations, and voilà, a business was created, unregulated and with zero oversight. My argument continued that if someone wanted to open a summer business, then they should start as early as possible, prior to summer starting, to get themselves in a regulatory position to open up. Background checks, as well as other appropriate and necessary safeguards for "our most vulnerable," was just one of the areas that was left to chance. Desiring to run a business for a designated period of the year shouldn't automatically preclude exemption from oversight that the exact same businesses are having to adhere to, just because those businesses run all year! In fact, it would seem that a pop-up business would have a far greater chance of being guilty of all sorts of unsafe practices affecting our most vulnerable than a full-fledged legitimate business that runs year-round. I, as well as all other day-care centers, had to start planning and preparing for summer camp in January. Why couldn't they?

Instead, what we saw were twelve-hour-a-day (which was allowed) summer camp facilities opening up in small storefronts, basements of churches, people's garages, whatever, with who knows who taking care of these children. In a televised interview, I believe in 2017 or 2018, with a head official of Bright from the Start, when asked about this lack of oversight on summer camp programs by the state of Georgia and the safety concerns inherent with this lack of any oversight, she basically responded, *"Parents need to do their research before they leave their child at summer camp."* Well duh . . . if that's the standard, then that should be the standard for parents to follow for the remaining nine months of the year on where to leave their child. How trite and dismissive of the problem put before her. A problem somewhat *created* by the bureaucracy of BFTS by changing the law that legitimized these unregulated places to operate twelve hours a day! *Of course* parents should do their research before they leave their child *anywhere*—licensed and regulated or not! What a foolish statement.

To be clear, I had no problem (as it seemed none of us at GCCA did) with parents enrolling their child in a three-to-four-hour summer camp as something to do to break up their child's otherwise at-home summer day. Gymnastic facilities, karate clubs, church programs, and art studios, just to name a few, are welcome outlets for children to go to during the summer to have something to do instead of just sitting at home. There is certainly a place and a market for these types of activity centers for children whose parents are not in need of "day care." However, for parents who need, or maybe just desire, to have their child attend something that is a *full, supervised day,* these type of pop-up, unregulated day-care centers (and that is what they are) should not be allowed *unless* they are willing to adhere to the same rules and regulations that other full-day day-care facilities are required to implement and maintain. A day-care center is a day-care center is a day-care center! How many months of the year a business *chooses* to operate is not the point. It's just that simple.

But as are so many other things that involve government, it's not so simple. It gets muddled and bogged down in all sorts of legalese and, in my opinion, buffoonery. I submitted these arguments to the government agencies involved, and part of their answer and reasoning was that they just did not have the manpower to license (which means to visit) the number of summer camps that pop up during the summer. My argument to that is 1) they should *never* have changed the law to allow twelve-hour days to be adopted (which was done fairly recently) for anything other than a licensed day-care center under their jurisdiction, and 2) they should make a one-time visit to shut these unlicensed summer camps down once they are reported as operating more than three to four hours per day. Believe me, owners and directors of neighboring day-care centers would absolutely get back to the state if these camps didn't close once they were told to do so.

Years ago I attended an employee conduct seminar and the presenter told us we should put employees in charge of "policing" each other as far as being late, calling out, etc. He said that usually directors are way too lenient on these matters, and if employees held each other accountable, there would be "blood on the floor"! That was a hoot, and so *true*! This would be the same situation for legitimate day-care centers to "police" the pop-up camps on behalf of BFTS. A grassroots effort so that BFTS really wouldn't have to do that much at all except enforce compliance or shut them down.

Of course, there is the issue of YMCA and Boys & Girls Clubs that may serve lower-income, rural, or at-risk communities of children. I can easily see the avenue of exemption for these types of full-day summer camps, which provide a valuable service for so many families and historically run very solid programs. What I (we) was targeting is the *for-profit* entrepreneur looking to make a fast, unregulated buck on the backs of our most vulnerable.

Stories of children left in vans and dying of heat stroke, being left at field trip sites, or wandering off from a nature hike and drowning are just several of very recent events that happened during my last year or so of owning PPP. What a devastating thing to happen to a child and to a family, and yes, even to an untrained summer camp counselor (possibly a teenager) who might not have realized the severity of their responsibility. In some of the cases of these terrible happenings, parents were not even aware they had enrolled their child in an unlicensed, unregulated camp.

Most parents take for granted that if a camp is operating to take care of *children*, then they *must be* regulated in some way by someone. This eye-opening revelation was echoed in the exposé on television when some of the parents interviewed said they had found out their camp was unlicensed, either by pure chance or because of a serious issue that had occurred that could not be hidden. A concession that was made by the state of Georgia to all the concerns brought forth from licensed day-care-center owners was that camps must disclose and parents needed to sign that they were enrolling in a camp that did not hold liability insurance (or maybe just post this notice somewhere). But again, if a state official didn't have time to make a licensed visit to certify a summer camp, then there certainly wasn't the manpower to go visit an unlicensed facility to merely see if they had the right postings. Please . . .

Total form over substance, as a lot of things concerning the government are, is unfortunate, especially when it involves the safety of children.

Another consequence of this lack of oversight comes with a lack of reporting and being accountable, summer after summer, from parents' knowledge of issues that may have come up at these camps in prior years. Example: One summer day, I was sitting at a drive-through bank near a "pop up" summer camp. All of a sudden, I see three young children running from this camp into the street! This was also noticed by two other adults unrelated to the camp. All of us left what we were doing to get the children out of the street and safely back to the camp.

I proceeded to the camp to find someone in charge. Young people and a couple of adults were "lounging" under a tent area. I approached them in quite a confrontational way to tell them what had happened. They were unaware, of course. They said they would handle it—"We're sorry"—that's about it. I asked them if the parents of these children would be made aware of the unsafe situation involving their child and the possibility of what could have happened. I mean, there were parents out there who trusted this camp with their very young child who was running out in the street totally away from this camp and no one was even aware, and now these parents would *never* know! Unacceptable.

They said they did not know the answer to that. I went back to the bank to collect my paperwork, drove back to PPP, and called the camp's office. They said they would handle it, and I asked the same question about the parents being notified. No answer. I was

99 percent sure this would never reach the parents. I then called BFTS to report this incident. I followed up a couple of days later to see if anything had been done about this camp and this unsafe situation. Bottom line ended up being that this camp was *exempt* (and this was a camp that ran *hundreds* of young children through the weeks of their summer camp) and therefore not under the jurisdiction for BFTS to get involved. So, that's just one story of so many things that happen at these unlicensed, unregulated summer camps.

> A funny (?) aside: One year the SCHOLARS went on a riverboat cruise in Chattanooga, Tennessee. We rented (as we did each summer) a luxury charter bus with plush seating, bathrooms, movie, etc., and it was full enrollment on these charter bus trip days wherever we chose the destination to be.
>
> So, the SCHOLARS were on the boat, gliding down the river, enjoying a full lunch buffet, when we were notified that there was an active shooter situation going on at (I believe) a naval base in Chattanooga. The phones started ringing off the hook! The teacher chaperones on the trip had no idea what was happening on land. We reached them by cell phone to let them know what was going on. We talked with the cruise operators and were fully confident that the children were safe. We were advised that this situation was not near the river site but that they would continue local monitoring of the situation to ensure that the children were safe at all times.
>
> We were glad to get the SCHOLARS back to PPP, to say the least! When I got home that day, I said to Steve, "Where is the worst place that the SCHOLARS could have been today?" He didn't really know what I was talking about, so I said, "Chattanooga, where an active shooter situation was going on!" He was glad

> he didn't know that during the day! But knock on wood, we never had an incident that compromised the safety of the children during all the PPP years—thank goodness.

As I said one year in an information email on the safety of summer camps to my parents, it's bad enough when something happens to a child in a camp where regulations and safeguards are in place; but when something happens at a camp where safety measures and qualified people are not in place, that turns from being an accident to being negligent, and really on everyone's part, except for the affected child. Accidents can happen and have happened at some of the very best of schools or camps under the care of very qualified individuals with every measure of safety in place—*that's why it's called an accident.*

This was exactly another reason for safety oversight in summer camps—the accident quotient goes up exponentially due to the activities engaged in by children attending most summer camps. Swimming pools, rock-climbing walls, trampolines, mostly outside-based activities—even when supervised by *qualified* people, these are a challenge. But couple these very physical and sometimes dangerous activities with supervision by teenagers or others who are just looking for some sort of summer job, it's a recipe for disaster. Does this position of the state regulatory agency for keeping Georgia's most vulnerable safe during the very physical-based summer make any sense? No.

So a losing battle I waged. This battle was more or less my signature issue as a board member of GCCA, but one that was never resolved. My last year on the board, enough accidents involving children in unlicensed summer camps had occurred, and BFTS and the state of Georgia were on the summer "hot" seat once again. They commissioned a review, a survey, a study—you know, what governments do—and we eagerly awaited their findings and a resolution. As of this writing, I have not heard of any changes that came out of this study, even though just the few of us on the board of GCCA could have given them enough information to come to a safe conclusion and solution without wasting time and money on a meaningless study. The summer after selling PPP, I heard another heart-wrenching story of a summer camp accident involving an unlicensed summer camp. My heart, as always, ached for everyone involved in this tragedy.

Summer camp is one of the most memorable events in a child's life. We all have our own fond memories of summers as we were growing up, either involving day camp, sleepaway camps, or riding bikes and running through sprinklers in the yard. Good times all.

As a parent, please ask the questions necessary to ensure that your child is involved in safe summer activities in the summer camp of your choosing. There are so many wonderful options available for children these days—it's a little overwhelming! But the best way to make sure your child makes fabulous summer memories that will last a lifetime is to make sure that they are *safe*.

CHAPTER 22
IT'S OUR TRADITION

Does your family have traditions? We have quite a few. We have a tradition of celebrating birthdays—or maybe that's not really a tradition, maybe it's just our way of celebrating. Our birthday tradition is gone now in the new house, but when we lived in the Grizzard house, the kitchen was the "birthday spot" every year. The photos of all our birthdays could be interchangeable, so similar was everyone's birthday table. But during the holidays, from Thanksgiving to New Year's Day, we have honored traditions that I think everyone in our family depends on and enjoys as well.

> A funny aside: There is a photo of me, Hayden, and baby William, just barely a month old, at my birthday table in July 1993. I had received a phone call from the neighborhood grocery store the day before with a confused baker wanting to talk about the birthday cake order. Steve had taken Hayden to order a cake for me, and Hayden chose a sheet cake with Ninja Turtles (his favorite) and a Cinderella carriage (for me—and maybe for him too, as we found out later in life . . . insert giggle giggle). Steve allowed this choice, of course, because Hayden (going on four years old) was thrilled with his selection. I giggled on the phone and told this confused baker to go ahead as ordered—I would act surprised, of course. It is a really cute photo; Hayden was so happy with himself!

If you are a mom like me, you are probably the "Keeper of Traditions." Dads and husbands may sometimes act like it's silly or maybe a drudge to have to keep up with these traditions, but we know they depend on us to keep these family traditions and acts of love going. I have a very special card I have kept for many years that Steve wrote to me and sent with a bouquet of flowers. I have no idea why he gave me the flowers, but I kept the card. The card thanks me for always making celebrations and holidays special for him and our boys. He may not even remember giving it to me, and I'm sure he doesn't know I kept the card—well, now he does (insert giggle giggle)! He's given me so many wonderful and extravagant gifts over forty-three years of marriage, but this card is one of my prized possessions.

When the boys were growing up, everything from Halloween through New Year's Day saw our house decorated. As we decorated for Halloween, Hayden and William both had special decorations that they knew just where they went. Some things had new places, and sometimes I purchased new decorations, but the old tried-and-true decorations were placed in the same place. The miniature witches that went in the kitchen on the baker's rack, the lighted pumpkin that went on the side kitchen counter beside the fridge, the monster trick-or-treat bowl that went by the door, and some of their school artwork from over the years, saved and taped up in certain places. All of this delighted and cemented in them not only the nostalgia of the holiday, but a sense of joy and anticipation. When it was time for Thanksgiving, the salt-and-pepper Publix Pilgrim people were special to Hayden, and in later years, when Publix added the Pilgrim little boy and girl, his holiday heart was complete (insert a sweet giggle giggle).

But nothing could compare to the holiday decorations of the Christmas season. Through the years, the outside of our home took on many different looks. Steve sometimes did something small with the outside trimmings, and sometimes it was a lot! Picking out the Christmas tree each year was also a *huge* family affair. Everyone had to be involved. Usually it was a visit to Pike's

Nursery. We always let the boys decide if it was a year we got a white-flocked tree or went with the standard green tree. One year our cat, Chopstix, climbed inside our tree, and during the night, the tree toppled over. If you have never had a tree full of decorations fall, you cannot imagine what a terrifically loud sound that makes, especially in the middle of the night (insert giggle giggle)!

And of course, there was the standard Southern look of candles in each window, and always a wreath on the door. (If you're from the South, you can totally picture it!)

> A funny aside: One year Steve and I hosted our administrative staff on a holiday trip to Biloxi's Beau Rivage for a long weekend of celebrating. One of the nights we went to see Jeff Foxworthy's comedy show. I had never seen him perform before or knew very much about him, but this night, whether it was the atmosphere or the cocktails, I was in complete stitches! One of the funniest things he parodied was what Steve and I, solemnly and lovingly, did *every year*! We always went outside after the tree trimming to see how it looked from the street and made the comment, "It's the prettiest tree we've ever had." We always said it "for real" until Jeff Foxworthy made fun of Southerners doing this (sort of "You might be a redneck if . . ."). Now we say it in jest. (Because we are rednecks? Insert giggle giggle!) I know most of you have probably said this exact same thing, year after year, about your own tree.

We had so many Christmas decorations, some years I decided to not put some of them out, and the next year it was even more special to see them back in their spots. Sadly, when we moved out of the house the boys grew up in, and Steve and I became empty nesters, a lot of the decorations from our holidays just didn't make the move. Our new house did not have the same vibe as the old house and I really could not see it decorated in the same holiday manner, so it was time to move on. I think in some regards I was so wrong in this. Maybe in my desire to start a new chapter in our lives, I did not honor what we had created as parents with our two boys, no matter what their age. Home is always home, no matter if the physical address has changed or your children don't live with you anymore—they always come "home." This is especially true of the holiday season. So maybe live and learn from this chapter if you are a new mom/dad starting your family traditions.

But wait a minute. Traditions *are* very family specific, and maybe even generation specific. Years ago my best friend Felicia told me that when her children started having their own children, she and her wonderful husband decided they would not put the obligations on their growing family that they felt (as we all did) when they were a young couple and had small children. She explained that (like all of us do) when she had her three small children, every single holiday they had to pack up the kids, toys, necessary items, etc. to spend the day at her mom's house—grandma's house—as tradition. She said she didn't understand why her mom couldn't just pick up her purse, get in the car, and come spend the day with them! Wow! This is so logical, right?

Recently, she and I were revisiting this. She used the word *fluid* to describe their family's holiday traditions. I can't remember the exact situation, but it seems I remember her telling me that a couple of the past Christmases, as a family, they had a fabulous gathering on Christmas Eve, or maybe even several days before, and then everyone did whatever else was necessary with "other" family gatherings. I know that one Thanksgiving, they were able to take a fabulous trip to London because her three children had other family and travel obligations that year, so they celebrated their family Thanksgiving early. She said she leaves it up to her three adult children to decide who will host the holiday get-together, and if it's her, she's thrilled—if not, she grabs her purse and dish and goes where she's told. I think this is wonderful, and I bet her children feel blessed and thankful for this "fluidity." I hope that, when the time comes when my family's traditions need to change and become more "fluid"—maybe when travel is a concern or when my boys have another family to factor in—I can embrace this situation as graciously as Felicia does and enjoy whatever becomes our *new* family tradition.

> A holiday aside: When Steve and I moved into our new home, and my mom had by this time become almost completely blind and unable to clean or cook, the holidays shifted from always being at her house to either my or my brother David's house. He started hosting Easter, Mother's Day, and Thanksgiving. I hosted Christmas Eve and Christmas Day and loved it!
>
> So, for the first two years that we were in our new house, that's how it was. Christmas of 2020, my mom decided to throw a wrench in that. She wanted to have Christmas Eve back at her house, and instead of all the traditional snacks and bites that we have had for thirty years as tradition, that she was now unable to do, she decided we could just make it simple and order pizza.
>
> I was not happy. For one, we have pretty much the same thing to eat every Christmas Eve. Now we were going to have takeout pizza? Two, even with ordering pizza, everything else from drinks, ice, desserts, alcohol, you name it, would have to be brought over, and then the cleaning up after—who was going to do that? Why was she insisting on this burden to all of us when I had the means and place to have a beautiful evening?
>
> So, she sort of dropped it but was not happy about it . . . so I gave in. At Thanksgiving I told her we would all come to her house for Christmas Eve—the look on her face was a gift for all of us, but especially for me, who had been the main holdout. But what happened was my loving aunt (who lived down the street from my mom) and my brother (who lived with our mom) decided they would handle the *entire* event

> with *all* the traditional food. All that the rest of us had to do was show up—and that's what we did.
>
> It was a beautiful evening, they did a fabulous job, we all had a blast, but most importantly we honored our mother's wish. She said she thought it was one of the best Christmas Eves ever. The next day, at my house, was even more special for this reason. It's almost a year later and it has become necessary to move our mother into assisted living. Thankfully, we will always have the fond memory of this past, but last, very special Christmas Eve at Nana's.

Two of my family's traditions especially stick out for me, and, I hope, for Steve and the boys: First is trimming our holiday table and setting the table in our dining room with the gifts given to me each year by my stepmother-in-law—Nandy to our boys. For me to try and describe how festive her house is from Halloween through Christmas is something I cannot do. Her home has been featured in magazines! She has a holiday open house every year that people can't wait to see. Her home, beautifully decorated year-round, is stripped pretty much bare starting in October and the decorations appear. From kitchen decorations, bathroom, bedroom, and the living area, almost everything but the furniture is replaced with holiday décor specific to Halloween all the way through Christmas. I mean everything! It is stunning, it is tasteful, and it is over the top! I can't imagine that there is anything left that she can purchase to enhance what she already has, so she started purchasing for me.

Each year I unwrapped a decorative item to put around our house. She would also give me a special dinnerware item. As the years went by, the table I and the boys set was unbelievably gorgeous. Sets of plates, cups, stemware, serving-ware, utensils, linens, pitchers, candy dishes, and all other sorts of items went on this table. When we were done, we just stood back and admired. It wasn't until both boys were in college that I ever did the table alone. While they were growing up, it was the three of us pulling all the boxes out of the hall closet, stacked like a puzzle each year, and emptied out to place all the items where they belonged. The boys didn't need any guidance; they knew where everything went. Then off to play, their job was done, and it was up to me to put the "puzzle" boxes back in the closet until it was time for *me* to get it all back out to repack and put back yet again. Several years ago, I wrote an article about our holiday table and Nandy's part in it. I framed a copy of that published article for her as a Christmas gift. She was so touched with this published article. She cried, I cried, and then we admired the "new" gift of that year that she gave me for the table.

As I mentioned, the first Christmas we were in our new house, I didn't really decorate with anything at all from our past. Poinsettias and candles were placed throughout the house and I thought everything looked lovely and festive. The second year, however, I *had* to get back out the holiday table items. It wasn't everything, but it was just enough to remind us all of how beautiful and traditionally important to us it was to see these holiday items out again and enjoyed.

Second is the traditions for the New Year. For many years, we would pack into the car during the day of New Year's Eve and head up to the border of Georgia and South Carolina, where it was legal to purchase fireworks. This always included a stop at Cracker Barrel for lunch. Steve and the boys delighted in picking out the fireworks for the evening's show. I mean, it was a *show*! What I am trying to explain here is that Steve bought fireworks that were shopping-mall or ball-park show quality! And of course, there was always the pop rockets and sparklers too.

> A sweet aside: I have mentioned our old house and our new house. What I didn't mention is the house we had in between. When we sold the Grizzard house after twenty-four years, which Hayden lived in since he was three and William was born in, we lived for a little

over a year in Steve's mom's, "Maja" to the boys, condominium while we were renovating our current home. Steve had beautifully renovated this condo after Maja's passing and we only expected to live there a few months tops, but as anyone who has ever gone through a major home renovation knows, a few months can stretch into *many* months.

Because we got rid of most of our old furniture and were buying mostly all new furniture for the new house, and the condo was empty after renovating it, we didn't really have anything to move in to the condo with, so we just didn't do anything to the condo—and I mean not anything. We had the two bedrooms decorated (meaning mattresses on the floor and a dresser), and we had a small love seat in the living room with a TV sitting on a plastic box—and that's it. Don't think I am exaggerating! We ate out *every meal* during the year we lived there. The refrigerator never had a thing in it but drinks. Again, I'm not exaggerating (insert giggle giggle).

So Christmas 2017 rolls around and we are still in the condo, and I am in desperation mode. What are we going to do? Where are the boys going to sleep? Is anything going to be decorated? What about a tree?

Everyone who knows me knows that Christmas is a big deal and that this situation was really a problem for me and a source of sadness. So sweet that the ladies at the school, as a Christmas gift to me, gave me an ornament inscribed with the year and the sweetest letter about what makes a home during the holidays. We didn't have any decorations, but we got a small tree and decorated it with some bought ornaments, and it was lovely.

The Christmas I am describing has been four years ago since this writing, and both boys mark that Christmas as among their favorites. But why? There was absolutely nothing about this particular Christmas that was anything like all the Christmases of their life. No decorations, a baby tree, no special food sitting around, and not coming into "Santa" together on Christmas morning. *Could it be that for all the time and effort and joy spent in creating traditions, that really the only tradition necessary is to be together?*

Okay, so, back to traditions, and ornaments! I have shared this tradition with more than a few of the young parents through the years at PPP, and I know a lot of them adopted this and still carry this on. In a nutshell, we would think of something special that the boys participated in during the year and that event would be memorialized in an ornament left for them from Santa as a thank-you for the cookies and milk left for him (yes, on the cookies-and-milk set Nandy purchased for us). And yes, Hayden and William are, as of 2021, thirty-two and twenty-eight, and they will be getting their special ornament!

Their ornaments are stored in a special box for each of them, and these are the ornaments that they concentrate on putting on the tree each year. It may be a special adventure they undertook, an honor they received, where they worked, collegiate ornaments when they left home for college, or when they bought their first car, dog, home, etc. Steve and I have always had a lot of fun trying to determine what will be captured each year with their ornament. Steve has even handmade a few of them when we couldn't find that exact piece to showcase what was needed.

It's sort of silly, but we seem to reminisce about the same things each year as the boys place these ornaments on the tree. I hope one of the things that makes this important to the boys is what Steve and I see as special in each of them. Wouldn't that be the best gift of all to Steve and me?

To end the traditions, a few years ago I decided to conclude our family Christmas gift exchange with the whole family with "Kay's Favorite Thing." Some of you may recognize this adopted tradition from *The Oprah Winfrey Show* (insert giggle giggle). This idea came to me because of a snack mix I make that my boys really like. They call it "legit"! So I made each family a huge bag of Kay's Snack Mix.

Now, each year, I choose something that has made an impression on me during the year and I give that to each family. This past year I decided that my favorite thing was *each* member of my family. So I chose a photo representative of each person (thirteen people in all), made a copy, got a one-dollar frame, and wrapped them up. It was the best (I think) Kay's Favorite Thing ever! Everyone opened their package at the same time, and they were delighted at what I had chosen for them as special to me and to them.

As I say in some of the holiday articles I wrote through the years, your children won't recall some of the items—in fact, most of the items—they received through the years or why, even though, at the time, the gifts they received each year were *exactly* what they wanted and *had* to have. Now, there are just a couple of gifts that stick out in my boys' minds, and we talk about these sometimes. But I know they will *never* forget the special ornaments that depict their lives or the mornings spent decorating the Christmas table or the hot chocolate after the four of us decorated the Christmas tree. The gifts may have been enjoyed and forgotten, but these memories will live on.

> A sweet aside: One year Hayden was really into video games. He *had* to have the new Zelda game. This was mentioned at some family function and Steve's mom decided this was the gift she was going to give Hayden. She searched all over Atlanta for it and finally found it. She was thrilled beyond measure that she was going to be his hero that Christmas season. I was not happy. His "big" gift should be from us—from Santa. But I kept the peace and let her give this gift. Of course, he was over-the-moon happy when he got it, and ultimately that was all that really mattered, even at the time.

Now, years later, Maja has passed away and we can all recall the year that she was the champion with the Zelda gift. If not for *her* giving him that special gift, it would be among all the other great gifts we gave the boys for Christmas or birthdays, and he would not really remember it. But the fact that *she* gave it makes it memorable and very special.

To continue the sweet aside: Maja—she has been mentioned several times in the book. She is Steve's mom and love-laughter-giving grandmother to our boys.

Here's how she became known as Maja: My brothers and I called our paternal grandmother "Grandmother" instead of some nickname. Annette (Maja) told me she always liked the way that sounded. So when we had Hayden, she decided she wanted to be called "Grandmother." When Hayden was around a year old and beginning to babble a little, she was babysitting him at her house one evening. When Steve and I arrived to pick him up, she greeted us at the door giggling a lot! She said, "I'm just going to have to tell a tale on myself! During the evening, I was determined to teach Hayden how to say Grandmother." (Hayden had been saying "Nana" for a few weeks, which is what he called my mom and was very easy for a baby to say).

She continued, "So I kept saying, forcefully and over and over to him, '*Grandmother, Grandmother*.' He finally looked at me and said, just as forcefully and probably in baby aggravation, 'MAJA!' So that's what I'll be—Maja!"

So Maja it was and, boy, did my boys love their Maja. I also think that the Christmas I talked about in 2017, the one that was the boys' favorite, had a lot to

> do with being at Maja's condo, where they had spent so many wonderful times with her. She had only been gone a couple of years at that time, so her presence was still felt and her absence felt even more.

To *wrap* up this chapter, maybe it's not actually the tradition itself, not the actual material thing that makes a tradition, of getting a great tree or having a beautifully decorated house or a special ornament, but instead just the thought and the love and the *desire* to create a tradition and keep it going. Maybe this is what makes the memories special *or* maybe it's the love and respect you show your family to embrace the changes necessary to create new traditions when that time comes.

The year I described when we didn't have any of our traditions present at the condo still rates as one of the boys' favorite Christmases. They knew that the special Christmas traditions would return, and just the memories of all the Christmases past, and all the Christmases yet to come, made this particular Christmas its own type of special. That meant everything to me that year. No one was upset over what *wasn't* going on, we just enjoyed the morning, the gifts, and each other.

So, as with the boys, that particular Christmas, with all my beforehand anxiety, will always be among my favorites as well, because I had the only gift I needed—Steve, Hayden, and William.

CHAPTER 23
THANKFUL IS AS THANKFUL DOES

What are you thankful for? Does your family sit around the dinner table on Thanksgiving or stand in a circle holding hands and recite thanks? Is it largely "we are thankful for our family" or "we are thankful for good health"? Of course, these are wonderful things to be thankful for and not everyone can be thankful for these two fabulous things, so if you are healthy and surrounded by a loving family, it's certainly worth acknowledging and showing thanks. But as I questioned in my "Thankful," Kids & Kay, article, how do you show thanks every day, or maybe not every day, but certainly more than at Thanksgiving? Do you truly ever think about being thankful? I know I don't think about it very much. You know when I think of being thankful the most? When something bad happens.

Several years ago, one of my boys had a friend involved in a fatal car accident. So many times since then, when something happens that aggravates Steve and I with one of our boys, we think, and have even said out loud to each other, how these parents would give anything for the opportunity to have this aggravation with the son they no longer have. Is that morbid to have these feelings? Did it mean we let our boys get away with any type of behavior? No, but it did sometimes put a situation in a different or proper perspective.

There are so many times when some people look on a situation and are thankful for it, while someone else may look at the same situation and not have these same feelings. My brother and I had a conversation recently with my eighty-five-year-old mom. She's in fragile health and feeling that the life she once enjoyed and all the things she used to be able to do are no longer a possibility. The only thing she can still take joy in is being around her children and her grandchildren. When we aren't able to visit her as often as she would like, we get an earful from her, believe you me (insert giggle giggle).

I am sixty years old, and I have one slightly older and one younger brother. One of my brothers lived with our mom, although he traveled sometimes, and my other brother and I would visit her once a week usually. We tell her how thankful she should be that she has her three children live around her and are able to visit so often. We tell her how lucky she was that her two sets of grandchildren were born far apart, so she had the benefit of having one set of grandchildren, watching them grow up, and then having another set she got to enjoy all over again! We try to make her feel thankful about the quality of life she has, acknowledging, however, that it is very much less than the life she would like. And now that she has moved into assisted living near me and my younger brother, we see her every day.

Nevertheless, there are so many parents her age who do not have the surrounding love of their children and grandchildren as she does. While she can understand this reasoning, she one day told us, "I know what you are saying, but I'm lonely, and I can't help the way I feel no matter how thankful you all think I should be." I mean, what can you say to that? We are absolutely correct in our reasoning to her, but she is absolutely right about her feelings. It is not typical of her generation's attitude to "take control of your feelings" or "control your destiny" or stuff like that that is the parlance of our times, if you will.

> A funny aside: As I said, my mom (not unlike most moms I hear about) can make us feel very neglectful of our duties to her as her children, which is very frustrating to myself and my brothers.

Before she moved and was still living in her home, she was having a very sad day and letting me know "she *never* sees anyone, just sits by herself *every* day." In my frustration I said to her, "Emma just freaking (friggin'? fricken? freakin'?) spent part of the thirty-six hours that she had at home from college with you *yesterday*!" Emma is my younger brother's oldest child who is a freshman in college out of state. What a testament it is to how much we all love our mom/Nana that she would take that precious time she had at home and, instead of visiting with friends, choose to go spend time with her grandmother.

Anyway, my mom had never heard the word "freaking," and after our strained phone call, she called my brother to ask him what that meant and why I had said that to her. My brother, without even knowing the context of why I had said that to her, delicately tried to explain it was just a slang word and really didn't mean very much.

A few days later, I returned from a trip and called Mom to tell her I was home. Immediately she went back to that word "freaking." She told me I had said that to her (I really never gave it another thought) and that she had written it down and then asked not only my younger brother, but she asked my older brother too! We then went on to rediscuss the situation of *why* I used that word in frustration, but then I told her that sometimes it is used in excitement about something as well.

Obviously I shouldn't have said that word to my mom, and obviously both I and my brothers were delicately hiding from her the other F-word it's most often associated with . . . (insert a sort of sad giggle giggle!). But we all ultimately got a good chuckle out of it. A few months later at Christmas, my brother's family gave Mom a hand towel that said, "Happy Freaking

> Christmas"! It was the hit of the family Christmas-present openings, and a huge laugh was had by all, especially by me and my mom (insert a real giggle giggle).

Onto the issue of being thankful. As a small-business owner, I always tried to show my administrative staff as well as my faculty how thankful I was for them. I tried to think of ways to show my gratitude in small ways as well as large ways. During the 20th Anniversary of PPP, Steve and I decided to give each employee $100 for each year they had worked for us as a Christmas bonus. This resulted in bonus packages as small as $100 up to $1,900 for over thirty employees! The staff was shocked and thankful for this gesture on our part. They knew that, being a small business, it was a huge financial commitment for us, and this made it extra special to them. Their reaction gave Steve and me so much joy at the time. A year or so later, one of my teachers, who was the recipient of one of the larger amounts, showed me a beautiful campsite with her small grandson playing, and she told me that this setup at her campsite was how she had spent her 20th Anniversary bonus. I was blown away to think that Steve and I had helped in a small way to create a place for her to relax and make beautiful memories with her grandchildren. The monetary thank-you to her didn't compare with the gift she had given *me* of being able to watch her teach young children for seventeen years and for the loyalty she had always shown to PPP. And then, on top of all that, to give me this feeling of pride when she shared the campsite photo with me. I remain ever thankful to her for that moment.

I was very proud of and thankful for the longevity of our teachers and administrative staff and used this in marketing strategies, tours, even putting teachers in community advertisements with their years of service noted. In one of these ads, I headed it, "Are You Happy?" The gist of the ad was, if you are not happy at the preschool you are working at or that you are placing your child at, come to PPP because obviously it's a great place to work (i.e., the tenure of these fabulous ladies shown in this ad).

In the day-care industry, the *average* tenure of our PPP teachers, which was over ten years, was an unheard-of commodity and was one of the important items, among many, that set us apart from other preschools in our area. It was painful to hear from parents, during their tour of PPP, how many teachers their young child had experienced during the span of a few months at other preschools. Day-care workers are typically on the lower range of salaries, have long hours, have a lot of responsibility, and in some cases have a thankless job from a parent perspective as well as an employer perspective. I tried, and it seems I was successful for the most part, to establish my gratitude to my employees. I know the teachers felt this thankfulness from the majority of the parents as well.

PPP was a successful business venture for my family. But what made it most successful and joyful for me and Steve were all the extras we could provide to the students, families, and faculty. Yes, of course, we could afford to spread around a thankful spirit in part due to the price we charged our families. The parents of PPP knew their "education dollars" were always at work! However, we knew of competitors who charged the same as we did that had nowhere near the "thankful spread-around spirit" as we had at PPP, based on information from parents or faculty who came to PPP from these other places.

Sure, we could have made a larger profit by not doing a large portion of the thankful gestures we did, but that was one of the joys I had for twenty-five years. I even mentioned this to one of the people involved in the acquisition team when I saw some of the corporate cost programs of efficiency that were being put in place when we sold our schools. What works for an individually owned business usually doesn't translate into a corporate culture, but sometimes it can be just the opposite. One of my directors had a saying between her and her husband, "corporate vs. private," when I did something so "out of the realm of a corporation" and she wanted to brag to her "corporate" husband.

Making a much larger personal profit was not as important to Steve and I as the reputation PPP enjoyed of always being "over the top" in customer service, child development, as well as a place of consistent "spoiling" of our faculty. We even had a professional development seminar with actual state- and nationwide data compiled by the presenting trainer, comparing wages, bonuses, and childcare perks that were enjoyed by the faculty of PPP as compared with other day-care centers. It was mind-blowing and eye-opening to the faculty, but not to Steve and I. Everything we did to take care of our faculty was carefully planned and thoughtfully implemented.

Could *all* these things I did for my teachers also be looked at as self-serving? No doubt these acts of gratitude, either monetary or in spirit, kept my teachers happy, but did it keep them at PPP for my benefit? I don't think so. I mean, it's not like if I didn't do these things for them they could go elsewhere and be rewarded in these ways. As I said, anyone who came from another preschool couldn't believe the dream they were living at PPP, in *many* ways. Anything I ever did for my teachers or admin staff was always made from the heart, and I think it was received as such. The natural, "intended" consequence of faculty retention was a bonus, but one that was not left to chance.

To illustrate: I once attended a director-only seminar with my fabulous director of twenty years. Part of the seminar topics was to brainstorm ideas to retain your faculty. So she started in and it went something like this: "Well, at PPP we have monthly faculty meetings with catered lunches. The teachers receive bonuses for completing training. Kay takes her administrative team shopping once a year as well as providing other admin lunches and dinners and gifts of gratitude. We enjoy traveling all over the United States, hosting two teachers, all expenses paid, to the NAEYC conference. Kay gives gifts to the teachers for milestones reached in years of service—embroidered scarves, engraved bracelets and necklaces, Tissot & Michele watches, bonuses, etc. We have monthly faculty appreciation with gift cards, treats, thank-you notes, and, maybe more importantly, Kay treats all of us as professionals and gives the faculty all the tools and support necessary to do a great job in their classroom every day, giving them a sense of true achievement and accomplishment."

Her description of what all I did to make our Fabulous Faculty happy and feel appreciated just went on and on. At the end of the conference, the facilitator said we were going to go around the table and everyone had to say one thing they learned from the conference. Out of the ten or so who were there, more than half of them said (and it was said jokingly by these directors and in the spirit of knowing that PPP certainly is not the typical day-care center) that what they learned was, "I want to work for Kay!" It was a very proud moment and one I *thanked* my director *for giving me. This made* me *feel so appreciated.*

I know a lot of this chapter sounds like I'm patting myself on the back—but not so. It's all to illustrate thankful *is* as thankful *does*. Keeping your thankful feelings to yourself does no good to anyone. You have to show your thankfulness, in business and in your private life. Believe me, there were times I was so busy with so many things, professional and personal, that I had to be reminded to be thankful for my Fabulous Faculty. I am a baby boomer—you get paid to do a job, you shouldn't have to have continual praise in order to do a good job was the way I was raised and the way *I* operated in my corporate life, no matter how much I wished I was praised more. But now, as the business owner, I didn't want my employees to feel that they were not appreciated, every day. I remember one Valentine's Day I had forgotten to get something special for the staff as in years before, so I sat down and wrote each and every one of the teachers a "love" note. I can say sincerely I got more appreciation back from the teachers out of that gesture than a lot of the monetary or gift things I gave to them.

Appreciation and the act of being thanked is what we all seek . . . even though cash and gifts are always nice too (insert giggle giggle).

These examples of how to show gratitude and how thankfulness is necessary illustrates an important component in today's workplace. Unless you own your own business and are able to make the financial concessions necessary to provide perks and gifts to your staff, your hands may be tied in some ways. But whether you are a small-business owner, a CEO of a large company, a supervisor of an office team, an at-home, volunteer-involved person, or retired like me, you have many people you are thankful for each day.

At that same aforementioned director seminar, the facilitator said she had worked for the same man for over ten years and she *never* left a day of work where he didn't say *thank you* to her. He didn't give her a gift or a note every day. He let her know he was thankful she was working with/for him, and this obviously resonated with her. Maybe that wasn't really necessary. Maybe there were days she may not have really done such a great job. Maybe it's not necessary to say thank you every day. Maybe that would become too mundane or may be looked at as disingenuous. People know when they should be thanked. People know when they have made that extra effort in whatever the task is, and people also know that sometimes the fact of just "being there" was enough for that day. I know there were many times when several people called out and I was worried about how we were going to support our ratios and make it through the day, and I was incredibly thankful to all those who were "just there." Maybe I brought in lunch for everyone on those stressful days. Whatever your business model and needs, we all have those stressful staff days, and it shouldn't be hard for us to see the dedication shown by our staff or team and to be thankful for it, but to more importantly *show that thankfulness.*

On a personal level and on how each of us looks at similar situations differently, when Hayden was born prematurely, I felt that it was unfair that I had done everything expected of me but didn't have the outcome I wanted, *what I felt I deserved* when this complication occurred. I had followed all the rules during my pregnancy, but when the rubber met the road, I was denied or cheated out of the outcome it *appeared* everyone else was having with their baby. He didn't have any health issues, just needed to stay in the hospital and get a little bigger before we could take him home, that's all, of which I should have been incredibly thankful. But I was not grateful for my situation *until* I looked at my situation in relation to others around me in the neonatal unit. When looking at these families and their babies facing operations and unsure outcomes, I instantly became grateful and thankful for my situation. This lesson has stuck with me my entire life. No matter the situation, there is always someone who would trade places with you, gladly.

I think before we feel angry, sad, cheated, or ungrateful, look to what we *do* have and give thanks every day.

CHAPTER 24
MIGHT AS WELL FACE IT . . .

Love—what a lovely word. It makes you *feel* good just to say it. It makes the person you are saying it to *feel* good. But did you know that your body actually has a *physical* reaction to love? A series of hormones are secreted that makes us literally addicted to love!

As with most addictions, you have a physical as well as emotional craving to experience this feeling over and over, sometimes to the exclusion of all else. I mean, what would the movie industry be if we weren't obsessed with love? What would the music business be without our addiction to love? In fact, what would the human race be without our devotion to give and receive love? The human race could not have existed or evolved without love—and if there is someone out there who feels that they don't have an outlet for their love or doesn't have love incoming, you can rest assured that their life is in dire straits, not only emotionally but, in fact, *physically*.

Without the release of the various hormones I noted in my article, which you can easily research yourself, published each February—the "love" month—your body function is not as optimal as it should or could be. In most books or manuals on how to be your best self or how to be successful in relationships, both personal and professional, you will see a common theme of the most successful or happiest people being those who have the ability to make *others* feel happy and successful, to make others feel that you see and appreciate their worth. If you are a person who can genuinely pull this off, you not only give that hormonal secretion "high" to others, but if it is sincere, you will feel that "high" physically yourself. And believe me, that's a gift that will keep on giving in so many healthy ways.

> An aside: I have been a runner since my twenties. The "feel-good" hormone (endorphins) that runners, or any person who exercises, experience not only helps keep your body fit but keeps your mind fit as well, both body and mind working at optimal levels. I have often laughed at myself that while on a run, I have come up with a solution to a complex problem or I have come up with some sort of great idea and I can't wait to get back home to tell Steve or call my admin team. I have jokingly told numerous people that I don't know how any corporate executive or business owner can do their job effectively without running! Of course, what I thought I meant was putting yourself in a situation of being able to allow your mind complete freedom to wander and digest all sorts of possibilities without being subject to interruption. For me, that time was only when I was running, and there is certainly something to be said about that alone time. But what I didn't realize is that my endocrine system kicked into gear as well. I didn't realize that there were actual hormones coursing through my mind and body that provided an outlet for these successful ideas and solutions to form.

For years and years I resisted having any sort of telephone accessory with me while running, because I knew that if the phone rang or a text beeped I would feel compelled to stop and see who needed me. I used to tell my boys, when they lived at home and needed me a lot, they could easily do without me for the twenty-five or so minutes it took for me to run three miles. It wasn't until I fell a couple of times while on a run that I started using a phone accessory for safety reasons, and for my sixtieth birthday, the boys gifted me Air Pods and an Apple Watch, so that takes care of music, phone, texts, and a host of other exercise tools, and the inherent interruptions (insert giggle giggle).

Endorphins also work with your brain receptors to decrease feelings of pain, almost like morphine. Being a runner for so many years, and also, I think, due to a hereditary trait, I have very "bad" feet. I have undergone many cortisone shots and surgeries on my feet and I still have pain. Funny enough, my feet *never* hurt when I run, and that's a fact!

Doctors verify and support the hormonal secretions of appropriate exercise not only for younger adults, but also to aid in health concerns for senior citizens. Have you ever been involved with an aging family member leaving the hospital after almost any type of illness, accident, or surgery? Almost without exception, they are discharged to a rehabilitation facility where physical therapy is at the heart of their recovery, even though their original hospitalization may have had nothing to do with a physical injury.

I give the rundown of the hormone download when we feel love (either giving it or receiving it) in my published article. It's very complicated and involved—our body is an amazing machine! Some of these same hormones secrete when someone gives us praise, that "feel-good" feeling that gives us a literal high. At PPP, we could see the children glow when they were praised for their achievements in the classroom. We saw this same glow when their parents would come in the classroom for afternoon pickup—that's love, and it's physical. You can see it in children when beloved family members come to visit. In fact, children glow *a lot* due to their innocent nature of thinking everyone loves them, and they love everyone and everything (insert giggle giggle).

In adults we glow a lot as well. In fact, the level of our hormones is sometimes in overload due to a host of emotions. The biggest "high" is love, but this hormone overload is also seen when we lose love. It's a scary thought and a physical reaction like no other when our addiction to love is not reciprocated or satisfied. This emotional addiction is also a wealth of material for the movie business and music industry—see Glenn Close's portrayal of unreciprocated love in *Fatal Attraction,* or listen to the destruction unleashed in Carrie Underwood's song "Before He Cheats"! The hormone secretion in the case of love's destructive power is similar to one's destructive addiction to alcohol or drugs. You will do almost anything to get that "high" back, and some of these actions can push the limits of acceptable or safe behavior.

Children *require* unconditional love; they do not understand anything else. For most children, the only love they know how to *give* is also unconditional. It's not until the late teen years or young adulthood that we learn to reserve parts of our love as conditional upon another person's actions toward us. Wouldn't it be nice if none of us ever had to learn that love is or can be conditional? Wouldn't it be wonderful to always be able to count on feeling love from those we love?

Sometimes we call a teen's first love "puppy love." I think that's really a nod to the unconditional love we receive from pets. The healing powers of a pet's unconditional love is well documented in the medical field, in children and adults, as our bodies secrete these important hormones that can aid in the rehabilitation of our bodies and minds after a medical event, a loss of a loved one, or other emotional stressors just by the presence and love of a pet. We can always count on the love and comfort of our pet. We also see these "feel-good" hormones associated with a pet's ability to make happier and possibly sustain the life span of senior citizens. It's more than just a societal thing that so many senior citizens have pets. It's not just for the companionship component. It's a physical and emotional healthy *necessity* to those seniors who have a pet.

> A loving pet aside: Steve and I have been blessed over the years with so many wonderful pets. When Steve and I were dating and I was twelve years old, Steve showed up at my house with a little black peek-a-poo

> puppy for my birthday. He didn't ask my parents, he just arrived with it! Who does that? (Insert giggle giggle!) Anyway, we named the dog Spanky and my family loved that dog.
>
> When Steve and I married, we got our own dog, a cute Lhasa Apso. We named him Catfish because he had fur down his tiny face that reminded us of catfish whiskers. When I got pregnant with Hayden, we had had Catfish for many years and I cried one night, with Catfish lying between Steve and I, thinking that he didn't know his life was about to change dramatically. Believe it or not, I was also emotional wondering if I would love the baby as much as I loved Catfish! I mean, I had a studio portrait photo shoot as a gift for Steve featuring me and Catfish (insert giggle giggle)!

Through the years, we have treated *all* our dogs like a true member of the family, like a person even. Funny, when we had the exchange student I mentioned in another chapter, one Christmas I was sad we weren't taking Catfish to my mom's on Christmas Day. She didn't understand my sadness and made a sarcastic joke about it saying, "It's Christmas . . . and he knows!" Of course he did! After Catfish died, we went several years without a dog.

Then, when the boys were around ten and twelve, we got their first dog, a white bichon frise. We named him Chicklet. Chicklet rarely went by "Chicklet." We called him Chippa Fish (in honor of Catfish), we called him Chick, Chip, President Puppa, and, in later years, Poke (because he moved so slowly). We mated Chicklet with a bichon from a family who lived in the house behind us and we got one of the puppies—the runt of the litter, a little bitty doggie we named Chocolate. She was anxiety-ridden and Steve was her protector. He couldn't *move* without her, and he loved it (most of the time). Chippa and Chock Chock (Baby Girl to Steve) died about a year apart when they were both around fifteen years old. We loved those dogs fiercely, and Steve had a really hard time after losing his Baby Girl. He still (two years later as of this writing) has her collar and heart-shaped dog tag hanging from his rearview car mirror.

Then there is Crash, our granddog that I have talked about in other chapters. He is the smartest dog Steve and I have ever run across. He's a Lab mix rescue and loves our son William to death! Steve and I spoil him a *lot*, but he always prefers to "hang" with William and William's friends (insert giggle giggle).

As an update, we now have our second granddog: a long-haired, English cream miniature dachshund named Coconut. His cute name checks a lot of "family" boxes for us (mainly about food names), and we have already resorted to various pet names for him as well, rarely calling him Coconut. We miss him a lot when he and Hayden are home in New York City and look forward to whenever they can visit and we can get our "nut" fix (insert giggle giggle). *Okay, when you don't have grandchildren, you take what you can get (insert a huge giggle giggle)!*

But back to people. I am certainly one of the lucky ones—really among the luckiest! I have been loved my entire life. I was blessed with wonderful parents who loved me and with grandparents, siblings, aunts and uncles, and friends who showed me love. I was also blessed at the age of twelve to find the love of my life. Looking up from my seventh-grade graduation ceremony, I saw Steve enter the auditorium. I had the same physical feeling then that I have now, forty-eight years later, when I see him. I have told more than one person in a relationship they were a little unsure about continuing, and even one situation involving a person who was about to get married but felt unsure about, that if you cannot recall, when the going gets tough, *and it will get tough,* that tingly feeling you got in those early-dating days, your relationship will not make it.

Okay, to be fair, during these forty-eight years (forty-three of which we have been married, as of this writing update), Steve and I have had our ups and downs, of course. The one year we attended the same high school, we sometimes broke up several times during the same day! Before Steve was old enough to drive, he would call his mom to come pick him up at my house because we were mad or broke up, and *before* she could get there, we were back together, so she just had to turn around and go back home (insert giggle giggle)! There was the year he went away to college, before he returned to attend Georgia Tech, and that was tough. And, of course, as we grew into adulthood with each other, we weathered some relationship storms that thankfully were not so severe that we could not remember how much we loved each other and were able to get through them. We grew up together and no one knows me the way he does, and vice versa.

We built a life, had two wonderful boys, built a business, and now are enjoying our retirement years together. There is no one I would rather spend time with than him. The adventures and experiences we have had together are vast, the memories precious. When I tell him that I love him, he always responds, "Love you more." And I say, "I count on that." And I do. He spoils me like you cannot imagine. He is an old-fashioned gentleman in every way, and I hope that trait lives on in Hayden and William toward their partners in life.

As Steve and I get older, our feelings of love are as much a part of us as our own selves—they are cemented in our brain patterning as a given; however, one of us will have to imagine a life without the other at some point. But when that time comes, hopefully many years from now, each of us will be able to continue to *feel* the physical and emotional benefit of the love we have shared for so many years with each other. Hopefully, we will not suffer this loss as much as some others might who do not share such a loving bond with another, because we do have such strong and enduring feelings. That sounds a little off kilter, doesn't it? If Steve and I depend on each other's love so much and have for so long, shouldn't we feel the loss of the other that much more? Maybe. But I choose *now* to believe that whichever of us is in the position of being without the other, we will be able to recall and actually still *feel* such loving and wonderful memories, and indeed see so much of our love in others in our family, that the physical and emotional feelings necessary to live a fulfilled life will continue as a constant, even without the other one's physical presence. This *feeling* of love gives me peace.

> A sweet aside: Steve told one of his cousins that when he and I die, we are going to be cremated and our ashes will eventually be mixed in the same container. She was so overcome with that feeling of love Steve shared with her, that she and her husband decided they wanted to do the same with their ashes and even had that desire written into their wills. That touched Steve and I.

Okay, enough of the "heavy lifting" as regards a life of love. The take on Robert Palmer's song to title this chapter was more prolific than might have been intended—or maybe not. It does seem that someone must have done the necessary research for this hit song in the '80s, so true are the lyrics!

So okay . . . I'm facing it, I'm embracing it . . . I'm addicted to love!

CHAPTER 25
ALWAYS REMEMBER TO INSERT A GIGGLE GIGGLE

I hope you enjoyed reading my book! I enjoyed writing it and remembering so many wonderful times from my professional and personal life. As in life, some of the chapters weren't always designed around a giggle giggle. But through it all, I tried to always see the "bright side" and giggle at myself.

After writing the book, I tried and tried to get my husband Steve and my boys, Hayden and William, to read the book. They either put it off with a shrug or out-and-out refusal! Why? Well, I think it came down to not wanting to criticize me (as hard as they saw me working on the book) if they thought it wasn't any good (insert giggle giggle!) or that they would be too emotional reading parts of it. I understood both emotions and tried not to push very much—only the few and far between sarcastic remarks about "Well, I wrote about that in my book . . . *that you haven't read.*" (Insert giggle giggle!)

After finishing the book, I started writing a blog, maybe to promote the book a little but also, I realized I had more to say, *and* I really enjoyed my "writing time." I hope you have a chance to check it out! It's sort of like the book, however, with vastly different topics—it's more about being a woman, a person, and being respectful of everyone's opinions no matter how different, illogical, or radical they seem *to you*. I generally think my point of view is the correct one—don't you? Well, everyone does, so let's try and put ourselves in each other's shoes and agree to disagree, as the saying goes. It's interesting to have different points of view around you. Who knows, maybe your point of view and opinion can change, *or* maybe by your actions you can sway someone else to change their viewpoint, if that's what you're going for. Whatever the case, different viewpoints were once looked at *as being interesting* instead of being *threatening*. I hope that we can somehow get back to that way of looking at people and the world.

It was tough editing the book, for me. I had to stop and giggle a lot at what the editing team may be thinking about the book—or, really, about me (insert giggle giggle). I have a huge box under my bed of two years' worth of manuscripts that I edited myself as I wrote the book before passing it off to the team. They would not believe those versions of the book! Even worse, I can't imagine what my first couple of readers thought before I even started editing—insert giggle giggle! One of my fabulous kindergarten teachers at PPP would tell the students, when they were doing creative writing exercises, to just get their thoughts down and worry about cleaning up the clutter and illogical thoughts later. So, I followed that advice (insert giggle giggle!), I'm somewhat embarrassed to admit from reading those early manuscripts.

In our first meeting, I told the publishing staff that they may have a tough time with my book (or again, maybe more honestly with me!) because I was aware that the obligation, of course, would be to edit the book to be grammatically and otherwise intellectually correct; however, that was just not the way (in a lot of instances) that the book could adequately be portrayed while being true to the way I wanted to "speak" to my readers—more as a friend rather than as a "self-help" (as the genre this books falls under) writer without errors. Believe me, no one needed more self-help and made more errors than me during my adult life, as a parent or businesswoman (and I still need that help as a retiree!), so I certainly didn't want to represent the opposite. And a little secret . . . for this final chapter I requested to be left "unedited," so I'm sure it is full of all the grammatical and word redundancies that were thankfully corrected in the hundreds of pages previous to this final chapter . . . *so read this chapter with the literary license that I gave myself (insert giggle giggle)!*

Through the editing process, I spent one whole day doing nothing but taking out exclamation marks—there must have been *thousands* throughout the book—so many because I put three or four marks after a sentence where (obviously) *one* would just not do (insert giggle giggle)! Was what I was "exclaiming" *really* that important (insert a huge giggle giggle)? Does anyone reading this remember the *Seinfeld* episode where Elaine was trying to explain to her editor why so many exclamation points were *needed*—in fact, *necessary*—and he finally had to *exclaim* (something like), "Get rid of the exclamation points!"? Surely with an exclamation mark in his voice, duly noted!

But truly, this book isn't solely about looking at situations and laughing them off. Each of our lives is full of tense and solemn moments that sometimes, with the advantage of time passing, we can look back on and realize they actually weren't as dramatic as we thought. I know that's been my experience. Sometimes in my professional life one of my employees or managers wanted me to be more involved or even upset with someone/something that was going on and didn't understand why it didn't irk me more, or even at all. Maybe because I was the owner and I had the luxury of knowing I was ultimately in charge and it didn't really matter what someone thought they had "gotten away with" as an employee. The opposite happens in my personal life, however. I giggled while on a shopping trip with my niece when I purchased a key chain that said, "HOLD ON WHILE I OVERREACT!" Yep, that's usually me—overreact first, ask questions later (insert giggle giggle).

But honestly, there are so many things—now as a sixty-three-year-old—that I wish I had done or acted/reacted to differently, either looking back now or sometimes knowing at the time. It's sort of like when you are about halfway through blow-drying your hair and you get interrupted and miss that critical point of no return. No matter what you do (short of re-washing your hair), you can't make it right. That's true of so much in life, isn't it? We can all relate to "I want a redo" in so many situations, yet it's most often not to be.

Unlike your hairdo, a simple shower cannot make everything right. Sometimes just a giggle will get you through a tough situation, and sometimes not. Sometimes you just have to muscle through, and maybe years later, how dramatic you thought a particular situation was, it is now a non-issue and finally a small giggle can come out. How wonderful if we could just imagine that possibility at the time.

I have reread this book, chapter by chapter, so many times it is uncountable, and no matter how hard I have worked to make it right, I still find things that need changing every time I read it. I think that happens in life as well. Work and work, think and rethink, and still it's not exactly right, not exactly how you wish it to be. So often we just have to let it go.

All this to say, a giggle won't get you through everything, and this book is certainly not a road map on self-help life skills to follow. It's more about all the mistakes I made and lessons learned that maybe others can see a situation similar and know we all go through stuff that makes up our life experiences. As parents we so often want, and try, to make it possible for our children to not make the same mistakes that we made, as generations of parents before us wanted to do for their children and generations of parents after us will continue to strive to achieve and will also fail. Relax and don't fall prey to this illusion. It didn't work with you, did it? It certainly didn't work with me, and I don't see my boys following each and every piece of advice I give them as their wise parent either—nor did the many parents of PPP—no matter how perfect I think that advice is!

I made mistake after mistake, and tons of them were what my parents or others close to me probably warned me of. Oh well. My life (and I'm sure yours) has been full of successes as well, and things generally turn out the way they should. And what's that saying, tried and true, about your failures being the most important part of your growth and future successes . . .

I recently said to one of my very accomplished nieces, who once again worked hard for something and once again got what she worked for, that success after success sometimes gets boring and the eventual defeat (which surely will eventually occur, unfortunately) will make all the future successes even sweeter. Of course, wishing all the while that this valuable life lesson will *never* befall anyone that I love (insert giggle giggle)!

So as I said in the first chapter of the book, but now metaphorically—relax, get a cup of coffee or a glass of wine, get in your comfy pants, *and go through your life*. Things *will* work out. Laughter is most always there, find it and cherish it. Share it with others, someone will *always* need it. Let those you love know that they can always count on you to show them the humor, the light at the end of the tunnel in the toughest of situations, and you know what, if that's not the case, show them that they have you and so many others to help them through. And who knows? Years later, just maybe a giggle will cross their lips.

My loveliest regards to you and your children, and always remember to insert a giggle giggle.

—Kay

ACKNOWLEDGMENTS

The Fabulous Faculty of PPP: My sincere appreciation to the ladies who worked for and with me through the twenty-five years of PPP. It was my privilege to call you my employees, my friends, and the foundation of the preschool. Your devotion to "Loving to Learn" was the cornerstone of the success of PPP.

The Administrative Team of PPP: My administration team throughout twenty-five years was a very small group of incredible ladies who assisted me in every aspect of building the PPP culture. Without your dedication, ideas, hard work, and fun spirit, PPP would not have been the joy to me that it was every day. I was very blessed to have you fabulously smart and loving women by my side.

The Preppies of PPP: The students of PPP provided all of us with so much joy through the years and continued to reward all of us by their achievements as they grew into young adults. Thanks for a wonderful year of "mystical connections" as so many of you helped us celebrate the 20th Anniversary of PPP. Keep wearing those "I WAS A PREPPIE" T-shirts! You have made us proud.

The Parents of PPP: Thank you for trusting us with your precious children. All of us at PPP took this responsibility with profound appreciation and sincerity. PPP's reputation was built through your positive voice in the community, and for that I will be forever grateful. I enjoyed sharing my boys and their stories through the years with you and I enjoyed you sharing your children with me.

My editing team: Thanks to my editors, proofreaders, and creative team for helping me see my book for the first time through the eyes of someone who didn't know me. I appreciate you printing the many edited manuscripts and letting me give them back with hand-written notes instead of through the internet. You all understood my vision of the book from our very first meeting and I appreciate you allowing me to keep a lot of the mistakes in the book (insert giggle giggle)!

Felicia: Saying "thank you" doesn't begin to express the loving gratitude I have for the support you've given me throughout my life in so many ways. You took on the task of reading my early manuscript and plowing through so much that was eventually cut out but nonetheless you read and supported it all. I'll never forget when, one day, you said to me, "This book must be published." Making your own notes in the margins with your own exclamation points (insert giggle giggle), it was obvious once again why you are my cherished best friend.

Hayden: Thank you for calling me your inspiration, your best friend, but especially Mommy. I look forward every day to our many phone calls and interactions. A huge thank-you for designing my book cover, setting up my website, and helping me understand social media! I couldn't have done it without you. You make me proud while challenging me every day, keeping me on my toes from world events to fashion. Your many achievements, fun spirit, and sense of adventure have made you a source of so much content in this book, and in my life.

William: It's been a joy to watch your free spirit while being the most grounded person in our family. You have provided so much play-by-play action and enjoyment for me and I have loved every minute of all the varied interests your life has taken you and our family. Thank you for always allowing my "mommy wings" to surround you and to participate in all your accomplishments, standing to the side, beaming with pride. I will always cherish the text you sent me after being the first in the family to read my book.

Steve: I hitched my wagon to your star at the age of twelve and you have taken me to the greatest of heights over our fifty years together. You are the rock of our family and you made it easy for each one of us to feel secure in anything we chose to do, knowing you are by our side supporting and guiding us. Throughout my writing this book, your encouragement was unwavering. You always made me feel like a best-selling author, which is even better and more important to me than maybe actually ever being one.

GALLERY

Hayden aboard a friend's boat in Naples, Florida.

Hayden and William —2017 family dinner.

My favorite photo of the boys in their great-grandmother's magnolia tree. Ages six and three.

William's college baseball team winning the A.I.I. Championship, 2016.

William, professional baseball umpire—2022

Hayden competing in World Irish Dance Championships —Glasgow, Scotland, 2007.

Family photo —Christmas 2020

Coconut (Hayden) and Crash (William), our granddogs

Hayden presenting me with flowers each year on his birthday.

Me and the boys at Hayden's apartment —New York City, 2018

Steve and the boys—2015

Family baseball photo—2016

Me and William—NAIA College Baseball World Series, Idaho, 2014

Snuggle time with Chicklet, Chocolate, and Crash—2014

Celebrating fifty years of friendship with my best friend Felicia.

Santa's "special" ornaments left for the boys — Christmas morning, 2020

High school sweethearts—1975

Our first toast at our wedding reception—August 1979

Honeymoon memories ❤ —Bahamas 1979

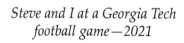

Birthday dinner for me—2016

Steve and I at a Georgia Tech football game—2021

First PPP
—August 1995

Second PPP
—January 1998

William proudly displaying his PPP 20th Anniversary T-shirt. He was literally our first Preppie!

Digital billboard in the community inviting all PPP Preppies to stop by and celebrate PPP's 20th Anniversary—2015

CPSIA information can be obtained
at www.ICGtesting.com
Printed in the USA
LVHW042250260323
742659LV00001B/163

9 781665 302937